The Nature
of Moral
Responsibility

The Nature of Moral Responsibility

Stephen David Ross

STATE UNIVERSITY OF NEW YORK, BINGHAMTON

Wayne State University Press
Detroit, 1973

57011

Library of Congress Cataloging in Publication Data
Ross, Stephen David.
    The nature of moral responsibility.
    1. Ethics.   2. Responsibility.   3. Liberty
I. Title.
BJ1012.R626   170   72-3399
ISBN 0-8143-1479-1

Contents

Introduction

It is odd that men seek to deny their responsibilities, for how they meet their responsibilities defines who and what they are. What men take themselves to be circumscribes the responsibilities they bear and how they meet them. What a man accepts as his responsibilities both represents what he takes himself to be and gives its character to what he will become in the future.

No wonder, then, that profound insights into human nature and the nature of moral responsibility can be found in great works of literature. In particular, consider the stories of Genesis and of Oedipus the king. They both reveal a monumental act of defiance of the Supreme Order of the universe, a defiance that is at once ignominious and truly human. Oedipus ignores the oracle's warning, and brings disaster on himself and his queen. Adam defies God and eats the apple. Both are doomed, and suffer for their transgressions. The doctrine of original sin, indeed, represents our continuing to bear the burden of Adam's fall.

Even literal interpretations of the story of the fall, as well as the version in the modern legend of psychoanalysis, should not blind us to the deeper hints they give us. Both legends represent a continuous and direct inheritance of guilt, and a pervasive sense of sinfulness. We are inflicted with a heavy cross, the burden of our humanity and its responsibilities.

Most important, our responsibilities are rooted in our manhood. They are not accidents of circumstance. The myths of the fall, of Oedipus, all dramatize the conception that man is in his deepest being burdened by his responsibilities—though at the same time his responsibilities represent the challenges that make his great achievements as a human being possible. Adam and Eve were doomed to fall. It was their very nature to disobey. Oedipus is the man who answered the Sphinx's riddle. He could do no other than become king of Thebes. It is our very humanity that oppresses us. The circumstances in which we find ourselves give us our being, and weigh upon us at the same time. In the more modern terms of Jean Paul Sartre, we are *"condemned* to be free."

But what is so burdensome about our responsibilities? As I see it, we are not condemned to be free, but to *fail*. The possibility of disaster haunts every moment of human life. That most of all is the horror and tension of the story of mighty Oedipus. What, after all, has Oedipus done wrong? His efforts to avoid the doom prophesied by the Delphic oracle led him to that very disaster. Oedipus is a mighty and exceptional man who has done everything right—but for something he "could not have known." The play is ambiguous on whether Oedipus *really* could have avoided killing his father—but that ambiguity too represents truly our typical condition. What we don't know about we usually can find out if we care enough. Townspeople in Dachau also "didn't know" what really went on in the concentration camp just outside the town, though prisoners were often marched through the town streets. Oedipus too "couldn't have known"—yet he is condemned nevertheless. If he can fail, none of us is likely to escape.

All too often it is the punishment that oppresses us, and makes us fear our failures and the weight of our humanity. Weak as we are, we could struggle with our feebleness and risk our failures if only we were not so vulnerable to condemnation by others. Adam may have succumbed to the beseechments of his wife—and what generous and modest man would not?—and Eve to the blandishments of the serpent. But the frailty of human spirit calls for correction and pity. Instead, for a single transgression, we have calamity visited upon us forever.

More striking than the story of the Fall is the tale of Job, for Adam and Eve did in fact sin against God. Job, however, is a deeply devout, pious man. Here it is not the man, but God who is tempted to display Job in his righteousness, and to make light of Satan. Job, in all his travail, does not defy the Lord, but he does curse his own life and his day. It is humanity that he scorns: "Why died I not from the womb?" The life of man is filled with the constant threat of woe, and the fall of the mighty from high places. Job is self-righteous, and asserts that he has not sinned!—but if he has not, then God has mistreated him without reason. How is Job to understand his plight? He has fallen into disarray and there is no way of comprehending it. He is rewarded in the end, but that does not make our understanding greater in the least. All men live surrounded by the possibility of judgment visited upon them; righteousness is of no avail. This is the truth of Job: that men may struggle and must endeavor the good; but nothing they do guarantees that they will achieve it. The curse of men is that they know of good and evil. Whether they will or not, men will be judged as moral agents, and condemned for their failures, without security or peace. Men know too much to be innocent as beasts of the field, but too little to be secure. The possibility of being brought to account haunts whatever they do. They bear on their shoulders a pervasive and unlimited range of responsibilities toward other men and other things, inescapably and unredeemingly.

Surely God is merciful as well as just: how then can men be just without mercy? If human life is a burden of responsibilities, it can be saved from impossible affliction only by mercy and the hope of redemption. The omnipresence of failure in human life must be balanced by an equal measure of the possibility of salvation. Men suffer enough the weight of their responsibilities; they must not equate their responsibilities with the prospects of punishment. Punishment and failure are separate and distinct notions. Otherwise mercy has no meaning.

This essay into the intricacies and confusion of moral responsibility is a study of the burdens of responsibility, of the condition of man as a moral agent held accountable for what he does and fails to do. The subject of moral responsibility divides in *two*—the responsibility of a *responsible person*, who is reliable, trustworthy, and mature; and the responsibilities that all men bear to something, by virtue of which they are judged and held *accountable*. Indeed it may be that a responsible person is one who *meets his responsibilities,* but for the ambiguity which pervades the notion of "meeting" a responsibility. Do we wish to say a responsible person is one who *does what he ought to do?* Colloquially, indeed we do, even if he does so automatically and unthinkingly. Kant's conception of responsibility entails that a responsible act is one which is performed in

obedience to the moral law. But what of Aristotle's point, that a responsible man must be able voluntarily to act wrongly as well as rightly?
What of the historical problem of freedom, that a man who is responsible must be capable of freely doing or failing to do what is right? My
concern is with these latter two aspects of responsibility, so I shall not
concern myself with responsibility as *doing the right thing*. Indeed, an unthinking man may act rightly irresponsibly—meaning unknowingly,
uncritically, insensitively.

The notion of "meeting" one's responsibilities suggests a manner as
well as a substance—a *way* of acting toward one's responsibilities. I shall
interpret the notion of a responsible person as one who adopts a particular manner of acting, a *method* of performance. Given that men are indeed burdened by moral obligations, what are they to do?—that is too
easy: the right thing, of course. But we do not all agree on moral principles and particular obligations. Let us then change the question from
what we are to do, to how we are to determine what we ought to do. A
man who makes that transition, who seeks to determine how to meet his
obligations and the nature of their claims upon him, is one seeking to
meet his responsibilities, a man responsible in his methodic activities if
not righteous in his accomplishments. That is the main substance of my
essay.

It follows from the shift in focus of concern, from *what* we ought to do
to *how* we ought to determine it, that punishment and responsibility no
longer go hand in hand. In fact, we do not always follow transgression
with punishment, though the association of punishment and failure certainly tempts us to simplify our conception of sin, and punish everyone
for what he does and fails to do. Where responsible action is viewed as
the following of a particular method, however, then it is easy to see that
one may follow that method successfully or unsuccessfully. No method
guarantees results. Furthermore, we may consider punishment, and
even simple condemnation, as dependent on methods used as well as
deeds performed. As I shall show, our decision to punish a man is quite
a distinct decision, not one that follows automatically upon his failure.
This is the solution to the unceasing burden of our moral consciousness,
where we may be judged at any time and found wanting:—that we
may have failed, but we are not necessarily to be punished, condemned,
even judged guilty for it. So separate is an act of punishment from the
original failure, that we may often not even be justified in considering a
refusal to punish a transgression to be an act of mercy. It is the punishment which requires justification, not our abstention.

The pervasive responsibility we bear at every moment of our lives is the *accountability* at the heart of moral consciousness; it is the ground of accusation. Each of our failures may be brought to our account. Others survey our actions and hold us responsible for them, and they may judge us to have failed in respects we never thought of. Blindness fills human consciousness, as it surrounds Teiresias and Oedipus. Psychoanalysis and tragedy give testimony to this. The light that is the focal awareness of consciousness is of narrow field of view. Most of what surrounds us, even of what we do and its consequences, remains obscured and hidden. Oedipus is the embodiment of reason, blind nevertheless to his own crimes, and blinded finally by his own hands to symbolize the sterility of his wisdom. Pervasive responsibility represents the ground of judgment within our blindness and ignorance. We may be judged for unknown failures as well as known ones, even for failures no one could have anticipated. Indeed, like Job we may be judged and condemned by others, and by our hidden selves as well, for lapses we have not in fact committed. Psychoanalysis is grounded in the perpetual condition of failure within human life, driven from consciousness yet operative in whatever we do. We hold ourselves and are held to account, for everything in our lives. Pervasive responsibility represents categorically the possibility of failure connected with everything we do, and the possibility of being brought to account.

As Sartre shows in great detail, psychoanalysis represents a considerable portion of our awareness of ourselves—but, he holds, always in bad faith. In particular, psychoanalysis captures our moral condition by a pluralistic and divided sense of human personality. We war within ourselves; we thus become unable to meet the call of our pervasive responsibilities. The fragmentation of psychoanalytic theory adequately reflects a disordered self that cannot meet its responsibilities; but there can be found no holistic self corresponding to responsibility in psychoanalytic theory. That is its weakness.

The very notion of internal psychic divisiveness, with its attendant excuses for our failures, makes plausible the conception of a holistic and integrated personality for whom no excuses hold—that is, one who meets and stands by his responsibilities. Such a man is a *responsible man,* one who *knows what he is doing.* He is conscious of his responsibilities to what surrounds him, and he methodically and knowingly acts consonant with his deepest needs and ideals, to meet the demands placed upon him. No one can fail to have pervasive responsibilities—no one is "not responsible" for anything, if that means "not judgeable" or "not accountable"—but most men are "irresponsible" in what they do, lacking sufficient self-knowledge and self-determination to make what they do count as representative of themselves. In that sense, they are judged and found wanting; they are incapable of ac-counting for their own deeds.

A responsible man stands by his own actions and declares them to be his. He allows no excuses; he did what he had to. It does not follow from this fact alone that he has acted rightly, particularly from the point of view of other men. Although a responsible man has taken steps to avoid the excuses which depend upon lack of self-knowledge, those steps cannot guarantee his success. The pervasive responsibility he bears is a burden of insecurity in action. A responsible man does the best he can, but that may not be good enough.

Conversely, a good man—one who does the right thing most of the time—may not be a responsible man, if he is uncritical about his own grounds of action and insensitive to possibilities which surround him. How then does he act rightly, in the complex and subtle affairs of moral life, if he does not know what he is doing? It seems unlikely to me that reliability in action could be maintained unless connected to profound self-awareness and sensitivity to the environment. Nor do I feel it likely that responsible men will act immorally and destructively. My point is only that it is possible for them to do so. Responsibility entails only the use of a method, which cannot guarantee goodness, no matter how carefully applied.

In this essay, I seek to analyze the concept of responsibility, not of goodness or righteousness. Responsibility is connected with the obligations of men, not their success in meeting them; while mercy entails that we separate failures of men from condemnation and punishment. We seek the nature of the accounts under which we hold other men and ourselves responsible, and which are grounded in methods of judgment and action. It will take another work to analyze the consequences and results of such a method in application, to show its connection with ordinary moral judgments.

1

Responsibility in General

Responsibility in Fact

Although the fundamental concern of this essay is with moral responsibility, it is advisable to begin with the general notion of responsibility, independent of moral matters. The moral elements do not affect the crucial issues as much as might be supposed. This will be made clear by the prior consideration of responsibility in general, and most of all by the investigation of what I call "responsibility in fact," which at first blush appears to be nothing other than the laying of a claim. When asked about the cherry tree, George Washington is supposed to have replied: "I cannot tell a lie, *I did it.*" And truly, he *did* do it! Is it not precisely this sense of responsibility that underlies the legal maxim that parents and children are responsible for each other? If you have a child (in fact), you are responsible for him. Sometimes the fact that a choice was made is of great importance in making judgments of responsibility. But we should not forget that a child is also thought responsible for his parents should they become incapacitated, though no choice of any sort is involved here. Moreover, parents who have children by accident are nevertheless responsible for them. Perhaps there are cases of responsibility that are nothing more than the realization of the facts involved in the situation at hand.

Let us begin with a simple case: a man comes home after a long day at work, tired and weary. He sits down for a moment's relaxation, and his wife asks, "Did you buy the groceries?" He replies, "Yes, I did"—a simple claim of fact. Either he did or he did not. There seems to be no significant problem here. Indeed, I suspect that the statement "I did" would be considered by most readers to be essentially a matter of fact, a simple assertion to be verified or refuted. To this extent, it may be considered plausible that an assertion of responsibility in fact is just that— *in fact*—by which I mean that there is no question here but that of whether the deed in question was performed or not. Either the man did or did not commit the act in question—just as it is a matter of fact whether a rock did or did not roll down a hill, whether an elevator safety mechanism did or did not fail to function. The correct response in this context, if a person hesitates in replying is: "Come now, just tell the truth. All we wish to know are the facts." The word "just" in the preceding quotation, however, is far more important than it seems, as will be shown by the next example, for it marks the fact that the speaker is well aware that telling the truth is not really what is desired, that acceptance of responsibility is not simply a matter of telling the truth.

Suppose in the above case that the man's wife had requested that he buy some things, and had also told him that if he were late or found it inconvenient simply to forget about it. To the above question, he would reply without hesitation, "No, I couldn't make it." This is not a simple fact; it is an excuse. For one thing, he might have been able to do the errand; it would just have been extremely inconvenient. Still, the excuse may well be accepted as legitimate. An untrue statement may sometimes constitute a valid excuse.

Suppose, however, that the man had forgotten the errand completely, that it would have been quite simple for him to do, but he was concerned about other matters. The question "Did you buy the groceries?" here evokes a mixture of guilt and embarrassment. The man does not simply say, without hesitation, "No, I forgot." For one moment, indeed, he is ready to say "Yes" (which is false, so it won't suffice), or "No, I did" (which is quite confusing). The problem is that *in fact* he has not done what he promised he would do—at least, it was not done—but for a silent moment, he wishes to say "I couldn't have forgotten." If he couldn't have forgotten, in a factual sense, then he did what he intended. Though he in fact didn't do what he said he would do, he is nevertheless a responsible person who keeps his word. Somehow a man is at stake here in a way that the mere facts hide. Simply stating the facts of the case obscures the relevance of these facts to judgments about the kind of person who is involved. The only correct description—"I couldn't have forgotten, but I did"—is paradoxical.

Often what a man wishes to do in such a case is to deny that he is to be blamed for what he did or did not do. Somehow it happened, but he was not responsible—at least, not in the way that he would have been responsible if he had done what he should have, or if he had remembered and chosen not to. It is not correct, it seems to me, to say that in such a case a man wishes to *lie*. That view is based on the incorrect belief that "I did it" is nothing but a factual assertion. Although the man is ready to admit that in fact he didn't do what he said he would, the mere fact omits something essential about the situation which he wishes to point out, but cannot find words for. He wishes to deny something, not merely out of fear or guilt, but because he forgot; and his forgetting made him not responsible for failing to do what he promised—at least, not as he would have been if he had remembered and still failed to keep his word. Somehow his failure of memory changes him or the situation. Although in both cases he would not have kept his word, in one his definite choice makes him responsible in a way that his lapse of memory eliminates. What is embodied in the agonized "I couldn't have done that" is one's entire self-image, presented as testimony that one couldn't have committed the lapse, though one knows that *in fact* one did. By the time one has said "I forgot," or "I made a mistake," he has completely reoriented to the new data with its moral implications.

On the surface, the hesitation evinced when a man is challenged for having failed in some way does seem to be due to his implicit or explicit wish to lie. Perhaps we learn early in life that one way to avoid punishment is by lying. Our later experience can show us the practical folly of telling lies, but cannot overcome the momentary relapse into older modes of response. Faced with the accusation, "You did this terrible thing," is it not reasonable (or at least natural and simple) to lie: "No, I didn't." Then, of course, we realize that the lie will not be believed, and refrain from speaking. Why then do I assume that there is more here, involving the person's sense of himself?

The reason is very simple. If guilt is nothing but a response to expected *punishment*, then by the evasion of punishment through lying one may also escape guilt. Under such circumstances, a lie serves the purpose admirably, as long as it eliminates punishment. It fails when it is not only not believed, but recognized for what it is and the punishment increased. If our every action were directed toward escape from externally imposed sanctions, it would be very likely that our momentary disorientation and desire to escape blame would be but an imagined lie, rejected because of its implausibility. However, we not only fear punishment, but experience guilt and remorse, even in the absence of punishment. The view that a lie could serve the purpose of forestalling such reactions is clearly inadequate. It is one thing to say to another, "I didn't do it," so that he will believe you and not condemn you; it is quite different to say it to yourself. We cannot lie to ourselves the same way we lie to others. Yet we hesitate to admit the truth to ourselves as much as to others. What is involved is clear: we seek excuses, not the "facts" alone.

This notion of lying to oneself is at the heart of the notion of bad faith in Sartre's *Being and Nothingness*. Sartre too realizes that a gap exists between a simple factual account and one faithful to the issues of responsibility. We can lie to others and escape their censure. But we cannot lie to ourselves—at least, not about the facts. We can be mistaken or correct; but we cannot be simultaneously correct and also mistaken as a lie to ourselves requires—such a notion entails a completely incoherent sense of personality. What we require are excuses for our failures; and we confuse the giving of excuses with lying about the facts. The key confusion here stems from the supposition that responsibility rests upon facts alone, from which it would follow that all we need do to escape guilt is to carry off a lie. Sartre, however, led by a clear insight into the nature of this confusion, concludes that facts about the past are irrelevant in cases of moral agency. This I take to be his fundamental error. Facts about the past are not completely determinative of responsibility, but they are very important. The problem is to determine just how.

The examples I have presented so far all take for granted a simple act, the commission or omission of which involves guilt and blame. And even here the denial of responsibility is a complex and far from straightforward matter. The facts at issue often seem almost irrelevant, or at least quite unimportant. If so, then the realization that in most cases which raise questions of personal responsibility, the act in question is never simple and complete in itself, but is related to fairly remote consequences, provides further complications that tend to render the whole subject rather bewildering. The relationship between responsibility for an action and something *else* an agent has or might have done will be developed later.

I suspect that my suggestion of the difficulties which arise in appraising a person's guilt will be thought somewhat artificial, particularly when we emphasize not guilt so much as innocence. Deciding whether a man is guilty and to be punished may be a difficult and complex matter. But surely deciding that he is completely innocent is clear and straightforward. If he did not commit the act of which he is accused he is innocent, regardless of anything else. This is not so simple as it appears.

Innocence

Much of the literature of the past hundred years or so has been deeply concerned with the nature of human guilt and the possibility of being innocent. In *The Brothers Karamazov*, Dostoievski has Dmitri say upon dreaming of a starving child: "Why is the babe poor? It's for that babe I am going to Siberia now. I am not a murderer, but I must go to Siberia." We are guilty for *all* the evil in the world. Kafka, in *The Trial*, portrays his hero K. as continually protesting his innocence in the face of general and vague accusations, convincing a thoughtful reader that no one can be as innocent as K. claims to be. Erich Fromm, in *The Forgotten Language*, maintains that what K. is guilty of is his refusal to face himself and his failure as a person—in other words, of failing to realize himself and his potentialities. The problem with such an interpretation is that the statement of what K. is guilty of transforms the nature of his guilt completely. If he can discover the accusation, he can transform the question into one of *fact*. It is precisely the factual nature of the problem that Kafka wishes to avoid. Both Dostoievski and Kafka represent, as a genuine part of human experience, the prospect that no one can ever be completely innocent, that each of us is guilty for some lapse or failure.

The other side of the issue is revealed in the occasional case that comes to our attention in newspapers, or perhaps even more forcefully in mystery novels, in which an innocent man is accused of a monstrous crime and watches the moral and legal forces mustered against him condemn him. So Dmitri stands before the court *innocent* of the murder of his father (though of little else), and finds it possible to come to terms with the accusation only by facing the nature of his real (rather than his alleged) shortcomings. He did not kill his father, but he threatened to, even intended to. He debauched and degraded himself. The very thought of being accused unjustly makes it necessary for him to find something of which he is actually guilty. If innocence were merely a matter of fact, such behavior would make little sense. This above all is what K. fails to understand: he seeks only the factual basis for the accusation against him. Can we really believe that on the Day of Judgment we will be held to account only for the crimes manifest to us? Our most devastating sins may well be those we never knew we committed, or committed only as uninvolved bystanders. On the pathway to hell that is paved with good intentions, do all the penitents understand the nature of their sins? The excuse "I tried, I did my best" is all too often a disguise for evading blame in the very teeth of the facts. Has our century genuinely come to grips with the principle of psychoanalysis that parents are contributory causes of their children's failures and misery, that in the fulfilling of their own needs, conscious or not, they harm their children irreparably? Are such parents truly innocent, even if they did not know what they were doing?

The horror we feel when confronted with a man unjustly accused of a crime does not and cannot stem from the nature of the facts involved alone. (And why do we say "unjustly" rather than "incorrectly" accused except to emphasize the complexity of the moral issues involved?) In contrast, the blind and purposeless workings of nature, whatever catastrophic effects they entail, are neither unjust nor evil. To stand in Pompeii and imagine the sky black with smoke and red with flame leads to horror and pity, not outrage and indignation. The so-called "problem of evil" takes its meaning from the view that a divinely just intelligence orders all things, whereupon nature takes on an aura of malignity that she otherwise does not have. We are outraged at the injustice of God, but only resigned to the inclemency of events. However, a man wrongfully accused of a crime—especially wrongfully convicted of a crime—need conceive of no malignity to feel the horror of his condition, and that quite independent of the punishment proposed. Injustice is hideous where facts are merely indifferent, however hard they may be.

The innocent man cries out his innocence. Can we say that he speaks to the heedless stars, to the immutable laws of nature, even to the cold and fact-oriented court and jury? Would he be saved by a mere fact, a piece of information? The evidence stands against him; the facts are gathered and interpreted, and he is accused. Is he accused by the facts? Facts cannot accuse and blame. He is accused by men, and held to account for the facts. Accusation is not merely a factual assertion, nor is a claim of innocence merely the assertion of its logical contradictory.

Yet we settle claims of innocence by explicit appeals to fact. "The de-

fendant could not have committed the crime because he was with me
when it was committed." Agency entails enactment. Without enactment, we have the absence of agency and release from blame. When
guilt is laid for the performance of a specific act, then innocence is simply having failed to perform that act. "I am innocent" seems to speak of
facts, then, as "I am not guilty" may fail to do; for there is clearly more
to guilt than the simple performance of an act.

If only the performance of an act were a simple thing; then perhaps
innocence would be nothing more than a matter of fact. The problem is
that once the question has been raised as to whether a man has actually
performed a given deed, it becomes extremely difficult to answer. What
is the act which constitutes patricide—the will, the decision, the motive,
desire, or imaginary enactment? Or is it but the final physical deed? Is
Dmitri Karamazov really innocent? The driver of a car which struck a
child who ran suddenly in his path protests his innocence, though he
knows only too well that without the physical event he rejects, there
would be no question of guilt or innocence. He did it, but he is innocent! Is it perhaps only because he did not *intend* to strike the child?
What then of the drunken driver whom we hold completely responsible? He did not intend to run off the road. What also of the busybody
whose existence is a constant attempt to interfere with the lives of others, from the best of motives, but without concern for the pain and disturbance such interference creates? Or the parent, who continually protests that he seeks the good of his child in his constant manipulation and
domination: can he too protest his innocence when his child rebels
against everything his parent thinks good? Consider especially the over-
protective parent, who fails to develop in his child a regard for others:
may he claim that he is innocent because he did not intend harm, that
he too could not know or anticipate the consequences? Do we ever
stand before an evil deed having done *everything* we could have done to
prevent it, thus completely innocent of it? Is anyone so innocent as to
deserve the "complete acquittal" that the painter Titorelli tells K. in
The Trial will certainly be given to an innocent man?—though no one
to Titorelli's knowledge has ever been completely acquitted. Is it not remarkable that it is the Raskolnikovs and Dmitri Karamazovs who may
be on the path to redemption when they admit guilt, regardless of the
actual status of their actions, while those who plead innocence simply
evade confronting the quality of their actions? It may well be that a
claim of innocence is at its heart only a self-righteous denial of one's
moral nature.

Unquestionably, facts are necessary to the existence of situations in

which matters of guilt and innocence arise. Questions of guilt and innocence are rooted in genuine existential conditions. But it does not follow
from this that guilt and innocence are matters of fact. Indeed, the facts
set the stage upon which guilt and innocence are decided, but they are
tied to issues which go far beyond the mere facts involved.

Perhaps the distinction I have made, between being *not guilty* and
being *innocent,* merits further examination. Clearly the complexity of
being not guilty is very great, for it is precisely the same complexity as
that of being guilty, and I have shown some of the difficulties involved
here. But is it not true that one can be innocent in a very simple and
straightforward manner, by not having committed the act in question?
Put another way, may we not say that innocence and guilt form the two
extremes of a scale whose middle region is of primary interest to us?
They are not complementary terms; there is a middle region—of being
neither guilty nor innocent—that gives rise to the problems I have mentioned.

If so, we may be tempted to relegate all the complex issues to that
middle region, assuming that simple cases of guilt and innocence—at
least at the very extremes—can be found without difficulty. Perhaps
most actions of men are neither necessary nor sufficient conditions of
their consequences, but some examples can be found where things are
much simpler. For example, a hired assassin shoots and kills his victim
from a rooftop. He is unequivocally guilty here, and it would not seem
that complicating factors need be brought in. On the other hand, a man
accused of a crime may be proved innocent by evidence that he was in
another city at the time, so couldn't (and therefore did not) commit the
crime he is accused of. Surely such cases are clear and straightforward.

Unfortunately, actual situations are complicated by factors not taken
into account in the above simple portrayals. For example, what if the
assassin had had his life threatened if he did not carry out the murder?
Or if his family were held hostage? Or if he had been taught that only
success and wealth mattered in this world? Or if he believed that a better world would result from his act of political assassination? Surely the
quality, nature, even the extent of his guilt is not the same in all these
cases. But I have dealt with these complexities already: guilt is a very
difficult concept to deal with in real cases involving moral judgments.

The same issues arise concerning innocence, though. Suppose the
man in question had been out of town but had hired an assassin to commit the crime? Suppose he had fired a gun with intent to kill, but
missed—and the victim died of a heart attack? Suppose a man in another town had overheard the plans being made for the murder, but

said nothing? What if but a couple of votes might have led to the passage of a gun control bill that would have made the assassination unlikely? Who was truly innocent of the crucifixion of Christ? In *The Brothers Karamazov*, Dostoievski makes very clear the fact that Dmitri, *who did not kill his father*, is nevertheless not innocent of his death, because of Dmitri's lack of self-control, his murderous intentions, and because his general behavior provided a means for the real murderer to escape punishment. Ivan too is guilty, if in a less direct and legally prosecutable manner, of having promulgated doctrines which could be expected to have murder as their consequence. Moreover, he was virtually asked by Smerdyakov in advance to accept or not accept the crime, and had only the excuse that he "didn't know." Like all men who blind themselves to reality, he should have known. Neither Ivan nor Dmitri is innocent, though neither committed the actual crime. Not even Alyosha is innocent, for he became so intent on his own needs that he neglected his obligations to those around him. Intentions, wishes, passions, and knowledge are the substance of which judgments of innocence and guilt are composed. It is true that in courts of law matters of guilt and innocence are often simplified. This is sometimes necessary if any judgment at all is to be reached. But the nature of such simplifications must not be overlooked.

The complexities of guilt and innocence no doubt stem from the complexity of human actions. There is no simple sense in which we may claim a given event to belong to one particular person, which is what is involved in assigning responsibility. Just when are we justified in claiming an action to belong to a particular person? Dmitri seems to tell us that all pain and anguish in the world belong to each of us. Donne's lovely Seventeenth Devotion speaks to the same effect:

> No man is an *Iland*, intire of itselfe; every man is a piece of the *Continent*, a part of the *maine;* if a *Clod* bee washed away by the *Sea*, *Europe* is the lesse, as well as if a *Promontorie* were, as well as if a *Mannor* of thy *friends* or of thine *owne* were; any man's *death* diminishes *me*, because I am involved in *Mankinde;* And therefore never send to know for whom the *bell* tolls; It tolls for *thee*.

Unfortunately, this seems to render the claim that a given man is responsible for something in particular quite as vacant as the claim that he is responsible for nothing. Many people interpret the claim that all are guilty to entail that therefore none really are. I shall argue that such an interpretation is illegitimate. A proper understanding of condemnation will show that what is of importance is the *act* of condemnation. Though all men may have failed in many ways, it is justifiable to condemn only some of them.

However, when nothing more is said, such passages as the above seem to render us brothers under the skin before a universal failure for which none of us is responsible. It is in this line that so many Germans would have us remember American support for Hitler and the refusal of so many Western countries to accept Jewish refugees when they could have saved them. We are all murderers, and therefore Cain was one no more than you or I. Until we know which are a particular agent's acts, by which he stands or falls, as against actions that belong equally to everyone, we do not quite face the complexities of responsibility. On the other hand, if we construe the possession of an act narrowly, so that it repudiates Donne's vision, we permit men to escape their responsibilities by simply neglecting them. Some initial impetus is needed to impel men to face the world with responsibility. The view that everyone is responsible for everything at least has the merit of escaping the claim that a man is innocent insofar as he was ignorant of what was happening.

Consider my friend who, in taking my well-meant advice, is thrown into financial ruin, and who in attempting to survive sets up a chain of events that results in someone else's death. I could not have known what would happen. I am surely not to blame for the death. Yet, can I really say that I am *innocent?* Was it not my act that was instrumental in the chain of events? I did not wish the death, intend it, nor prefer it; but I am nevertheless partly responsible for it. So also is the scientist responsible whose discoveries bear military fruit, the results of which are greater pain and suffering in the world—though he did not use the weapon, nor would he have condoned its use if asked. The consequences of one's actions are themselves events which belong partly to one; and if they were not anticipated, either they should have been, or they call for a reevaluation of one's moral attitudes and practices. Perhaps this latter judgment is too strong; but the point is that we must, if we are to judge guilt and innocence, take consequences of indefinite range into account. Furthermore, we cannot limit responsibility to immediate actions if we are to control and direct our actions into more productive channels. The remote consequences of our actions can be the most important. We often wish to say to a man who pleads generous intent and ignorance of the consequences of his actions: "You should have known—or at least thought about—what would happen."

Though I have criticized this view above, we often seem to judge a claim on the basis of *intent*. Kant in fact based moral evaluation solely on the maxim of intended action, for he construed the basis of moral judgment to be what he called the "good will": one which respects law for itself. This plausible view must be examined, through an analysis of intention and will.

Intention

In his *Grundlegung*, Kant points out that "in fact, it is absolutely impossible to make out by experience with complete certainty a single case in which the maxim of an action, however right in itself, rested simply on moral grounds and on the conception of duty. . . . In fact we can never, even by the strictest examination, get completely behind the secret springs of action; since, when the question is of moral worth, it is not with the actions which we see that we are concerned, but with those inward principles of them which we do not see." I am not at all ready to agree that we are *solely* concerned with inward principles in moral judgment, but there is little doubt that intention or will is fundamental to moral action. Kant seems to tell us that these can never be known.

Some effort might be expended in considering the words "with complete certainty" above, since perhaps we cannot be *certain* of a man's motives, but may come very close to the truth in surmising them. Kant seems to be asserting something stronger than mere scepticism, though, and this is that intentions and motives are thoroughly "inward" or "internal" and that our judgments of human actions are based on *external* manifestations of these original sources. Intentions are *states of mind;* and because another's mind is hidden from us, we can only use external indications of what transpires within. We may suppose a man to act out of simple moral conviction when at great inconvenience to himself, he assists someone who seems not to be gratified even by the act of charity. But Kant's view is that we can do so only hypothetically, since the evidence in such a case can never guarantee the presence of a given state of mind. It seems that to Kant, the presence or absence of intentions of a specified sort denotes an inward state of mind.

Let us, however, take into consideration three examples of intention to gain perspective on the issues involved. Consider again Dmitri Karamazov, who is enraged at his father for his past crimes as well as for his present refusal to give Dmitri money he needs for his honor; who comes to his father's house expecting to rob him; who strikes in his rage a servant who had befriended him; and who actually enters his father's room to kill him. We may, of course, view all of these as *evidence* supporting the view that Dmitri intended to (and did) kill his father. In this case, we must also envisage the possibility that our hypothesis is wrong. But how could it be? Is it not clear by Dostoievski's later account of Dmitri's sense of guilt that Dmitri is quite clear about his former intentions? Though he can deny the act of murder, can Dmitri genuinely deny his *intention* to kill his father? If he did so, would we not feel far more justified in responding, "I don't know what you mean when you say you didn't intend to murder your father," rather than, "I don't *believe* you when you declare that you had other intentions"? The latter is the only way to construe Dmitri's claim of innocence if his actions are but evidence of his intent. If his actions comprise part if not all of his intentions, then we may see by his behavior what he intended. Dmitri too accepts his guilt as a degraded, evil man—on the basis of his actions, not his thoughts alone.

Moreover, consider a burglar who *thinks* only of silencing an unexpected occupant of the house he has entered, but who strikes and kills him. Or similarly, consider the parent who thinks only of his child's ultimate happiness, but whose righteousness and restrictiveness drive the child to self-destruction. Sometimes we ask such men, "How can you ask us to believe your intentions?" But we often say also, "Your actions *are* your intentions: you stuck to silence, even if it meant murder!" "You failed to consider consequences of your actions that a reasonable man might have foreseen. Men simply do not do such things unless they intend to, though they may be ambivalent about them."

Here we are led into some of the considerations of psychoanalysis and its claims about unconscious motives and intentions. Typically a psychoanalyst, confronting a patient without friends, asks "What do you do to repel people?" and further, "Why don't you want friends?" The treatment is successful when the patient comes to the realization that indeed he has, by his actions, *chosen* to isolate himself. It would have been so easy for him to have won people to him. Only intentional activity on some level could have so successfully made him fail. Psychoanalysis preserves the identification of intentions with effective behavior, in judging that certain kinds of behavior on the part of an individual mark that behavior to be intentional. Therefore, if the patient has not been aware of "intending," in the sense of exerting conscious acts of will, it makes considerable sense in psychoanalysis to speak of "unconscious intentions."

The concept of intention is often considered to be defensible only

when entailing consciousness. Unconscious intention seems to be a specious notion, called an "intention" only out of some sense of analogy. As
a contemporary philosopher puts it, "there is no contradiction or conceptual confusion in the phrase 'unconscious purposes.' The confusion
arises only if intention is separated from consciousness." * The same
identification of consciousness, self-consciousness, and intentional action
is at the heart of Sartre's *Being and Nothingness*. Such philosophers hold
the notion of *unconscious anger,* and other types of unconscious feeling, to
be flagrant misnomers. Yet the justification the psychoanalyst gives is
simply that the feelings of which the patient is aware are often quite ineffective, particularly when it would seem that they should be most
efficacious. The patient who weeps when he is attacked may discover
that pain and self-pity are quite his last concern, that his momentary
(and suppressed) reaction, which emerges consciously in later stages of
treatment, is of an intensity of hatred and anger which he cannot endure or control, so he takes refuge in tears. The discovery of such unconscious mental qualities is based on the *subsequent* behavior and
thoughts of the patient, as he acts on the basis of and reacts to hypotheses proposed by the psychoanalyst. He *verifies* his judgments concerning
intentions by the feelings which ensue upon the promulgation of these
judgments. He learns, that is, what he is, what kind of person he is,
through discovering what he becomes. It is this peculiarity of the temporal relations of the psychoanalytic self that complicates the understanding of emotions and intentions provided by psychoanalysis.

More properly, however, this last claim should be reversed: it is the
peculiarity of the temporal aspects of a person and his intentions that
psychoanalysis throws into high relief. The intentions of a person do not
alone reside in his behavior or thoughts at a particular time, but in his
future as well—especially when he accepts responsibility or offers excuses for repudiating it. It is at once the great strength and overwhelming danger of psychoanalytic theory that it grounds the giving of excuses by human beings in the total conception of the agent's being as a
person. The simple equating of intentions with behavior overlooks
something that the mentalistic analysis of intentions recognizes the need
to preserve—the emphasis on the *will,* if you wish, or more accurately
on a dimension of human action above and beyond, though not independent of, behavior. I have suggested that it is often quite appropriate
to respond to a person's actions by saying, "so your intentions were so
and so," not as something else which his behavior is evidence for, but to

* Stuart Hampshire, *Thought and Action* (New York: Viking, 1960), p. 133.

show that his behavior *identifies* his intentions. The appeal to the concept of the will, however, to allow an individual to respond, "I admit I did what you accuse me of, but I didn't *mean* (intend or will) to," shows that something more than a person's behavior alone is relevant here.

The sense of a self existing and changing in time is what is required; and it is the strength of psychoanalysis that it seeks to explain and modify behavior by generating an organized (if theoretically incoherent) sense of a person as agent. The thread of unity in a person's apparently disorganized behavior may be far more apparent to an expert observer than to the agent himself, if psychoanalytic theory is correct. (And on this topic, most people would agree that it is.) Here it is clear that an agent need not necessarily "know what he is doing," nor even what he is trying to do. (He may, of course, have a goal in mind, or he may not. But he needn't know the "real" reason for his behavior.) If we proceed from this and identify intentional behavior, consciousness, and "knowing what one is doing," then what psychoanalysis suggests is that much if not all human action is intentional, but not conscious. In terms of his total personality, a man does not know what he is doing if his act fails to fit into a coherent set of policies exhibitive of himself. When the psychoanalyst reveals the unity of a patient's being to be related to elements of his past of which he has been unaware, the analyst casts serious doubt on the importance and meaning of the inconsistent and disorganized intentions that the patient is consciously aware of.

The unity of self involved here is something above and beyond a simple itemization of an individual's behavioral responses. Yet it cannot be dealt with solely by an appeal to a mental act or experience of will. A person may well not have thought in advance of taking action, "I intend to do such and such," and yet not wish to deny that he intended to do it. What is involved is clearly a matter of accepting or denying responsibility—therefore we will not be able to analyze responsibility in terms of will or intention, for all of these concepts are far too directly related and intimately dependent on each other for such an analysis to provide any but minimal intelligibility.

What seems clear is that a person who states his intentions, either for the future, or to explain his past behavior, is telling us to look at his behavior in a certain light—that cast by acceptance or repudiation of responsibility. He is describing to us the way in which his action is related to his total being. "I intended to do it, and take possession of the act and all its consequences." The claim that a person's behavior reveals his intentions generally implies that his behavior can be viewed reasonably in only one light. His denial—"I was careless and unthinking"—is an attempt to show us another, plausible way of looking at the same action, such that he is not to be held to account for it.

Appeal to excuses, will, intentions, or motives will not, then, save us from the complexities of the central problems of responsibility, for the former are all ways of dealing with responsibility, not its components. The fundamental issue generally is that a man stands before an event and is asked to accept it as his or to repudiate possession of it. We must turn to the notion of a self and its possessions and consider the analysis of how a person can be said to possess an event or action, or under what circumstances he can be said to have been superficially involved yet not to have been responsible for what happened.

It is worth exploring this point a bit further: the problem that confronts us is that a man's intentions are neither a simple mental state for which his actions are evidence, nor are they the actions themselves, at least in any simple equivalence. We might, of course, seek a way out of the apparent impasse by holding psychological states to be a *union* of action and feeling, but for the fact that such a union is quite unintelligible and as such indefensible. No doubt feelings are themselves part of or evidence for the existence of intentions or motives, and the actions which parallel or support them constitute the remainder of the evidence or are the motives themselves; but the union of these is no simple sum, nor does it offer a well-defined point of demarcation. Furthermore, our judgment of the motives of others would then be thoroughly crippled, since their feelings at least are hidden from us. On the other hand, if we repudiate the feelings altogether, by turning to behaviorism of one sort or another, we must cope with such pleas as that of the parent that his actions are not a sufficient account of his will, just as the footracer who loses may well claim that his failure is not of will or desire, but of body or skill. I may will an act, I may fail my intent, and I may altogether fail to intend by doing nothing. I may act with skill and grace, quickly and apparently with passion, but may fail when I should not have—to which others reply, "You didn't really intend to win (want to win)." Such an accusation may always be made upon failure. Under what conditions do we accept it?

It is a mistake to construe such an accusation to be without significant empirical content—that is, unverifiable. Although I tried (you can see my bruises), and wanted to succeed (measured by my anxiety), perhaps I failed because of some underlying negation of my overt state. I didn't want to succeed and become a spectacle; I didn't want to try with all my might and still fail, so I failed without trying very hard. The truth is not easy to uncover, but it is determinable, and measured by the realization of my *true* state of being. But what can possibly tell us the difference between felt and observed states and one's "true" state? I am suggesting that if there is any answer to this question, it rests in the total self under consideration, viewed in its temporal relations from past to future. I discover that I am genuinely crippled by self-loathing, that I so despise myself as to produce my own failures—which further substantiates my view of myself. I view my past in its total orientation to my present actions to discover just how these actions fit into it; and I discover in the future, in terms of feelings of relief or pain, whether this interpretation is correct or not.

I thus discover *myself,* and thereby *come to know* what is my intention. The latter is neither an isolated feeling nor an overt series of actions, but is my self in its moment of truth confronting the necessity of action. However I act, my intentions are bound within—though by no means as I may wish, desire, or consciously know. Neither the act performed, nor the feelings accompanying it, are quite my intention. There is always the possibility of failure, however worthy the intention, and I may fail to recognize my general being in the world. My intent is nothing less than myself, in its fullness, confronting a particular choice. The choice calls forth *my* action, and it focuses me upon itself. I intend to do what I, being who and what I am, am led to in this act. In this moment I stand completely summed up, adopting a point of view toward the world and toward myself that is my intention. Only this enables me to call it *my* intention, and the act *my* act.

*A*ction

An act of a person is an event which exists in space and time, characterized most essentially by the fact that it is an act of a *particular* person, which belongs to *him* in some special sense. Some events belong to no one at all and simply come and go in the flux of things; other events are guided, intended, sought, and achieved by men with purpose and desire. Many versions of the doctrine of divine immanence—God endowing every event with His presence and meaning—fail to make this distinction, and subordinate the simple and unguided event to an act of divine will. The mechanical model, particularly when viewed from without in an extra-natural perspective, does the reverse, by turning human actions into events which simply occur, which belong to no one. If the universe is a machine, run according to fixed and immutable laws, then any particular event belongs only to the universe as a whole, to space and time in their mechanical movement. If there are no purposeless events, then a science which eliminates human destiny and value from its significant variables is completely empty; if there are no actions, then the movements of men pale into mechanical rhythms and moral vacuity. At least, before choosing one or another of these extreme paths, let us determine what status of possession human actions have— what exactly belongs to a person in his experience?

The possessive in this case is by no means the possessive in phrases like "my land," "my legal rights," even "my job." The latter exist in a context of explicit social or legal conventions which define the act of possession. My property is registered in some official file in some governmental office—otherwise it is not fully "mine." Even where no legal structure defines the possession of property, some code is presupposed which may be thought to define possession—if only use, occupation, or an appeal to force. When Marx speaks of the labor theory of value in which a man at least can say that his labor is his, this is clearly meant to contrast a value judgment on the possession of labor and its fruits to the social convention that a man's labor belongs to the person he sells it to for wages. Even natural rights, though perhaps not formally registered with the proper authorities, are defined by conventional rules, though not necessarily arbitrary ones. My right to freedom of speech is defined by the constitution of the country in which I live. Without it I can only point to implicit social rules or the common law which define these rights as mine. This is why Hobbes is partly correct to deny the existence of rights apart from society, and yet oddly inconsistent when he speaks of the natural right of men to preserve their lives. Until such a right is formally accepted, it is no *right:* it is but a fact of life. On the other hand, if there are no rules controverting it, I cannot be denied the right either. I am therefore in an anomalous position in claiming any natural rights, unless I believe that they are inherent in the very character of my being.

The possession of an act may be thought of as the most fundamental form of possession, for it is presupposed in the rules which define other modes of possession. An object is mine if I claim it, occupy it, have built it, or the like—that is, if an *act of mine* satisfies whatever criteria are in force which define the possession of property. If I failed to file a claim properly, though I intended to, the property is not mine. If I make a will to leave my property to someone who has coerced me so that it may be shown that I was not responsible for that act, he may not claim the property as his.

Some fundamental sense of ownership is involved here, and it is not easy to determine what it is. The claim that a particular act belongs to someone cannot be said to depend on straightforward rules as do other modes of possession, yet the latter depend on it. Although some conventions exist for the determination of responsibility, only very few of them define possession. They implicitly assume the claim, and define the circumstances under which such a claim may be considered open to sanction. What then renders an action mine as against another's, mine alone, mine even though I repudiate it? And what does repudiation mean if an act seems to be or was in fact mine?

Traditional modes of analysis rely on two criteria, with an occasional attempt to combine them. An act is mine if it is performed by my body; or it is mine if it is antedated by an act of my will, created by a conscious decision inspired by a conscious motive; or occasionally if it is both willed *and* enacted by my body. I am inclined to consider these views of human action quite distorted accounts of responsibility and possession, arising from inadequate accounts of the human self included in the judgment. Man is neither entirely a complexly-behaving material object whose mind is but an epiphenomenon of no great consequence; nor is he but a mind inhabiting a body of another mode of existence; nor may he be viewed successfully as a combination of these once they have been freely separated. There are moments in all lives, though most often in what we consider cases of severe pathology, in which we virtually stand back from our actions and watch our own bodies with horror. A suicide is seldom of *one mind* while destroying himself. His ambivalence is experienced as a denial of the very act his body is performing. The shy and awkward adolescent, speaking to the pretty girl, may well think to himself that his fumbling is not really himself, that he is something more than this weak body which does things he does not approve of. So also the harshly-reared adolescent girl, whose sexual urges lead her to behavior she feels is wrong, often takes refuge in the claim that these are not *her* actions. Sartre calls this kind of denial an act of bad faith: one is free and responsible for whatever one does, and a person who denies that his deeds belong to him is lying, to himself and others. I believe that Sartre, disturbed by the plausibility of excuses which depend upon the complexity of human actions, arbitrarily simplifies the latter notion and introduces bad faith to account for the difficult cases. Some very clear cases are very like the ones above—for example, where our bodies are appropriated by others against our de-

sires and will. A woman who has been sexually assaulted denies the act
to have been hers, despite the violation of her body. Some people, it is
true, judge an act to be nothing but its bodily form; here the form of
virginity is considered essential, not the meaning or value of the sexual
act. But even in the Catholic Church, emphasis is placed on desire and
concurrence for an act to be sin. The man whose hand holding a knife is
forced back to his own body has not killed himself. My body participates in any of my actions; but it is not true that everything it does or is
forced to do by others is an act of mine. It often seems to be appropriate
to admit that one did in fact perform a given deed (meaning that one's
body was causally involved), and deny that one meant to. There is a
gap between the physical act and the act as mine, I who could not want
to, and therefore did not, commit the act. Returning to what was said
before, although my body was a causal factor in the event under consideration, I am *innocent*—the act was not mine.

The problematic character of such a claim of innocence is evident. It
is by no means clear that we are justified in repudiating an action as
ours when we have participated in it. Is not the fearful onlooker in the
mob, who participates in its frenzy from fear of reprisal, as much responsible for its actions as the leaders? There are complex and difficult
problems here, and bodily participation is only one of the factors to
consider. Is not a man who joins others out of fear, but suffers the
awareness of horror at his deeds, less blameworthy in some fashion than
the others? A man is always something more than his body, which may
be appropriated and manipulated by others. Some of its acts are not his.
Yet clearly we wish to avoid extending this notion to the point that no
action belongs to anyone, for where then would responsibility lie?

It is to place responsibility or possession of actions more clearly that
men have turned to the will, motives, or intentions: an action is mine if
I willed it, chose it, wanted it, or intended it. That there is often a mental component which accompanies actions we accept as ours is quite apparent, but it is neither decisive nor even necessary. I may will my hand
to move when it is exhausted from overexertion; the jerky, uncontrolled
motion is not what I willed, but it is my act. I may intend to be com-
radely and jolly by slapping my friend on his back, but if I hurt him it is
an act of mine. When a man consciously intends only to be clever and
charming in uttering cutting remarks and cruel thrusts, which nevertheless injure others and anger them, his (conscious) intentions and his
actions fall apart into discontinuity. When he says that he did not intend to hurt anyone, but his victims show that he nevertheless did hurt
them, we can interpret the situation only to show that a man may act in

ways he may not consciously intend. If we go on and claim that a man could not have acted so contrary to his overt intentions unless he in some way wished or intended to, this does not alter the quality of the original claim, since the impasse can be resolved only by introducing unconscious desires and intentions. The value of the latter is in resolving the feeling of incommensurability between the act and the agent in such cases as we have been considering. When a man discovers more to himself than he was aware of, then he begins to see (intuit or feel) how this act of his is indeed fully his—something he failed to understand before.

I can accept an act as mine only when I understand myself and how the action follows from what I am, both bodily and spiritually. My slip of the tongue is but a blind and meaningless event until it is made part of me by showing how it is a rational consequence of what I am. My stumbling and clumsiness are but empty errors until it is revealed that they are not merely physical events, but to be understood in terms of my feelings and surreptitious goals. When I discover in myself the source of my acts, then I can genuinely claim them to be mine.

On the other hand, I deny the claim and plead my innocence when my body was the causal agent but disconnected from my feelings and intentions. I may have committed the act in question, but I was somehow absent or unthinking. If I had thought more carefully, or if I had known more than I did, I would not have done what I did. I did it, but it was a mistake. Do not hold me responsible; I was not fully involved; the act was not really mine. I indeed stole the money—you found it in my pocket—but I was not fully myself at the time. My emotional state crippled me. I am, at least in this sense, partly innocent. I refuse to accept what I did as mine.

Such denials are common; yet it is by no means clear just what they involve. I intend in the rest of this essay to develop an analysis of what is involved in responsibility and the right to make and deny claims such as the above. Without doubt, what is involved in accepting or denying responsibility, even when there is no moral issue at hand, is wrapped up in the nature of man's conception of himself. This will be taken up in the next chapter.

The strength of psychoanalysis, in the face of fairly strong philosophic objections to its methodology and conceptual commitments, is that it develops a conception of a total person in order to explain particular events in that person's life. It shows that a person's actions indeed follow from his basic nature, and that the influences upon and patterns within his personality are always at work. The drawback of psychoanalysis is that it achieves a unified conception of a person's life and personality only by a theoretical framework that is fundamentally incoherent. It unifies the life of a person by an appeal to a fundamental disunity in its conception of the human being, by installing at the heart of human personality a pluralism of competing forces. This is a very serious fault, and will be analyzed in detail.

Before considering the notion of a unified human self, however, it is necessary to take up again the notion of facts and their relationship to responsibility. For despite the complexity of judgments of responsibility, there is some basis in fact for them. Causal information may not be sufficient as a basis for judgments of responsibility, but the latter must depend in some fashion on them. Certainly the sense of unity of the self is not independent of causal facts.

The Facts of Responsibility

The difficulties presented above concerning the ascription of responsibility on the basis of physical involvement in and causal relationship to a given act do not appear to do justice to the problems involved. It may be difficult to place responsibility on the basis of facts external to the life, history, and feelings of the person involved; but it is essential that we be able to do so, at least *prima facie*. The complexities of the possession of an action depend upon the existence of some simple characteristics of responsibility. We could not even begin to speak of responsibility if connections could not be made between the physical actions of a person and the events he is responsible for. What has been shown in the past few pages is that the nature, size, or causal significance of a physical act is not determinative of the extent of responsibility of the agent for it; but *some* physical contribution appears to be necessary.

On the other hand, placing the physical contribution is not as straightforward as it may seem. Consider the fact that we usually lay blame on a person only if his actions comprise part of the cause of the event we are concerned with. A parent is responsible for his child's later choices and mistakes only insofar as his own acts affect the behavior and character of his child. A murderer is responsible for his deed because the contraction of his finger is the cause of the gun firing, which is the direct cause of his victim's death. If there is no causal connection, there would seem to be little basis for a judgment of guilt. A plea of innocence often consists in the assertion, "I didn't commit the crime," which is a denial that any of the agent's physical movements is a partial cause of the crime. The agent may claim further that although his physical movements were causal factors in the event under consideration, they do not make him responsible; but he must first be involved in the mode of causal efficacy for that denial to make sense.

It is interesting that on this basis, Donne's assertion that "no man is an Ilande," and Dmitri Karamazov's plea that we are all guilty for the starving child, make no sense. It is quite clear that there are events in the world to which a man contributes nothing, which are causally independent of his physical actions. It is not true that there is always something that every man might have done to prevent or ameliorate every crime. May I not say that I am innocent just because my actions did not causally lead to the crime? If I am physically uninvolved, am I not fully innocent?

Two examples, however, immediately come to mind. Were there not Germans who did not join the Nazi party, who led simple lives quite unmotivated by hatred and dreams of world-conquest, who failed to discern the terrible events taking place in their country? Are they completely innocent? Can we not demand of them that they should have known? There are sins of omission as well as commission: can we not demand that men should act where they fail to—particularly when their actions might well make a difference? Here, of course, there is a genuine causal efficacy—their failure to act is a definite causal determinant of later events. But what if I believe that *however* I act, the results will be the same? Am I justified then in doing nothing? Hannah Arendt, in *Eichmann in Jerusalem*, discusses this plea with great force. She quotes a German physician who explained his lack of rebellion by setting forth the danger and meaninglessness of opposition: "None of us had a conviction so deeply rooted that we could have taken upon ourselves a practically useless sacrifice for the sake of a higher moral meaning," to which Miss Arendt replies: "The lesson of such stories is simple and within everybody's grasp. Politically speaking, it is that under conditions of terror most people will comply but *some people will not.*" Such rationalized cowardice is among the most destructive of human excuses. It promotes the worst atrocities under the guise of necessity. Only when it is accepted as a legitimate excuse does it become true that open opposition is useless and merely self-destructive; it is not true until most people believe it to be true; it possesses that sort of self-fulfillment at its heart. In fact, the plea that my action will have no significant consequences ("will be practically useless") is usually false—particularly if I

am not the only one willing to act regardless of consequences. Moreover, it simply does not relieve me of responsibility for the actions I
might have undertaken but did not. Dmitri discovers that he cannot remain uninvolved without concern for others. Ivan discovers that remote
and quite unintended consequences of his actions are brought to his account, from which he cannot escape. The man who, horrified at the
events surrounding him, becomes paralyzed and unable to act, is far
more responsible for the continuation of these events than the man who
struggles ineptly to improve them and who indeed may provoke retaliation. The man who refuses to oppose the invaders of his city cannot
plead less guilt than the man who, in rebelling, causes the murder of
hostages. The last thing I wish to do here is to legislate which of these is
the "correct" or "right" thing to do—indeed, both may be right, if enacted under the proper acceptance of risk, by different individuals—nor
do I believe it possible to legislate such matters abstractly. The point is
that both men are guilty or innocent, although only the fighter risks
causal involvement. One does not gain innocence by refraining from
risk. Direct causal efficacy is not necessary for the laying of responsibility.

Perhaps it may be felt that causal efficacy is at least necessary, as a
minimal condition of responsibility, in that unless something one could
do would accomplish the desired goal, one cannot be responsible for a
failure to reach that goal. Perhaps the German mentioned above was
certain and even correct that nothing he could do would have saved the
life of a single Jew. Is he still responsible for trying? Hannah Arendt's
second point is that if only a few had *tried*, in the teeth of evidence that
alone each would have accomplished nothing, then together they would
probably have been able to nullify much of the force of the Final Solution. The latter could have been so successfully implemented only if everyone involved was efficiently dedicated to carrying it out. A man *may*
not be responsible for a deed if nothing he could have done would have
prevented it. But he may be responsible for not trying. Moreover, his
trying may make like deeds possible for others. Finally, when can a
man be sure of impossibility? His tentative judgments may be implicit
cowardice. We may well condemn a man who offers impossibility as an
excuse for not acting on his principles, regardless of moral consequences. Causal efficacy is not a critical component of responsibility,
but only a factor to be weighed with others.

This becomes clearer if it is recognized that one's actions are never
necessary nor sufficient conditions of other events, that causal relations
among real events are usually so unclear and arbitrary that the ascrip-

tion of physical responsibility is usually quite insignificant. There is virtually no act which in itself has specific necessary consequences: something may always interfere. I may plan to rob a bank, but be in an automobile accident on the way. My plans for the improvement of society by revolution may be upset by the Army, even by reforms within society as it stands. My gift of charity may weaken and destroy those I wish to aid. At best, my actions are far from sufficient, only a contribution to the general flow of things. In addition, no specific human action is itself necessary to any other event, since there is almost always some other way of effecting it. If I refuse to fight for certain goals, there are others who may and will. I may not exercise my right to vote, but others will, and may elect the same man. What then can be meant by the claim that an action is causally related to its consequences, since it is neither necessary to nor sufficient for them?

This, it seems to me, is the central problem of responsibility: that a man is responsible for events of this world in terms of his own actions, and yet it is impossible to relate these to him causally in a definite and clear manner. On the most fundamental level of analysis, no single action by a person is ever the sole cause of a subsequent event. The future indeed comes out of the past in a definite causal order; but the world is a complex and interrelated system with no simple causal threads. Nothing exists alone, independent of everything else. No event has specific causal consequences alone, independent of everything else.

Thus, suppose I utter a cruel remark to a man who subsequently commits suicide. Surely my remark alone was not sufficient to lead him to kill himself. Moreover, he might well have committed suicide anyway. What factual knowledge can I collect which would aid me in determining my responsibility in such a case? Suppose I discover from his psychoanalyst that he would *probably* have killed himself anyway—am I relieved of responsibility? What circumstances and conditions are included in this judgment of probability? Is the psychoanalyst assuming that *nothing* could have saved his patient—no miracles, spontaneous remissions, or unexplainable cures? What is the relevance of the statistics he assumes concerning groups of individuals to this particular situation? I may decide that my remark was both warranted by circumstances and quite natural to utter, but am I thereby relieved of responsibility? And if I discover that this would-be suicide had tried but failed to kill himself before, am I really less responsible? Suppose I was not alone that day in displaying cruelty to him, so that if only someone else had shown kindness and support to him, he would still be alive—am I somehow then innocent, for he could have been saved by someone else who

did not save him? Often we evaluate responsibility by considering
events that it would have been rational to expect to take place, that
might be considered ordinary. But what have such generalizations concerning most men and their actions to do with me? Just why is the appeal to what is ordinary or expected so important in placing responsibility? In 1965, thirty-five people heard a woman being murdered in
New York City, and none of them assisted her in any way, even by calling the police. Thirty-five people cannot be all wrong concerning what
is ordinary. But they are all guilty for having not helped her. They are
all participants in her death.

Suppose I discover a psycho-physical law that uttering a few select
phrases to anyone will depress him and cause him to kill himself. This
law, of course, presupposes that no one else will restore my victim's
equilibrium. Nevertheless, to what extent am I responsible for his
death, when others might have saved him? If I calculate the probability
that he will die upon my manipulating him, at what point is responsibility mine—when the probability is .99, .6, .2, even .00001? Does not
anything I do create a small but finite probability that someone will die
or be injured? Am I responsible for all such injury?

Furthermore, the determination of the probability of an event is
never possible without judgments as to the relevant factors—although
under any but carefully controlled conditions, all factors must be considered. Only in scientific experiments can we ignore variables not explicitly taken into account, for the experiment is designed to that end. If
I test the results of mixing water and alcohol, and drop the beaker, I
don't assume a causal relationship, but redo the experiment. In moral
contexts, however, there is often no opportunity to repeat. What then is
the relevance of general causal laws?

It is plausible to suggest that my knowledge of the *likely* consequences
of my actions renders me responsible, that it is my *anticipation* of the consequences that is essential. I predict (or have good grounds on which to
expect) that my actions will lead to cruel consequences for another person: is it not the knowledge assumed concerning these consequences
that makes me responsible? Am I not responsible, therefore, for everything I do whose consequences I can reliably predict? Does it not seem,
then, that responsibility is a function of knowledge? This is a far more
complex problem than may appear at first.

For one thing, what of a man who simply repudiates any and all
knowledge? He will learn nothing, predict nothing, weigh no evidence,
foresee no consequences. He then acts in ways that hurt others, without

intention or malice. It may never cross his mind that harm would result from his actions. Yet we do wish to call him responsible for what he does—on what grounds?

If we say that his act *caused* the pain and suffering, we must recall that it is never the only factor in the situation, nor even the most efficacious. Furthermore, society as a whole may condone the result by not taking action to forestall it, and may have even permitted the conditions to develop that led to it. What then do we mean when we say that an act causes its consequences, and that one particular agent is responsible for them?

Often, reference is made in contexts like these to what is ordinary, natural, even reasonable. It would not be reasonable to expect anyone else to forestall the consequences of this man's actions; it would have taken far more effort than was justifiable. Adolph Hitler was responsible for the murder of six million Jews because he could easily have avoided it. The ordinary German could have prevented it or fought against it only at great risk of his life and the lives of others, and probably would have failed even then. We seem, then, to consider it reasonable to perform actions that are fairly simple to perform, while great inconveniences are not to be expected or judged harshly. Few men are heroes.

The difficulty here is that a judgment of what is easy or convenient is at best complex and difficult to defend, and at worst quite arbitrary. I hear screams from my window, but fear the *inconvenience* of getting involved with the police, so I ignore them. Surely this is not an innocent act. How then does it differ from the man who passes a beggar without helping him on the grounds that it is society as a whole which must be changed, and that accomplishing that is beyond him? Where shall we place innocence and guilt in such cases? And how then judge responsibility in its factual dimension?

It is possible that we may find it necessary to give up trying to make sense of responsibility, and settle for judgments related solely to the magnitude of the moral issues at stake, and which may depend on evaluations that are so personal as to be beyond rational analysis. We may hold Ivan Karamazov responsible for his actions because the very sophisticated attitudes he displays make us consider him culpable for not recognizing the possible consequences of his statements upon Smerdyakov. The simplicity of calling the police when hearing cries of "Help! Murder!", when compared with the consequences of not doing so, renders a man culpable if he refrains. It is not merely that his re-

fraining causes the murder to go on unabated, but that the simplicity of
his task, when coupled with the horror of murder, requires him to do
everything in his power to halt it.

The fact that our judgments differ concerning just where innocence
ends and guilt begins does not imply that such judgments are arbitrary,
but that in weighing such matters, each of us may emphasize different
factors because we have not settled things among us. So, upon hearing
screams we may agree that I should call the police, but it is not entirely
clear whether I should go down barehanded and risk my life against an
armed killer. Specific disagreements are bound to occur in such matters,
and they are important. They occur constantly, and they should not be
overlooked, but they by no means imply that moral considerations are
arbitrary and subjective.

They do reveal, however, that moral responsibility is almost never a
matter of circumstance alone. I can certainly be held innocent, whatever actions I actually undertake, if my sanity, manipulability, even my
intelligence or knowledge are taken into consideration. At other times,
even an apparently innocent act may be thought so consequential as to
be fraught with responsibility. G. K. Chesterton was fond of taking apparent paradoxes revolving around our judgments of actions viewed
from without, to show how absurd it is to view them in so detached a
manner. In particular, he portrayed an example of a man who, in a
thunderstorm, caught and bound another to a tree, not as it seemed, to
harm him, but to teach him a salutary lesson. The facts required for an
understanding of such matters are not general laws relating actions
causally to their consequences, but facts concerning the people involved, their feelings and intentions.

Yet I do not believe it should be concluded from what has been said
above that knowledge of consequences is not important in moral affairs,
nor that possession of such knowledge does not transform one's responsibilities. My knowledge that a particular drug is deadly makes my ad-
ministering it quite a different act from one where I only consider it
possibly dangerous, or do not have any such knowledge at all. This kind
of example suggests that it is not the real, but the entertained consequences that are essential to judgments of responsibility. Here, however,
Ivan Karamazov offers a counter-example, as do those parents whose
ignorance is of terrible danger to their children—as, for example, the
permissive parent who sees his son trapped in a terrible and irremedia-
ble crime, from not having been more carefully supervised. Is the parent not responsible, though he never for a moment entertained the possibility of disaster? And if we claim that he should have known, or at

least considered the possibility, we cannot make the case for this in terms of what everyone, or even reasonable men, know or imagine. The parent-child relationship is so intimate that a child may justifiably call his parent to account for failing to see something no one else sees either. The Communist parent of the 1930's, who out of deepest moral conviction abandoned his children as well as the entire family system, may be condemned for this by his son, regardless of the rest of the world. To be a parent is to incur certain obligations, whether or not anyone accepts the obligations. Causal facts and predicted consequences form part of the context in which blame is laid; but the laying of responsibility is nevertheless often virtually independent of such facts.

The resolution of such difficulties will be pursued in later chapters by the consideration of the character of a responsible person, and the nature of his understanding of himself. I shall argue that a conception of oneself as responsible, when warranted, implies a concern for factual consequences and the justification for the appraisal of such consequences in judging one's responsibilities. The point is that facts begin to count only under special conditions. When these conditions fail to hold, other factors bear greater weight. It all depends on the nature of the person involved in the moral situation.

2

The Self

Preliminary Considerations

Man discovers himself in a variety of forms and guises, and upon a number of different pathways. Every man sees himself sometimes as innocent, sometimes as guilty, as strong or weak, praiseworthy or despicable; he faces his anguish or flees from it; he submits to his pain and weeps, or struggles to control the twitch of his lips; he shudders in ecstasy and rejoices with pleasure; he humbles himself before the Almighty, or arrogantly defies it as an instrument of his will. Every act, desire, movement, or thought marks the evidence of a man, determines and reveals the kind of man he is.

We might adopt the view, then, that a man is but the sum of his actions, the upshot of his manifest choices, a career of doing and undergoing. Such sequentialism is suggested by William James's neutral monism in which the things of our world appear as histories or sequences of drops of experience, each sequence constituting a different natural entity. Such a view, however, neglects the essential structure of things, replacing the intentions and goals of purposive action, as well as the causal links of motivation and habit, by the history of their manifestation. The simple sequence of a man's actions lacks the tensions and connections provided by intention and guilt. Man cannot escape his history, but neither is he its experienced skeleton. His history reveals himself, but it is something different from, though an aspect of, that self. The view that men, like all things of the universe, are but *histories of affairs* neglects the particularity and individuality of things in their relations and temporality. It is altogether too easy to commit what Whitehead calls the *Fallacy of Misplaced Concreteness* and reduce actualities to universals or histories, neglecting their particularity, their concrete existence. It is true that men live in time, and their affairs form histories. But there is an irremovable individual focus to such histories, something more than the mere sequence, that is the self in question. The conception of a "history" can suggest chronology and sequence, and fail to allow for direction, purpose, and intention. A history is the objective residuum of the living self in time; it fails to include the subjective forms and qualities, the impetuses and dynamisms found in human life. A human being is more than its objective aspect—it includes subjective order and response to the objective data available to it. Put another way, an exclusively behavioristic psychology fails to include precisely those dimensions of human experience that render that behavior *intelligible* as against *predictable*. There is more to the understanding of human behavior than rendering it predictable and controllable; there is more to human life than the causal movement from past to future. Human events are more than physical movements; they not only include emotions and aims, they are directed and channeled by them. I may retrospectively examine myself and discover only my overt acts and consequences of my past motives and desires, but it is the latter that provide my experience with focus and integrity. The scientific analysis of the self characterizes the movement from actions to feelings as inference. It is this claim in particular that has so confused the proper understanding of the moral person.

I am not rejecting psychological behaviorism as a scientific theory on the logical grounds that its vocabulary fails to include the ordinary vocabulary of psychic states. Scientific vocabularies often serve their particular purposes best when they abstract from the richness of experienced events. Psychological behaviorism viewed as the development of instruments and laws for the scientific or determinate understanding of human actions and behavior may well turn out to be invaluable, or it may fail utterly in determining important laws of behavior by its own standards. In neither case can it hope to satisfy our need for an adequate conception of the human person because it, like physics, simplifies the richness of experienced events to gain predictive power over them. Just as ordinary objects are usually not usefully characterized as assemblages of atoms and molecules, so (for purposes other than scientific), a man is quite inadequately viewed as a history of his behavior. Purposes, desires, and conscious appraisal endow behavior with a direction which science rejects as irrelevant and which permits only dubious inference from available data. This confusion of evidence with what it is evidence for parallels the confused epistemological claim that the proper understanding of the self is exclusively a scientific one in which evidence plays a central role.

To give up mere history or sequence as inadequate to understanding the human self is not, however, to eliminate the temporal and cumulative nature of the human person, nor of anything else in concrete existence. The search for the human self in a momentary, if constantly shifting, center of consciousness is equally an epistemological subterfuge to simplify unduly the relationship of the person to what can be discovered about him. It is a poor view of evidence to think of it located forever in a momentary present, forever fading into a lost past; but it is even poorer to seek evidence of the self *as a self*. Descartes may be understood to have shown the complete implausibility of engaging in an investigation to determine if any investigation is possible at all, at least so far as the agent is concerned. The discovery of moments of consciousness provides us with another factor to cope with in our theories; to place the self altogether in these moments is as much a repudiation of the direction provided by appraisal and motivation as of the causal effects of the past self on the present and future. Perhaps I may choose to do something different from what is expected; but *I* choose, and it *is* different. The concept of choice is too strictly located in the context of a past from which the choice stems to permit its analysis in terms of a momentary self located in a present moment of consciousness.

The Cartesian elements in Sartre's existentialism are not the result of an epistemological concern for the human self, but an emphasis on the irreducibility of some aspect of the self viewed as a moral agent. This element for Sartre is "consciousness," but it is not consciousness as an attribute of a particular person; rather it is selfhood as the condition of agency. Human beings as agents make choices, have intentions, seek goals, and remember their transgressions. No image of man which fails to make a radical distinction between man and the nonhuman can capture such dimensions of moral experience. Rocks and clouds make no decisions, have no purposes, and do not *act* in Sartre's sense. Some fundamental attribute of human experience is missing for things which are not agents, which no strict behaviorism can capture, since behaviorism is a view of man in which he is regarded as one thing among others.

The difficulty is to develop a theory of the self that makes no reference to some mystical quality that renders man unique, yet which does not treat men in terms that render them objects like all other objects. We have here the metaphysical correlate of Kant's second form of the categorical imperative: *So act as to treat humanity, whether in thine own person or in that of any other, in every case as an end withal, never as means only.* We can make such a distinction between means and ends only if we have a conception of man as significantly different from all other beings that we treat as means; it is unquestionable that we are morally committed to some such imperative and its correlative distinction. Yet the scientific view of man rests upon a conception of men as experimental objects. This is incompatible with an ethical conception of the person. To Kant, we can be moral agents only under the presupposition of freedom. This is Sartre's point also, and he argues that this recognition must be embodied in our very conception of humanity. Still, he does not analyze the nature of the human self in its ties to the rest of the world, and it is this lack that renders his analysis of the actions of that self inadequate.

What then is the human person? In this chapter I will give only a very general account of the nature of the self, leaving for a later chapter the analysis of what is discovered when one seeks self-knowledge. Before examining the kind of self-knowledge that is essential to moral conduct and responsibility, we must have a fairly clear overview of what we expect to find. What sort of thing is the self? What are its generic properties? Above all, what can be meant by assertions about oneself: *I* am innocent; *I* am sorry; *I* do not remember. How can a man properly judge himself innocent or guilty, *given his actions,* if they do not determine the judgment?

Man as Experiencer

Our major problem is that the moral sense of man—in that broadest and most comprehensive sense of the moral that includes all appraisal of decision and action—is the richest and most comprehensive one possible. We seek the widest and most complete sense of a human being, one so wide as to render a perfectly whole and consistent sense of personality impossible. If a person is part of a unified and directed order of natural events, there are always surds and incoherences within that order, particularly insofar as a man changes from what he was to what he will be. Some part of that change rests upon the relinquishing of his past self and the generating of a new one. The becoming of a person always takes place in a partly incomplete order of things—and it is the becoming of the self that is essential to moral action. The moral self is unbounded, in the sense that its purview is forever shifting, expanding, encompassing new possibilities.

The main point to make clear is that the human self is never bounded by clear and definite lines. When we view a particular person and attempt to understand just who and what he is, there is no particular point at which we can draw a clear line and say, "here he ends." Once it was thought that it was possible to sever a man from his own body; his person terminated at the borders of his soul. Such a view is not only incoherent in a metaphysical and epistemological sense, but fails to make clear how any given act of a given body may be held to belong to a particular person except by appeal to a Divine Judgment that can see into a man's soul—and even here we wonder if that insight can possibly be independent of the man's behavior. It follows from such a conception that nothing is any particular person's; he is responsible for nothing. Since he is not thoroughly endowed with his body, but is only inexplicably or incoherently attached thereto, his acts cease upon his willing them. Circumstances over which he has no control enter thereafter. The terrible dangers men run in willing actions that may involve them in dire failure and even catastrophe are eliminated in a single stroke; on this view a man can never try to will without success. Such a view may apply well to such instances as my willing my arm to move, but surely fails to grasp the agony of my will to help my child suffering from an affliction of the soul which leads him to self-destruction. If my body is not fully mine, why have I sinned when my will was good?

This view finds guilt only in a guilty will. It neglects the terrible cases in which a man's apparent will is good but his actions bring destruction. Psychoanalysis, by introducing the notion of the unconscious will, seems to save this view: one is guilty only for his will, unconscious or known. But psychoanalysis does not succeed once we realize that the grounds for supposing that the unconscious will has so willed are often nothing but the behavior which follows from the supposed act of will. There is no escape from the realization that a man's behavior and actions are fundamental to him, and that no purely psychic conception of a man can do justice to his moral needs.

✓ The extension of a man's being to his body, then, is quite simple and straightforward, though the very nature of the extension suggests that one's body does not terminate at a clear and definite line. If I will my finger to pull the trigger of a rifle in war, am I quite free from the consequences of my act? Are not these consequences *mine*—the sundry dead, the gasping wounded? Do they not belong to me as thoroughly as my arms and legs? Technology strengthens and develops our wills, and extends our capacities beyond the natural force of our arms and legs to unlimited regions and remote events. My rifle is my good right arm. The bomb too, that I release upon my enemies in war, is unquestionably part of my will. What I am, therefore, is at least what I do and the consequences of my actions—though, of course, I think and feel as well. I am not neatly tucked away in a narrowly circumscribed body, but extend into indefinitely distant regions, a participant in events remote in space and time. I am the record of my doings as well as of my thoughts, and my deeds extend virtually without limit in time and space.

A man is not limited by his intentions or conscious choices either—he cannot hide from judgment within a circumspect region of his own narrow situations. He may find himself upon the pathway to hell, upon which his consciously well-meant desires and intentions have left a mark of suffering and pain. A parent can never simply plead the excuse, "I did not wish or intend that." The further consequences of his actions for his children reflect back upon and provide the grounds for appraisal of his original intentions. My conscious will may be weak and shallow; the cruel and vainglorious consequences of its fitful acts come back upon me. How else understand the psychological claim that a destructive person's actions stem from neurotic feelings of self-inadequacy? His life has been a search for adequacy. What then are the hurt and wounded to him?—they are the echo of his passing.

A man is his thoughts and his actions, his assertions and his withdrawals, his judgments and his reflections, his submissions and his denials. The world stands before him, and he marks a history within a larger temporal order, a point of view forced upon its grossness, and makes judgments carved out of only partly yielding materials. Things of the world enter his experience and are rooted therein as his very being and personality. He is much more than he knows, and everything which surrounds him contributes to his nature. The friendly act of a forgotten time lingers on in the friend who remembers—or even he having

forgotten, is nevertheless an unwitting reflection of sacrifice and friend-
ship. Men can never avoid seeking, nor can they escape a direction to
their lives. Their experiences move from past to future, embodying the
very nature of their persons within the world.

   A man's personality, then, in the sense that we speak of his being a
person and having a person-ality, is simply everything relevant to him
in the structured order of his experience and self. As a person, he is the
focus, direction, or impetus that the events of the world relevant to him
contribute to. As Whitehead and Dewey recognized so well, a being
that experiences has a definite and irremovable complexity at its heart.
To Dewey, experience is a "double-barreled word" (really triple-bar-
reled), reflecting the essential complex unity of subject, object, and
manner of experiencing in a single process. To Whitehead, every act of
experience is a concrete unity that can be analyzed into objective and
subjective aspects, though the latter may often be negligible in any particular concrescence. Preserving this insight, I am suggesting that a person must be thought of at once as his mark upon the world and as the
source of that mark; as a trace of the effect of the world upon him, and
as a directing and transforming of the material given to him to work
upon; objectively as a history or career, and subjectively as a unified
appropriation, organization, and direction of the components of that
career. The scientific conception of man looks to the objective elements
of personality, a career in time. Sartre and other existentialists place the
essential aspect of personality wholly in its subjective or directive dimension, neglecting the place of a given person in the world, the social
aspects of his environment that become part of him, the fact that a man
is what he is only in terms of his appropriation and organization of the
environment surrounding him which he makes part of himself. ✓

   A person is indeed part of a history of affairs, but he is more than a
sequence of events. A personal history is ordered and focused, with a
unique integrity. Within it new possibilities are resolved, and events of
close physical proximity ignored as meaningless. Out of a history of
events constituting a dimension of the person, new intentions and goals
come to fruition and are realized. I am everything that is "mine"—but
the order of choice and the transformation of self effected by such
choices are essential. The indefinite character of the self within the
world-process is not simply an assemblage or even a sequence of events
within that process, but is unified by a direction, an order, focus, or
point of view, from which and within which we assert a person to have a
particular *character.*

   The recognition of character in a person, that he is a particular *kind* of person, is a realization about his personal history and its internal propulsions. It is an affirmation of a coherent continuity or order which prevails throughout the various aspects of a man's life, through the many roles he plays and actions he undertakes. A person's life is more than a mere history—that is, a listing of events in sequence. His past is caught up in a propulsion into new situations that arise. Some (perhaps very few) events enter a person's life unexpectedly and adventitiously; but in the moment they, with all the rest of his experience, become enlaid with the structure of his purposes as well as his habits, conscious and unconscious. The history of a man is the constant regeneration of experience out of an older history into new and fresh events. Nothing ever simply "happens" to him that is not incorporated into and suffused with the qualities of his own personality. His own personal history is directed and structured—he possesses character and personality. In knowing a person in either sense—by acquaintance or discursively—we recognize the structure and strength of this personality as well as the events that have contributed to it. We "feel" the direction of this person and the thrust of his actions. A person's life is a subhistory of the world-history, one which has taken on momentum and direction.

Of course, inorganic things are also subhistories, and in a somewhat more trivial sense they too possess a character or direction. This recognition underlies Whitehead's cosmology. A snowball rolling downhill is without a doubt becoming something, and every moment that occurs is a product of what has come before. The incorporation of elements into a coherent and directed history is often a natural and unintentional process. The sweep of a man's habits and unintended responses constitutes a directed and ordered history as much as (and perhaps even more than) the few acts he endows with forthright and direct purpose. It is the routine of habit and the unexamined stream of behavior in human life that most resembles the complexly ordered sequence of inorganic events. The point is to recognize the fundamental character of such unexamined and unquestioned causal histories beginning in the earliest stages of conception and continuing almost unabated throughout the life of the person. The fact that causal order is so fundamental a determining factor in the constitution of the human being neither minimizes nor trivializes that order; the self has a direction and character whether known or not. The blind habits of a man totally enslaved to his causal past may be more thoroughly determinate and focused than any intentional purpose could be. What is essential in an unbreakable compulsion is that it is rooted in forgotten and unknown depths of personal history. What is most important in the Freudian view of man is not the notion of psychic determinism but the extent to which unrecognized events in a man's past render him enslaved—a slavery which permeates every new entry into his experience with meanings that are rooted in quite past but still influential events. On the level of unexamined and unintended responses, the only difference of note between human behavior and the behavior of ordinary inorganic objects in novel circumstances is the extent to which events remote in time from the present are causally influential. In the purely physical realm, remote history is of little impact; the object here and now is subject to bounding conditions and behaves lawfully. The acts of a person when his conscious attention is removed often refer back to relatively ancient personal history and cannot be understood without it. To this extent the human self carries its history with it, floating in the immediate background of every act and situation. It is this which permits us to speak of the *cumulation* of experience rather than the mere accumulation of event upon event in a mere sequence where each term reflects only the preceding one. The human self is sufficiently complex as to incorporate its remote past into its present responses, often without diminution or exhaustion. To be oneself is to be like one has been, to preserve the habitual and regular responses to the things which surround one, or else to have changed in one's being by changing in one's sense of and incorporation of one's past into the present. The source of ruling habits is often rooted in the early history of the person. Amidst the trail of common and regular actions every person carries with him to insulate him from the onslaught of new experiences, the causal determinants of behavior extend indefinitely in time and space. There is nothing that cannot be incorporated into any particular self as significant for it, nor is anything necessarily part of any particular self. However immediate its impact upon his physical being, a man can always fail to heed it. The habits and structures created by the past define the self, and the constantly-changing character of personal history forbids us from ever precisely defining any given self at any moment. It has new roles to fill; new possibilities for action arise, calling for the expansion of powers and commitments.

The self is on one hand its entire history, the assemblage of all the events and things which have contributed to its being and upon which it has left its mark, and on the other, it possesses a rather definite structure or direction which is of fundamental importance in its momentary activities. This *momentary self* is what may be considered the upshot of a person's life to the present, the available resources and principles which are drawn upon in any given situation. It is constantly being modified, but it possesses considerable inertia in its habitual constituents. In general it is this inertia we refer to when we speak of the personality or character of a person; it is not his entire history all at once, but the residue that history has left behind, the directive order defined by it. Every situation of a person's life involves him in it as a "floating" being, available for response to and in that situation. The character of his life-history has a form or structure left by the sequence of events within that history. Certain resources, abilities, habits, and ideas are available in particular patterns of response which he may draw upon. This is his momentary self.

I have not attempted to define the human self in terms of consciousness or cognition. It seems to me quite essential to avoid doing so, for while conscious of and knowledgeable about some things, most men are not acutely aware of what they do or who they are in any deep and significant sense. For most men consciousness is a trivial element in their lives. They think almost without effect upon the critical moments of their lives, at which time habits and blind prejudices emerge in full force. If consciousness is the capacity of the self to transform itself upon the emergence of novel circumstances, few moments in many lives are conscious. Alienation here may be thought of as the quality of a self not open to self-transformation, by the absence of any but trivial self-awareness (such as that involved in moving one's arm), sometimes by the inculcation of empty and formal responses in a way that is so devoid of interest or appraisal as to be wholly impossible of examination. The alienated man is not alienated alone by virtue of an internal division which he takes to be himself. He is alienated when he is so benumbed and confused as to have no sense of himself at all, split or not, from which to act. His activities comprise no continuous interrelation. Ivan's greatest problem in *The Brothers Karamazov* is that he acts without knowing it, and the discovery that sends him into collapse is that he actually is what he thought he was only pretending to be—a dangerously hypocritical and destructive person. His alienation consists in his not possessing sufficient awareness of himself as well as critical tools with which to examine himself to determine whether he is worthy or lacking. It is not that Ivan is unknowing—for he possesses a first-rate mind—but that his consciousness fails to touch on himself in any significant way. Too often men blind themselves by the adoption of a narrow conception of their own being, denying their wider ramifications and influences.

Something must be said about the role of consciousness in moral life, if only to prepare ground for the analysis of self-knowledge. Without recognition of the unconscious elements of the person, we will not be able to understand judgments of guilt or innocence nor be able to grasp the quality of moral responsibility. But it is impossible to determine when judgments of responsibility are warranted unless we take into account the unique properties of the self constituted by consciousness.

Consciousness and Self-consciousness

Two opposing traditions have developed in which self-consciousness is considered important and worthy of concern. One takes its departure from Descartes' *cogito* and the method contained therein that views the beginning of all philosophy and all knowledge as the scrutiny of self and the discovery that "to speak accurately, I am not more than a thing which thinks, that is to say, a mind or a soul, or an understanding, or a reason." Thinking here carries its own warrant as well as clues to its own nature. To be conscious is to be capable of engaging in reflection on oneself as knower. To know is to know that one knows; knowledge of oneself is coextensive with knowledge of the world. In more recent times this tradition finds its expression among phenomenologists and existentialists like Jean Paul Sartre who claims that "Every conscious existence exists as consciousness of existing." Every consciousness of an object also has itself as object. Every consciousness is a self-consciousness.

The equation of consciousness and self-consciousness is fundamental to Sartre's view of responsibility and freedom. Men are responsible precisely insofar as they are self-aware in their projects and therefore free. However, though Sartre is Hegelian in his view that consciousness and self-consciousness are fundamental categories for moral analysis, he omits a critical part of Hegel's position—that there are stages of development in conscious life, and that the higher stages of self-consciousness come to be from lower stages of consciousness. Moral self-consciousness is a late and sophisticated stage of self-consciousness to Hegel. His dynamic analysis of self-consciousness makes clear how seldom are men fully aware of themselves, and how multifarious and complex are the various stages and types of self-awareness.

The terms in which I wish to capture this recognition are that self-consciousness arises fully in the moral sense only in adherence to particular *methods*. Methodic self-consciousness, the self-consciousness essential to freedom, is a particularly important and valuable part of human experience, something to strive for rather than something easily come by in all conscious experience. It is a higher and more complex state than simple response to or awareness of things around us. On this basis I must begin by refuting the view that self-consciousness is always present in every conscious thought and make clear the nature of my objections to that view.

Descartes failed to see that he was presupposing a very advanced type of consciousness in proposing a method for the solution of philosophic problems. No wonder he discovered in his *cogito* that he was indeed conscious of his own thoughts and attempts at knowledge, for these were presupposed in the attitude that made the *cogito* itself possible. The "I think" of the *cogito* is a highly sophisticated and complex form of consciousness, as well as the self-consciousness of meticulous examination and reflection on the contents of the mind. It is by no means the fitful and intermittent state of everyday awareness in which we undergo the events that come upon us. Sartre, in taking the attitude of the *cogito* as paradigmatic of all consciousness, is led to the claim that "the necessary and sufficient condition for a knowing consciousness to be knowledge of its object is that it be consciousness of itself as being that knowledge." If we take "knowledge" to be the entertaining in thought of an object, then it may well be that self-awareness necessarily involves the entertaining of an object other than oneself—one may scrutinize oneself only in the process of acting upon or thinking of an object, thus in consciousness. Kant certainly maintained that this is the case; we discover ourselves through our consciousness of other things. The crucial question concerns the *necessity* of self-consciousness to consciousness—whether we may not well be conscious without awareness of our own participation in the process. Sartre states further: "every conscious existence exists as consciousness of existing. . . . This self-consciousness we ought to consider not as a new consciousness, but as the only mode of existence which is possible for a consciousness of something."

On the surface this last quotation is certainly false, so far as some obvious cases of consciousness are concerned. For example, a man may distractedly wander the streets after an emotional blow and find himself home again without self-awareness or even awareness of having directed his steps there. Was he not conscious? Did he not see where he was going? But he was not aware of having made a *choice,* and it is where choosing, deciding, and *knowing what one is doing* are paradigmatic that consciousness entails self-consciousness. It is by conceiving of consciousness as the defining human trait, and coordinating it with choice, that Sartre is led to the identification of self-consciousness and ordinary consciousness. Purpose and intention are the paradigms rather than awareness. There may well be a mere awareness of things (such as the awareness of an infant) quite distinct from an awareness of self.

"Consciousness" is an ambiguous word. It can be thought of in an active sense derived from sentences of the form, "X is conscious of Y," as a form of awareness which reflects the joint activity of Y and X. The key notion here is of an *activity* connected with an object, as we speak of "consciousness *of*" that object. But "consciousness" can also refer to that quality of humanity which underlies *agency*. Sartre conceives of consciousness as an entity or state, not as an activity, and separable in thought from its object. It is hypostatized into a stuff, a kind of being, an order of existence. In this latter sense consciousness is taken to be the distinguishing feature of men viewed as moral beings, not as organisms or creatures. When awareness is taken to be a form of consciousness, we are reminded that animals and insects certainly are aware and therefore conscious in this sense. If we wish to stress the uniqueness of men as moral agents, it is plausible instead to ascribe to them some attribute which we call "consciousness," and which distinguishes men from beasts. There is, however, a quite arbitrary element to the supposition that men are indeed conscious where animals are not. Sartre shows how committed we are in understanding man as a moral agent to his freedom and self-consciousness. But he does not prove that freedom to be genuine. He does not even try to show that men are indeed conscious in his sense of that word, only that we are committed in our conceptions of action and responsibility to thinking of them as such. What Sartre shows is that no purposive consciousness (which he takes every consciousness to be) can be divorced from a consciousness of oneself as decisive or at least as instrumental in the action undertaken. It is *moral* consciousness that interests Sartre, and he argues that all purposive consciousness is reflexive and conscious of itself. I agree, as in the case of his example of counting; one can count only insofar as one is aware of oneself counting. But Sartre certainly means by this that one can be aware of being engaged in a *purposive* action, as against merely running through a sequence 1, 2, 3 . . . purposelessly as a child might in memory, only insofar as one is aware of oneself as the agent with purpose. Perhaps Sartre's point can be put most clearly that embodied in our very conception of purposive activity is a conception of self-consciousness that entails that the agent has the freedom to choose from alternatives. If so, then these pages can be understood to show that the distinction between mere wishing—without plan or real purpose, when means are lacking to produce ends in view—and planning or intending—

which is based on an intelligent appraisal of means to achieve desired ends—does in fact narrow severely the range of purposive activity; and to suggest further that the Socratic quest for self-knowledge was nothing other than the quest for the conditions under which responsible choices can be made by men. Not everything a man *does* is a *choice.*

The analogue of the latter view is that the self-consciousness necessary to moral responsibility is not something possessed by all men but is rather something won from passive awareness and slothful indecision. In line with Kant and especially Hegel, I shall adopt the view that self-consciousness is not found in all human awareness but only within carefully controlled activities. In ordinary experience men regard the passing of events and objects before them without a passionate regard for just how they themselves participate in and contribute to them. An automobile passes before my window; I may remark on that without reflective awareness that "I" saw it, nor is my noting at the same time necessarily a noting of myself as observer. I simply note the event. I listen to a late Beethoven string quartet without scrutinizing my own tools of analysis; I listen and it passes. Without self-awareness, am I aware at all?—surely, for I am lost in the music, too engrossed to worry about myself. Even a most sophisticated mode of consciousness can be without focus on oneself. Self-consciousness arises only when a person addresses himself in particular.

The sense of consciousness as awareness or attention is a radically different one from the hypostatized consciousness of Sartre and Descartes. From the standpoint of a particular individual, consciousness is an activity of mind under which events and things take on special qualities of feeling and attention which blend without sharp demarcation into activities and states which clearly lack consciousness or awareness. This active sense of consciousness must be distinguished sharply from the sense of consciousness as a property not of events and things actively responded to by an organism, but as a defining property of humanity, as the essential characteristic of men. Perhaps from the active sense of awareness we may gain some perspective on the question of whether indeed there can be found a definite distinguishing characteristic of human beings in the sense that Sartre assumes. Although he shows, it seems to me, that our very conception of man (and consciousness) entails self-consciousness, freedom, and responsibility, he does not examine the possibility that such conceptual relations are without corresponding instances—that although we must think of moral agents as free, no justification in fact can be found for this supposition from the standpoint of rational analysis.

Another way of putting this is that Sartre presupposes that there exists a substantive analogue to the moral distinction between men and all other beings. By calling this state of being "consciousness," Sartre endows it with a substantial being virtually independent of the organic aspects of human life, which it would seem he supposes are dealt with only in causal terms. There is little sense in Sartre's work of a holistic conception of man; he begins with a dinstinction that divides man from nature, and repudiates his organic dependencies. Everything other than consciousness is part of the environment in an extreme Cartesian fashion. Being-in-itself and being-for-itself are exhaustively distinguished; yet the human body is then placed in intimate relation with consciousness, where it certainly belongs, but only in an integrated conception of the human person. To Sartre, "consciousness" is another name for the being of man, not an aspect or part of him. The very notion of a "pre-reflective consciousness" suggests that Sartre seeks an analysis of the being of man, not of an occasional aspect of his being. In critical passages, Sartre speaks not of the activity of consciousness, but of "human reality" surpassing being. The key hypothetical is "for man to be able to question, he must be capable of being his own nothingness." This is certainly true, but it is equally true that many men do not question many things. If Sartre means that *when* men question, they are their own negations; and if he means as well that *when* men question purposefully they are aware of their own being from the aspect of nonbeing; then if both statements are true, there exist few moments of genuine interrogation in most men's lives. If there is a necessary relation between consciousness and humanity, it is not that men are always conscious, even nonreflectively (in the sense of performing or participating in conscious activities), but that all men are sometimes conscious, or at least demand that they be thought so in the respect shown by others for their wishes, purposes, and goals. Sartre shows that one cannot both demand consideration as a person or agent and yet deny his freedom and responsibility. He ignores several of the primary characteristics of excuses—that they are often inconsistent, and that they make reference to particular times and places. "Yesterday I couldn't help myself; today I am alert and responsible." The refusal to consider an analysis of the activity of consciousness leads Sartre to a view of man that fails to include room for important excuses. Indeed, his sense of being-for-itself in effect makes all excuses irrelevant and acts of bad faith. Such a conception is far too limited for his and our purposes.

The Cartesian sense of consciousness is the having of particular thoughts, beliefs, images, or intentions. Consciousness is identified with "noting" or the awareness of objects as data. Although Sartre to some extent preserves this view, by conceiving of consciousness as a defining human trait, he avoids the far too narrow conception of consciousness as the entertainment of data in the mind. The conception of a prereflective consciousness marks this most clearly.

It is quite commonplace by now that the conception of consciousness as mere "noting" in a visual, sensible, or mentalistic sense is not broad enough to do the job required of it. The tennis player who makes a magnificent save does not "note" his own actions; he simply acts. But it would be ridiculous to maintain that his stroke was remarkable in being not conscious. So also, the artist who, in working on a canvas without self-reflection or any mental act of noting, simply fills in a particular area with a particular shade of color, does so quite consciously. Here too it would be ludicrous to call the act unconscious; but it is without the verbal reflection upon an object that is often taken as the paradigm of consciousness. These examples suggest that consciousness is often something other than covert discourse. The tennis player is conscious, at least visually (not "mentally"), of the appropriate act under the given conditions, if he can only perform it. Reflection and examination may follow the very conscious act of leaping and striking. The artist takes the unbalanced canvas as an indication or sign of further action, and responds thereto, without verbally examining the situation itself to see if such acts are appropriate. Consciousness, when released from the bonds of self-awareness and over-reflection, reaches quite deeply into affairs.

But if consciousness is not the entertaining of particular thoughts or images, what then is it? One conception is Sartre's, which identifies consciousness and purpose, and allows for the possibility of a prereflective consciousness where reflection is lacking but purpose is not. The problem with this conception of consciousness is that it has been turned into a pervasive human trait rather than an activity or occasional state. Questioning becomes paradigmatic of human life, at least unreflectively, and Sartre fails completely to allow room for the frequent lack of concern, interest, and interrogation in most men's lives except as acts of bad faith.

Another possibility can be found for preserving consciousness as a particular mode of activity, yet which avoids its identification with particular states of mind. That is, the realization that consciousness is a genuine *activity*, not a state or condition, whose nature resides in what it promotes or leads to. What is required is that we move from the item or thought *in* consciousness, to the whole system of thoughts or actions that constitute a person's conscious awareness, a process which develops and changes in time.

It is neither possible nor necessary in the limited space here to develop a full analysis of consciousness. I shall instead address myself to but a single characteristic of human consciousness without unduly pursuing the question of whether it is indeed necessary or sufficient in itself. My intent is to show that consciousness is something other than mental "noting," yet need not involve the intentionality that entails self-consciousness. Consciousness is a complex mode of experience, but its complexity is other than the complexity of self-consciousness. What I wish to do is to show how self-consciousness brings with it particular changes in consciousness, which are essential to responsible actions.

To begin, let me propose the hypothesis that to be aware, or conscious in the simplest sense, is to experience things as leading outside themselves to something else. Consciousness is not to be found in a thought or idea in isolation from its surroundings, but within a whole system of thoughts and actions. This is the truth inherent in the associationist theory of mind—thinking in the broadest sense always leads from one idea to another. I am aware of an element in my visual field only insofar as I "notice" something about it. The word "about" here signifies nothing less than that my responses to whatever I notice move from one point to another, in a whole series of interconnections and relations, with a common focus. I note that the elephant is gray, a bit like the color of slate in the quarry I visited last summer, and his skin is wrinkled like some of the textural lines in slate also. But the flexibility of that incredible trunk is quite different from the hardness of slate and is a bit like a snake or rope. Perhaps I imagine an elephant frightened by a snake, or a huge snake eating an elephant, think of some elephant joke, or remember feeding peanuts to an elephant when a child. But the *stream of consciousness* in which my thoughts lie continues to flow unceasingly around the focus of the elephant just so long as I am aware of him. And when the focal point of this cacophony of awareness shifts to some inward memory, or to the giraffe in another part of the zoo, then I cease to be focally aware of the elephant. (I might be peripherally aware of him if, throughout, thoughts of the elephant broke into my new focus of awareness, and were in that way part of this other stream of consciousness. I am totally unaware of the elephant when important aspects of his being fail to break into my new focus of awareness.)

It is not easy to draw a clear line between states of consciousness and peripheral states of awareness, those states when we are half-asleep, distracted, or ill. Moreover, borderline cases of consciousness do not appear to be of great relevance to the subject of moral responsibility. Unfortunately, that appearance is rather deceptive. The point at issue is precisely whether the average human being is sufficiently alert to the circumstances and conditions that surround him to make his moral decisions responsible and efficacious. A distracted or half-conscious man is not a full agent—at least not to the extent that we can easily justify holding him fully responsible for the consequences of what he does. The state of passive routine to which we, alas, are so susceptible, that dulls our minds and hobbles our good intentions, separates us from what we do. Diminishing our power over our actions, such passivity isolates us in our unawareness and subjects us to the impact of events over which we have little control. We live most of our lives in an unalert condition, at least with respect to much of our surroundings. Our claim to be responsible agents for what we fail to recognize the existence of or consequences of is empty.

What, then, constitutes the conscious alertness that underlies responsibility? My claim is that the self-consciousness of responsible agency is a rare and highly sophisticated mode of consciousness. Our lives are filled with the passage of things we barely notice, if we are aware of them at all. We are by no means agents in control of them. Yet they may dominate our lives or endow our more explicitly conscious states with significance and meaning. Consciousness and causal impact fade into each other, and the latter may hold the greater sway over our lives. If so, we are not agents responsible for what we do and what happens to us.

A newly-born infant cries upon being held upside down and slapped; his pupils contract upon being exposed to bright light; he shudders and draws his first breath. These are clear and definite responses to particular stimuli, yet they are not conscious. They are crude and immediate; they amount to nothing; they lead nowhere. The stream of thoughts and actions that are part of even our somnolent states of awareness is not to be found here. The infant's responses are discrete and distinct, without the complex interconnections that are part of consciousness.

In all unmistakable states of consciousness, we find connections and relations. Even to note the existence of something is to note it as being a certain *kind* of thing, like or unlike other things. Consciousness is a constant movement, connecting things together in varying ways. It is the qualification of causal responses by elaborate replacements and substitutions. When an infant cries from hunger, simply as a response to feelings of discomfort, there is none of the awareness inherent in a cry em-

ployed as a signal for the alleviation of the discomfort, part of a whole
context of pain and soothing. There is, of course, no clear line between
such a case of mere causal response and conscious alertness, for we are
forced to surmise much of the content of an infant's experience. But the
working criterion seems fairly plain: an event, object, or thought which
comes and goes without becoming part of the connected and ordered
stream of events and actions that is the course of a person's experience is
not part of his conscious awareness. What he is alert to sufficiently to be
capable of varied and multiple interpretations is a firm part of his consciousness. Causal impacts comprise a single mode of relatedness. Human experience, as it becomes laden with multiple habits and meanings, is enriched with multiple possibilities of response and many and
varied systems of interconnection. Our conscious thoughts lie in the
complex realm of interconnectedness where any item brings with it
multiple meanings and significances. What we are conscious of we may
develop in a wealth of different directions and systems of relations, for
our conscious experience is imbued with the richness of its past associations and implicit meanings.

A cause indeed has its effects, with its further consequences, but in a
relatively linear order of sequence with rather undifferentiated patterns
and structures. The meanings and associations of conscious experience,
however, ramify each other and reflect upon each other. Structured,
highly ramified, and systematic orders of response underlie our conscious experience. Awareness coexists with dispositions of recurrence
and deeply intertwined patterns of thought and behavior. All the difference in the world exists between a dog's obedience to the command
"lie down!" and a child grasping both the command *and* that it is a
command, a sentence in a language, an aspect of social life. The complex ramifications created by the latter orders of response as they condition and qualify the responses made within them are the heart of conscious thought. Causal impact goes no further than its effect. Further
consequences do not affect the character of the original causal relation.
The burning of a candle which causes a fire is not affected in any significant way by the deaths of the inhabitants of the dwelling. Conscious
awareness always resides in the further ramifications of the order it ar-
ticulates. The understanding a child has of the meaning of "No!" is intimately bound up with an entire pattern of parental behavior and is
heavily dependent on other meanings as well—such as the meaning of
"You're a good boy!" and "We love you."

Two aspects of consciousness seem to me most essential: the mediate
or indirect character of conscious response to things as they lead beyond

themselves; and the capacity we have of expressing in words or some other form the content of our consciousness. We can always tell what we were thinking of, however incompletely or distortedly. Our inability to follow a thought by another, a major break in our train of reflection, is the termination of our conscious awareness on a given topic and its departure from our awareness.

Conscious awareness is always part of an ongoing and interconnected domain and is never complete in itself. One of the reasons why language is so inextricably part of consciousness is that language provides us with a system of interconnected meanings that makes the rich fabric of our conscious life possible. The grasp of a linguistic system of meanings guarantees that any item of consciousness may be elaborated upon by further thoughts within that language.

In our everyday experience we continually meet with borderline cases of consciousness to which we apply the criterion I have proposed. A man leaps reflexively away from an oncoming car; a tennis player swiftly and without thought returns a volley; the driver of an automobile swerves suddenly away from a pedestrian who appears in his path. These are unquestionable cases of consciousness. On the other hand, an infant cries "Dada" upon seeing his father—is this to be considered a conscious act, or a mere causal response?

The point is that the tennis player may remark to himself, "Wow, what a shot! I never thought I'd get it"; the driver of the car may stop, wipe his brow, and pray silently to himself; while the infant may make no further response to his own actions. Let me, before examining this, take one more example, from psychoanalysis—of a man who never "feels" anger, but who possesses an ulcer, and who is told by his psychoanalyst that the ulcer is an expression of "unconscious feelings of anger." How can a feeling be unconscious? The man reaches within himself for some feeling but finds none. On the other hand, he finds that he undergoes an ulcer attack whenever he might have felt anger but didn't, in cases where anyone else would have become angry. Moreover, at such times he also becomes depressed and anxious without knowing why. It is impossible to doubt under such conditions that the events which evoke such responses are meaningful to him, however unconscious he is of them. Sartre concedes at least this with his notion of a *prereflective consciousness*. What is most significant here is the agent's complete inability to recognize what is happening to him. The tennis player can relate to himself his own actions; the automobile driver may respond at first without thinking, but immediately thereafter is aware of what just happened. The infant and unconsciously angry man cannot think further about what they do, the infant because he does not possess the equipment for such a development, the man because some mechanism is at work inhibiting his recognition of the nature of his own feelings. When fairly clear and obvious modes of response are eliminated from a person's experience, and he becomes incapable of making common and natural connections, we doubt that he is fully conscious of what he is doing. A person is fully conscious only when he thinks about what he does, and when what he does is part of a complex order of interconnected meanings or habits that allow him to explain or tell what he is conscious of.

Consciousness, then, is like a personal dialogue, one which a person has with himself about the object of his thoughts. This is not to be taken quite literally, yet it should not be interpreted too loosely either. The dialogue is "personal" in that only a single individual engages in it. It is not particularly private, for the articulating behavior may be quite overt and physical. The dialogue is person-al only insofar as the same individual plays both parts. It is not personal in the sense that it is private or hidden from others. What I am most concerned with is the notion of a dialogue, for without the give and take of acts in an interconnected series, there can be no consciousness. A man in sleep may repeatedly be bitten by a mosquito and respond repeatedly by toxic and allergic physical reactions. This series has none of the multiple possibilities made available by consciousness; the linear sequence of stimulus-response does not reflect back on itself in thought and action. The sleeping man is not conscious of being bitten; he sleeps throughout. He becomes conscious of what is taking place only when he notices the sting of being bitten and remarks on it, or slaps out at the annoying insect; or later, when he notices his own welts and remarks on them to himself or aloud. Moreover, he is conscious of his own actions only if they too become the source of further reflexive dialogue. If he merely slaps and does nothing else, then it may be involuntary, an act in sleep of which he is unaware.

The wealth of possibility within conscious experience is the source of both the sense and the reality of freedom. Even when we are constrained by force, the multiple associations of our conscious awareness create for us a sense of possibility against which our constraint is enslavement. Causal determination is a relatively determinate and linear order of possibility, and the sense of its constraint, which underlies the dichotomy between causation and freedom, is due precisely to its limited range of possibility.

A conscious man inhabits a world of interconnections which he can call upon at any time by acting with or upon them. A man engrossed in thought may look at the sky and consciously see nothing; he "sees" the clouds only by remarking on them, at least to himself—that they are very white, that they look like faces or animals, and so forth—or at least by actions in response to them in a ramified order of possibilities and alternatives. He may respond to a sudden chill by goose pimples, a slight shiver, or by calling attention to it and rising to shut the window. The last case is significant because the activity of focusing attention on the temperature renders a host of other activities or responses possible; while the unnoticed raising of the hackles of the skin cannot be the source of multiple associations. Language is often considered indispensable for consciousness because without it the range of possibility open for carrying on a personal dialogue is sharply limited, while to one who possesses a language, the natural response to meaningful situations is in some form of discourse. I think, however, that it should be clear that a good part of consciousness is simply devoid of linguistic attributes, though these may follow at some subsequent stage.

The activity of consciousness may or may not have consciousness itself or the person engaged in it as its object. There can be an ordered flow of associations, even an interrelated system of meanings, without focus on the person who responds to those meanings. In order of increasing complexity of behavior, we may distinguish three ascending stages: first, a direct and terminal response to a stimulus, virtually a causal impact, such as the shrug of a shoulder while sleeping, a reflexive slap at a mosquito, becoming angry when hot and weary; second, an ongoing reponse to situations in which one's own actions or thoughts lead to further responses, a dialogue a person holds with himself in activities with steps in them—such as repairing a flat tire—where each step performed calls forth the next; finally, the response, not merely to prior acts of the individual as stimuli to further action, but to an act *as* an act of oneself—in reappraisal, criticism, or appreciation—where the agent recognizes himself to be an active agent. The first of these is not conscious; the second exhibits consciousness as awareness, even purpose; while the last, of concern here, is consciousness of the agent *as* a self, thus self-consciousness. I shall consider this last stage in a moment. First, however, I wish to consider again the question of whether consciousness can be found without consciousness of self?

It is quite certain that *if asked,* a conscious individual would reply that he is aware of himself. But this is nothing more than a recognition that any awareness in a being with language can be brought to self-awareness, though the person may not have been self-aware before.

This only shows that a man *can be made* conscious of himself as an object among others, just as he can see a table, or can sit on a chair with awareness of doing so, though he may not have been aware a moment before. It is analogous to asking a man who is in a room with a pattern in the wallpaper whether he notices the pattern. The question brings it to his attention.

Nevertheless, there appear to be strong grounds for objecting to the restriction of the phrase "self-consciousness" to the third stage in that every consciousness entails the existence of an object of consciousness and a subject who is conscious. In taking apart and putting together an automobile engine, a mechanic surely cannot forget that he is the instrument and agent of his task, insofar as it is his own actions which are the focus of concern. In a more passive situation, such as viewing a program on television, one either responds to every event with attention and thought, or one is not attending to *it* at all. The continual response to events before one, however passively, is unavoidably accompanied by multiple associations and reflexive habits of thought. One simply cannot be aware of anything without being aware of one's own responses to it, at least by responding further to them. To repeat Sartre's example, a man can count only insofar as he is aware of his activity as counting. Otherwise it is mere activity without aim. Every consciousness of an act entails a consciousness of the activity as an act of the agent's; otherwise it is blind and unintentional, and, to Sartre, not conscious as purposive.

However, there is a considerable difference between responses to one's own behavior and responding to oneself as the doer of deeds—that is, by forming the notion of a self, acting in a patterned and intelligible way. Mere consciousness may well be the manifestation of rigid and unbreakable habits of thought without sufficient awareness of self, intellectual acumen, or methodic habits of thought to permit reorganization and challenge of the habits themselves. I may be tempted to tell a lie to spare myself embarrassment, knowing full well that lying is a poor choice. I may converse with myself concerning my prospective feelings, may predict the results of both courses of action, and even face the impending conflict. I am here quite conscious of the consequences of my actions, though in a routine and unquestioning way. It is this very routine that marks the absence of methodic self-consciousness—for I am here but a creature of habits developed long ago. That these habits may conflict is of little importance, as are the anguish and pain I feel in the conflict—they are direct and straightforward responses to the situations in which I find myself and the things I do. The stronger habit will triumph. My hesitations, false movements, and torments are fully conscious, if not entirely purposeful, but only that.

What is lacking is a direct confrontation of these habits and how they came to exist—that is, a conscious scrutiny not only of the content of the conflict, but of my own place in it as a human being faced with particular choices. A conflict may, for example, call forth investigation to resolve it; it may evoke the re-examination of the principles of evaluation which have led to such a conflict; it may, in other words, lead to methodic acts in which the very nature of the person involved is examined as a creature of habits and visceral responses. Such a state of self-examination is very different from a concern for another object of consciousness. On the one hand, I respond to a situation (such as visiting a museum and viewing a style of painting I have never before seen) by talking about it, experiencing certain feelings, speaking some more (describing how vulgar it is, unimaginative, or how it breaks all accepted rules) and so forth; or on the other hand, I may respond to the same situation by heeding my own responses, seeking an expression of the canons apparently broken by this new style, taking my total reaction as an object of attention, and seeking to understand or improve it. Surely the latter is a very special, rare, and significant form of consciousness of self.

One of Hume's most difficult problems was that of ascertaining the ground of memory and habit in his analysis of causation. His principle of separability—that what can be distinguished must be thought of as separate—left him with no thread of continuity in an individual's experience to ground the formation of habits and the truth of memory. What Hume failed to do was to recognize the Cartesian insight that there does indeed prevail throughout a man's experience, however diverse and heterogenous, a continuity of identity and focus of awareness that is his awareness of himself within the variety of his experiences that constitutes them *his* experiences. In this sense, it would seem that all experience is constituted by the presence of self-identity, even self-consciousness.

However, two points must be mentioned in reply. First, Hume's problem is a problem of inference, as was Descartes' and Kant's, a philosophic problem of considerable complexity. In such cases it goes without saying that the modes of consciousness appropriate to problems of such sophistication are the most sophisticated possible in return. Hume sought the ultimate grounds of inference from the past to the future, and of the continuity of our experience. It is no surprise that implicit in such grounds—which arise, it may be said, only in profound philosophical inquiries—should be a concession to self-consciousness. It is the same self-consciousness Descartes discovered: the consciousness of self entailed in any investigation as belonging to the inquirer. Knowledge of a considerable degree of assurance entails a commitment to the continuity of memory and thus to the continuity of the knower. What Hume and Descartes showed is that inquiry is a sophisticated mode of methodic interrogation, and thus presupposes a considerable degree of self-consciousness. They showed nothing about less perspicuous modes of experience.

The second, and more important point to consider, is that inherent in both Hume's and Descartes' philosophic analyses is a conscious and sophisticated conception of method at work which they apply to the analysis of the self and personal identity. Unfortunately, though they employ a method directed at the self, they fail to distinguish self-consciousness which is no more than a continuity of discernment from a self-consciousness methodically employed. Kant and Hegel took a profound step in realizing that the sophisticated mode of self-consciousness necessary to the highest human activities is itself methodic. No doubt in most human consciousness—though not in all—there can be found an acceptance of one's continuous identity through time. This may indeed be a kind of self-consciousness. But it is worlds apart from the self-consciousness which is the synthesis of multiplicity within one life methodically interrogated.

To claim that all forms of consciousness are self-consciousness is therefore either trivial—in the sense that they are personal dialogues—or is false, in that only occasionally are the self and one's own conscious habits of thought and behavior an object of conscious examination. Self-criticism, one obvious example of consciousness of self in the fullest sense, is very rare—as compared, for example, with self-loathing. The latter can be a direct response to the world and oneself; the former comes only rarely to some men who are willing to examine not only their actions, but their very being engaged in them. All forms of consciousness contain a dialogue with oneself, and in that sense a consciousness of (or *by*) the self; but consciousness of self in which one is taken *as* a self, in which one's responses are not mere stimuli, but are viewed as products of a person in time and space, with patterned modes of thinking and acting, is something very different.

One of the definitions of consciousness Sartre offers is that "consciousness is a being such that in its being, its being is in question in so far as this being implies a being other than itself." This attitude of *questioning* Sartre takes to be essential to consciousness. Negation comes about

through the posing of questions: "In posing a question, a certain negative element is introduced into the world." Central to Sartre's sense of
consciousness is questioning of some sort, though he emphasizes a consciousness whose very being is in question.

However, questioning *as an activity* is not always present in awareness.
In fact, it is not present in all cases of self-consciousness either. If it can
always be found in what Sartre calls "consciousness," then he has preconceived of consciousness as distinct from awareness, as a mode of
being in which projects, plans, and goals are not only operative, but intelligently pursued. The point is that when sophisticated questioning is
present in consciousness, then it is also true that "methodic self-consciousness" obtains. But this is a truism—there are cases of consciousness and even self-consciousness which are not interrogative and certainly not methodical. This has the most vital consequences for the
claim that men are responsible for what they do—for I agree with Sartre that responsibility arises as a form of interrogation; but I deny that
most men question their existence. It is by active interrogation, implicit
or explicit, that mere consciousness becomes a methodic self-consciousness. It is by casting into question either an object—by asking if one's
initial response to it was correct—or oneself—by seeking to modify one's
responses and behavior—that one is methodically self-conscious, and
eventually may come to self-knowledge. What is fundamental is that a
questioning attitude is essential to a moral being insofar as he can seek
principles by which to guide his behavior. It is to the interrogative consciousness that we may look to find the source and nature of responsibility—viewed as *responses* to questions posed.

The equation of consciousness with *reflection* is considerably more profound than is often thought—"reflect-ion" as the turning of thoughts
and actions upon themselves. It is precisely this reflecting of responses in
and upon themselves that is consciousness, the responding to one's own
actions as part of a connected system of associations and meanings.
When I am aware of my behavior, I think about it, I appraise my own
actions. For example, if I am engaged in sanding a block of wood, I
may begin in a careful and watchful manner, but after awhile become
distracted by my thoughts and the monotony of the task. In the latter
case I cease being actively aware of what I am doing, though the nature
of the project leads me to continue my efforts repeatedly and habitually.
The difference between the self-conscious and the habitual stage of my
efforts is that the latter permits no correction, since it is merely action
without attention to the meaning of that action. I do not study the
effects of each stroke and modify my efforts in line with what I intend to

do. Critical analysis depends on the existence of a consciousness which attends to oneself and what one does. My stroke of the sandpaper is a response to roughness of a part of the block of wood. Conscious *control* comes by noting the smoothness being produced, and its location, by consideration of the angle and rate of stroke that give the most efficient results, and by my modifying my actions suitably.

The latter is a highly sophisticated example of consciousness, containing methodic concern for relations between means and ends. Contrast it with the consciousness of strolling down a leafy lane on a summer day, noting the shady spots, the patterns of light and dark, the color of the sky. Here one does not intend the completion of a task, nor to correct his actions in line with it. He is conscious only insofar as he notes events. This noticing is more than a simple response (such as scratching a mosquito-bite); it is a response filled with the presence of other things, with the associations and interconnections such as can be brought by language. I notice the color of the sky when I not only "see" it, but think to myself "How blue it is," or that "it is the color of Wedgwood china." The advent of language permits the beginning of various trains of thought: blue like . . . ; Wedgwood china is expensive; and so forth. It is the continual interweaving of thought and action that is consciousness.

A particular object, then, remains in consciousness as long as the organism continues to respond to it in a network of associations, in which it is the central focus to which various actions continually return. If I walk around a horse, inspecting him from all sides, I remain conscious of all his failings if I not only converse with myself about them, but continually reflect upon my past responses as well (what I noticed about him five minutes ago) in such manner as to characterize my present consideration. What I completely forget about passes into oblivion, making it doubtful for me to say that I have been conscious for the past ten minutes of it. What I completely forget, so that it ceases to be meaningful now, I am not conscious of now.

To be conscious of *oneself*, then, is to pursue in one's continued responses an awareness of oneself in some definite and structured sense. I become the object of my own sequential actions. My own acts, as well as my character, self, goals, and desires, become the focus of attention. I pursue a discourse with myself upon them. That this is a fairly sophisticated activity should be rather obvious. I must first respond to the world in order to have my own responses as an object of attention. I may develop all sorts of habits of response, which may be filled with purposive qualities, without ever learning to examine the habits themselves, the goals within them, or even noticing that they exist. In order to be aware of myself *as a self,* I must have an implicit conception of a coherent and organized person who lives in a spatio-temporal world, subject to its influences yet capable of efficacious control and manipulation of his environment. The more confused or indeterminate my conception of myself, the less self-conscious I am in the full sense.

In consciousness of an object, the focal system of associations that centers on a given object may be distorted and noncognitive. The associations called up by the presence of a point of light in the sky may involve neither cognition of astronomy nor facts of navigation. A fundamental ambiguity is thus inherent in the claim that a person is conscious of such a point of light *as a star.* In one sense he is conscious of the star, but not *as* such. To be conscious of the star as a star unmistakably involves knowledge of some and perhaps many of the essential properties of stars. Yet without any knowledge of astronomy whatsoever, a person may be said to be conscious of a star if some of its direct causal effects are the focus of his attention. A person is thought to be conscious of the presence of a lion in the jungle if he hears the lion's roar, although he may have no idea whatsoever that it is a lion roaring nor even that it is an animal sound at all.

The same ambiguity is central to the issue of the relationship between consciousness of an object and the presence of self-consciousness. In a trivial sense analogous to the noting of direct causal effects, we are aware of ourselves in any act of consciousness in that our existence is a necessary condition of that consciousness. We observe a direct effect of our enduring existence, and thereby ourselves as well. We are conscious of ourselves insofar as we are conscious of something that could not exist without us—say a particular feeling or perception.

Such self-consciousness contains the most minimal cognitive commitments. We are not aware of ourselves as possessing any particular properties, nor of being any particular kind of person. Descartes followed his *cogito* with the question: "What then is it that I am?" and decides, "a thinking thing . . . a thing that doubts, understands, affirms, denies, wills" and so forth. He assumes too much, as does Sartre in supposing that the self-consciousness of all conscious existence is a form of questioning. In fact, we are conscious of ourselves here only insofar as we are conscious of something *else* which is dependent upon our existence. But we do not know the true connection between the object and our existence, nor even *of* that connection. If we are always conscious of ourselves when conscious of an object, we often possess that self-consciousness without knowing that we have it. In particular, we may know little about ourselves, and yet possess this trivial kind of self-consciousness.

The self-consciousness that is essential to moral responsibility is a very different kind of awareness than the trivial one I have been discussing. For one thing, it includes a consciousness of oneself as an agent, capable of effective choice and action, who is subject to influences that may aid or hinder him in achieving his goals. The system of associations that is ordinary consciousness becomes self-consciousness in the full sense only when the focus of awareness is a rich and full person who is capable of decision and action. A person can be self-conscious only if he has a fairly rich and accurate picture of himself as a self. As I shall show, a person is self-conscious to the extent required for moral responsibility only when he has rich and adequate self-knowledge.

One property of such self-knowledge has already been mentioned, though a detailed discussion will be provided later—that is, *methodic* self-consciousness. The questioning Sartre claims is essential to all consciousness and self-consciousness becomes genuinely interrogative only when methods of analysis and discovery are available and utilized. In the example above of sanding a block of wood, I may be conscious of my task and of the roughness of the wood by nothing more than the activity involved in sanding it. I continually respond to my own activities and to my projected goals by sanding without further thought or attention. Methodic self-consciousness obtains when I not only respond to the roughness of the wood, but to my own movements, or to the sandpaper I am using, critically or with satisfaction. In evaluating what I am doing, I consider the method I am using and my accomplishments. In asking myself if I am doing what I ought to be doing, I implicitly appeal to a method for determining the answer to my question. I shall argue that it is the presence of methods of self-consciousness and self-interrogation that brings responsibility and freedom into existence.

3

Reason
and Method

Ethics and Reason

The dispute over the cognitive status of normative judgments is an ancient one, captured eloquently and persuasively in the Socratic discussions on whether virtue can be taught. In recent times, however, the negative view has returned with great power. Drawing by implication from a successful science which they construe as totally empirical (or more recently, hypothetico-empirical), twentieth-century philosophers have reached the conclusion that knowledge and science are virtually synonymous—due to the unmistakable success of the latter—entailing that since normative judgments are unscientific, they must be irrational. The position that normative concepts—such as "good" and "ought"—may not be validly derived from purely empirical descriptions of facts supports this view. Recent papers in ethical theory have moved the common-sense doctrine that moral disputes are basically but "a matter of opinion" to a loftier intellectual plane, without disturbing the surds of that position, by straightforwardly denying the relevance of methodic canons of inquiry to judgments of value. Two people may dispute on a moral question only *after* having accepted the initial premises or values implicit in the argument. In A. J. Ayer's youthful and exuberant words: "We find that argument is possible on moral questions only if some system of values is presupposed. . . . What we do not and cannot argue about is the validity of these moral principles. We merely praise them or condemn them in the light of our own feelings." *

The pit lurking here is that of a violent subjectivism in which it is maintained that *no* critical modes of appraisal whatsoever may legitimately be applied to ethical judgments. Whether supported by the claim that a normative judgment is "nothing but" an expression of the agent's feelings, which may not be criticized insofar as they are his true feelings, or whether it is an expression of social or cultural norms, which again are just facts about human behavior or patterns of social adjustment; the view taken is that holding a normative position is but a fact, not open to criticism except from some other normative point of view, which is itself but a fact and so on. Thus, social scientists proudly display their data-collecting and empirical methods as value-free, maintaining all the while that they as men have particular values and hold certain moral principles that are quite separate from their professional activities, and that a person's moral attitudes are quite irrelevant to his carrying out scientific investigation.

The foundation of this view—that science and ethics are essentially disparate—is twofold. On the one hand, science has succeeded best when it abandoned values based on immediate needs or nonempirical cosmologies. As Galileo put it in his *Dialogues*, "It is the purpose of our Author merely to investigate and demonstrate some of the properties of accelerated motion, whatever the cause of those accelerations may be." It was the underlying causes that contained moral import. Giving up the search for a unified world-view containing both scientific and normative judgments was wonderfully productive for science. Positivism (in the looser sense) became the watchword of the empirical, the mark of the scientific attitude as against the superstitiously emotional. On the other hand, philosophy failed to satisfy the desire of men for *proof* that a given moral system was the best. Perhaps the desire for such proof is failed by science as well—at least Hume's attack on induction led many to think so. But the constant search for new evidence, for theoretical order and economy, for empirical vindication, made science difficult to oppose. To repudiate science was to refuse systematization and order as

* *Language, Truth and Logic* (New York: Dover, 1952), pp. 111–12.

well as its obvious fruits manifested in technology. Science cultivates the
proofs in things, notwithstanding the distance to be traversed at any
time to reach evidence at the frontiers of science. One can always repudiate any moral principle or value-judgment by the claim that it cannot
be proved. How prove that a Nazi war criminal or an American soldier
engaging in atrocities in Vietnam, *who obeyed the laws of his country*, nevertheless did something wrong? Is it not a matter of opinion?

It is well-known in value theory that this "matter of opinion" need
not pervade all one's normative judgments, that there is a place in morality for factual knowledge. *Given* a basic set of values or normative
principles, one may seek to determine the most efficient means to desired ends, what Kant called "hypothetical imperatives." The quest for
means is the quest for knowledge, provided that ends are taken on mere
inclination or feeling. I may be *persuaded* to change my basic values, but
I cannot be objectively compelled to. Once I have formed them, however, empirical knowledge is important to me in determining courses of
action.

The fundamental questions of value theory I wish to avoid here.
They complicate the analysis of moral judgments to an extreme. I shall
therefore argue in the rest of this chapter only that the impossibility of
proof exists in science as well as in ethics, that rationality and cognition
are not "built in" to human life, but depend as well on some basic value
choices, and that the unavoidability of such choices does not imply that
logical compulsion is nonexistent or illegitimate. In short, I shall argue
that the methods of ethics are rational, quite as much as are the methods of science and philosophy, but that reason in ethics is quite different
in important respects from reason in science.

In beginning, it is necessary to avoid the identification of "reason"
with "science"; otherwise the claim that there are other uses or kinds of
rationality than the scientific becomes trivially false. Some sufficiently
general conception of rationality is necessary in order that it be meaningful to investigate the relationship between reason in science and
morals. Here we might think it useful to consider a historical account of
conceptions of reason, but a cursory look indicates that history in this
instance will not aid us very much. The recognition that science is necessarily hypothetical and theoretical, that confirmation is not and cannot be logically conclusive, has until very recently been considered a
cognitive liability. It is a relatively new conception that the struggle
within science for tentative hypotheses, theoretical systems of varying
degrees of confirmation, and the minimization if not the elimination of
risk, is a pervasive characteristic of science, and one of its strengths

rather than a weakness. The great problem for Hume and Kant was to reconcile in some way the logical gap between scientific conclusions and confirming evidence with the claim that knowledge is certain or necessary in some sense. They recognized the existence of a problem which contemporary epistemological theory completely dismisses. Under these conditions we cannot hope for aid from the history of philosophy, for it was involved for too long with overly "necessary" conceptions of rationality.

Validation

Perhaps the place to look for a more general theory of rationality is to the act or process of confirmation. I suggest that the mark of reason in science is to be found not in speculative thought—for fictional imagination, artistic fantasy, even theoretical mystification, all are pervaded by and depend upon the excitement and satisfaction of an inventive imagination at play. What is crucial in science are theories that are capable of test and confirmation, which order data into new and more illuminating patterns, and which themselves are open to test. In other words, the mark of scientific reason is its ability to respond positively to the demand for proof (or, if "proof" is too strong a word, suggesting logically determinate arguments, to the demand for substantiation, confirmation, or more generally, *validation*). An imaginative speculation remains only that, without cognitive value or control, unless it is submitted to test, often indefinite further test. The purpose of this test is to determine if the speculation is "merely" a speculation, or whether it is "valid"—that is, whether it has met and will continue to meet further tests. (In science, we often call a successfully tested hypothesis "true"—at least tentatively.) Invalid or nonvalidatable (meaning nontestable) hypotheses are not of scientific value, and are called respectively "false" and "noncognitive." The verifiability criterion, whatever its faults, marks the introduction of a test for determining whether cognitively significant statements are capable of validation or not.

My main thesis here is that there are many forms and types of validation, of which scientific confirmation is only one, and that some analysis of validation in general is worth pursuing in order to avoid lapsing into the stultifying identification of validation with confirmation, and rationality with scientific method. I suggest that the mark of cognition is not so much the existence of *logical* criteria as it is the existence of criteria of appraisal of any sort. In science certain judgments are considered valid (or most valid) if they have been directly or indirectly confirmed, if they produce (or at least do not violate) systematic order and organization, if they contribute to certain aesthetic criteria of simplicity and elegance, and if they are capable of promoting intuitive satisfaction or "intelligibility." The incorporation of logical structures and principles into methods of confirmation is essential only by stipulation. The important element is the criteria of appraisal which permit the determination of some judgments to be valid and others not.

It is probably worth, then, taking a number of examples to investigate the role of validating criteria in different areas—indeed, within what may be considered different *methods*. Methods of science are but one kind of method; other methods have their own means of validation and their own kinds of test. I suggest, however, that unless there is method—that is, control, order, purpose—there cannot be validation. An action becomes capable of validation only within an order with determinable goals and ends. It is either valid because it is good for some purpose, or insofar as it satisfies implicit or explicit criteria of appraisal. (These conditions may well be identical.) Validation cannot exist without an ordered sense of means for achieving ends. If I am hungry and seek some means of relieving my pangs, I do not consider the accidental state of nervous exhaustion into which I may fall and which terminates my pain a valid achievement. Nor will taking a quick-acting poison be valid, though both of these achieve the gross end I have in mind. The *accidental* relation of means to ends here renders the achievement of the end unmethodic and therefore invalid. Put another way, the claim "It worked" is not significant if it worked by chance. If there is method, it is legitimate to ask "how?" And the sense of this question is, "How did you do it? Can you do it again?"—implying the existence of a method. If there is no answer available to these questions, tests for validity are empty. The reply "It just did" is simply unintelligible, in having no connection with validity. If it just happened, it may have satisfied us, but it is no achievement. Of course in this light, trial and error is a method, and if one employs it one may recognize which particular act produced the intended effect and when.

A general definition of method may be useful here, and I offer one from Justus Buchler's *The Concept of Method*: "A method is a power of manipulating natural complexes, purposively and recognizably, within a reproducible order of utterance; and methodic activity is the translation of such a power into the pursuit of an end—an end implied by the reproduction." * What is important is that there are good and bad, rational and irrational, defensible and indefensible methods. Not all methods indicate rationality; some methods are hysterical, superstitious, even chaotic. However, methods are reproducible—in being *powers* of manipulation—often at will under appropriate circumstances. There are habitual methods without interrogation or control, as in domestic rituals (Which sock goes on first?), even controlled activities like farming (My father farmed that way and so do I). There are methods which are themselves the object of investigation in which there is questioning, criticism, and test. It is the latter with which we are most concerned.

It would not appear that habitual or uninterrogative methods permit concern for validity. Yet in at least one important sense every methodic act can be valid or invalid—and one might say that to this extent every methodic act raises some questions. A given act may accord with the method employed or may fail to do so—as a pipe smoker's lighting his pipe cannot be accomplished if he uses both hands to deal a hand of bridge. The method in this case is the use of his hands in well-defined ways, and we simply deny that he is employing the method, or doing so correctly if he claims he is. A chef following a recipe may put in too much butter, indeed twice the amount specified. We usually consider this a special kind of error, that of *not following* the method correctly. He made a *mistake;* what he did was *wrong*, but by virtue of misemploying the method. This should be contrasted with the same chef inventing a new recipe. Here there is no recipe to follow, but there is certainly a method he employs, based on his experience and knowledge of other recipes and styles of cuisine, for developing a new and satisfying combination of tastes. Here he may put in too much butter also; but the amount is not specified in advance. His "mistake" is not that of failing to *follow* a method, for the method of invention has been carefully adhered to. (He may, for example, utilize the same amount of butter used in a similar recipe for chicken only to find that it doesn't go with lobster.) Here we may speak of validation also, in recognizing the failure of the proposed recipe; a correctly used method may lead to an invalid result. The method itself is interrogative, with built-in questions and tests. A well-defined means exists, with fairly definite criteria whether precisely formulated or not, for testing a product to determine if it is suc-

---

* (New York: Columbia University Press, 1961), p. 135.

cessful or not, if it accomplishes the end for which it was produced. The test here is that of simply tasting the end-product. This, coupled with experience and acquired skills of appraisal, determines the validity or success of the enterprise.

Validation depends upon the existence of a means for testing an object or action as to whether it meets particular standards; and such tests exist only in methods framed by questioning—which at least seek results which pass the tests built into them. Consider an automobile mechanic given a car which will not start. He possesses a fairly definite and well-defined method for finding what is wrong and correcting it. He tests the electrical system first, to determine whether the starter is turning over the engine, if the ignition system is generating sufficient spark to ignite the fuel. If they seem in good order, he turns to the carburetor to determine if fuel is being delivered to the cylinders, and so on. Eventually he succeeds, by finding some component which is not performing adequately and by adjusting it, in producing a car that will reliably start. Each act is tested by the total performance of the automobile, and the mechanic must continually ask himself if he has improved it. Without asking himself questions, at least implicitly, he cannot test what he does. The method is itself interrogative. In fact, implicit in its questions about the validity of actions and objects may well be questions concerning the method itself and its purported goals.

I suggest at this point that the notion of interrogative and inventive methods, with procedures of test and validation, may be used as a basic concept on which to build a general theory of rationality. I shall in the next section show that science, with all forms of "propositional" knowledge, is one example of interrogative methods with means of validation, and that this, more than anything else, determines its rational status. But it should be clear that many interrogative methods exist which can by no stretch of the imagination be deemed to be based on propositional knowledge. A brief example will suffice: consider a "natural athlete" learning to play tennis. Of course, some instructions are given him—to hit off the foot on the opposite side of the stroke, to change the position of the racquet depending on the stroke, and so on—but these are of relatively minor importance in his knowledge of tennis. Moreover, the instructions are not "propositions"—they are either normative judgments or commands: "You should keep your eye on the ball," or "Move to the right more quickly." What our sportsman must learn is how to move, what a proper stroke feels like; he must learn strategy and timing. He makes mistakes; he misses shots or returns them too softly. He changes his style of play to correct such errors—indeed, he may have to completely change his style of play if things do not improve. A clear test of his skill and method of play exists; he may constantly strive to improve himself in relation to this test.

It is sometimes said that such knowledge is "knowledge how," which is different from "knowledge that" or propositional knowledge, and that little is gained by confusing them. I hope it will be clear that I do not wish to confuse them, but only to relate them as methodic activities. For it is clear that the absence of statements or propositions is no liability to the presence of skill, training, or methods of validation and appraisal. It may well be maintained that what a scientist knows best is *how* to set up well-designed experiments, *how* to think in a logical and consistent manner, *how* to write effective and informative reports. The propositional knowledge embodied in the reports exists only by virtue of these other skills, and by other scientists' knowing *how* to read such reports intelligently. The function of propositions is to report *truly*, but they can do so only insofar as they are based on the methods of tests and analysis which are the heart of science. These issues are to be taken up now by the separate consideration of propositional knowledge.

Scientific Validation

I shall, for convenience, identify scientific and propositional knowledge in this section. This will permit me to emphasize what I have already indicated to be most important in such forms of cognition—the search for and exhibition of evidence on the basis of which hypothetical propositions are accepted as true. No doubt certain questions will be blurred by such an approach—*viz.*, concerning the ways in which some ordinary beliefs fail to depend upon secure evidential foundations yet are accepted by most people as true and therefore known. However, I cannot but feel that to take up such issues here would not necessarily illuminate the problems under consideration and would simply try the patience of my readers.

Philosophers are divided today into those who are very clear about what is meant by the word "proposition" and those who persist in their failure to understand its meaning. Sometimes propositions are defined as "meanings" of statements, so that two different statements may "mean" the same thing (i.e., "It is raining" and "Il pleut"). However, meanings are not simple and self-evident things, if they are *things* at all,

and certain obvious questions come to mind: When are two propositions identical? When do they differ? Here we find that all the interesting work in the analysis of identity turns to sentences and substitutabil-
ity, rather than propositions. Further, just how do propositions and facts
differ? If we hold that propositions are true or false by virtue of facts,
just how do we compare the two? What are we comparing or relating? I
can look and see that it is raining, but see neither a fact nor a proposition; nor do I utter a proposition when I say "It is raining"—which is a
sentence in the English language. It means something, but it does not
follow that it *has* a meaning except by extension from the adverbial
usage. Meanings are far too difficult to construe at all much less to identify as bare-faced entities called "propositions."

These difficulties, considered only as difficulties and not as sugges-
tions for solutions, make me reluctant to take the concept of *proposition*
as clear and self-evident. I shall, therefore, speak of propositional
knowledge by extension from the methods of science, as knowledge
gained by employing those methods. In this way I will be able to avoid
the difficulties of analyzing the concept of proposition. Moreover, I will
also avoid the too-common separation of propositional knowledge from
other methodic results by the supposedly intelligible claim that the
former involve propositions. Propositional or scientific knowledge is
unique as a form of knowledge because it is the result of methods of
definite and unique properties. It is important to avoid the hypostatiza-
tion of propositions in such a manner as to construe the ontological relations between scientific statements and the world to be much clearer
than they really are—that is, by taking the meanings of such statements
to be propositions, and by blurring the distinction between facts and
propositions into nothing, so that scientific statements become simple
cognitive accounts of the real world. Methods of test and verification
draw the connection between scientific statements and the world we live
in, just as methods of artistic manipulation and appreciation set the relations between the art object and the world the artist or audience live
in. Without such methods neither scientific statements nor art objects
would be what they are—which is but another way of saying that without methods of appropriation, they would not have the meaning they
do.

What then is essential to the methods of science? Sometimes it is
claimed that science is unique because it relies on observation. But art-
ists also carefully observe the world they live in, and claim that the significance of their work is that it reflects the world *as they see it.* The logical structure of scientific systems is paralleled by philosophy and

mathematics, yet few philosophers today would claim that these are sciences in the sense that they reveal new empirical information about the world. A remaining alternative is that science is unique in that it offers a combination of observation and logical rigor found in no other method. This is true, though by no means obviously so. Philosophic arguments also often tend to consider well-known observations without which they would lose much of their force, and logical rigor is essential to philosophical systematization and order.

If science offers a unique combination of observation and rigor, we must ascertain its nature. What is essential is the concept of *evidence*. Scientific conclusions depend upon definite evidence supporting them. Evidence is quite irrelevant to art; and although philosophers often turn to empirical observation in their arguments, they seldom offer hypotheses so conceived as to be determinately testable by the collection of evidence. Hypothetical prediction of observable events is often irrelevant in philosophy, while it is, at some point of the entire enterprise, *essential* to science. Indeed, scientific hypotheses are notable in that they *must* be experimentally testable, at least in principle and often in fact; otherwise they are without important scientific value.

My claim, then, is that science offers unique methods of test rooted in unique ideals and criteria of testability. Arguments, systematic rigor, and fruitfulness are criteria of validity in philosophy; exciting organization, vivid arrangement of material, to the point of evoking thrilling or at least eminently satisfying experiences, are essential to valid works of art. The difference among these various types of method comes down to their different goals and over-arching ideals, with corresponding differences in their modes of validation.

Science is permeated by an ideal of completion in its collection of evidence. If a "problem" does not permit a "solution," it is not scientific. Here what is meant by a "solution" may be one of a number of different items depending on the problem posed. It may be an experimental result which confirms a given hypothesis. It may be a hypothesis which is compatible with accepted or known laws and which explains given observations. It may be a suitable system of statements which "explains" (that is, permits, with appropriate boundary conditions, the logical deduction of) many laws and separate observations, and so on. The essential point in each of these cases is that every problem in science is posed in terms of evidence, and every solution either is the presentation of evidence or is a hypothesis presented in the light of available evidence for or against it.

What is the nature of evidence? I suggest that in science the concept of evidence rests upon an ideal of completeness and determinacy. However insecure and tentative a proposal or hypothesis may be, it is a *scientific* hypothesis only under the definite expectation that among its various competitors, only one is compatible with available evidence. Of course, it is always possible to construct many alternatives to an acceptable theory which may, for example, differ only in the twentieth decimal place, far less than can be determined by the state of science at the time—but then science turns to a principle of simplicity or some other principle of convenience or order. At any time, two competing theoretical systems may not allow for a determinate and grounded choice between them—but they are genuine competitors within scientific investigation only if it is possible within the domain of their incompatibility to find evidence which can ground a choice between them. It may not be possible for years to decide between two competing scientific hypotheses, but the decision must be possible in principle, and eventually in fact, or else the dispute will be rejected as unscientific. Every problem offered as scientific presupposes a *solution*—that is, a solution so determinate that everyone in the scientific community must eventually accept it. If logical criteria alone do not suffice, aesthetic criteria are likewise proposed, or else normative principles of method are found, as in experimental psychology and the disputes over methods of conditioning. Every definite hypothesis in science may be rejected by some pioneer on good grounds, but first the evidence must be collected to demonstrate that a new problem has arisen.

I am proposing that the nature of evidence is to be found in the scientific ideals of determinacy and resolvability, qualified by the ideal of theoretical generality. Evidence is that sort of thing which, within a system of observations and experimental methods, makes determinate answers possible to proposed questions. Instruments make new evidence possible, and give substance to what we consider to be evidence at any time, instead of being merely new techniques for finding older modes of evidence. Every new device creates new problems and new modes of evidence to resolve them.

It should by no means be thought that the definiteness of scientific discoveries implies either permanence or lack of controversy. Controversy arises at most stages of the scientific process in the various hypotheses, experimental techniques, even observational results, which may be attacked as inadequate. The point is that a solution to a scientific problem arises only within certain implicit and explicit, perhaps even unformulated assumptions. It is these assumptions that fulfill the ideals of determinacy, and the sense of the solution of problems. Mendeleev's proposal that chemical elements might be listed in order of increasing atomic weight, and that families of elements would then have similar properties, depended heavily on the *assumption* that two differing atomic weights denoted two different elements. From this he was led to change the conception of chemical elements—from weight to atomic number (the number of units of charge in the nucleus). However, in terms of chemistry and its problems at the time he was writing, Mendeleev resolved an essential problem of the interrelationship of chemical elements *on a false assumption*. When evidence arose to challenge that assumption, the periodic table was so well documented as to constitute an essential aspect of chemistry at *that* time, and isotopic variation had to be subsumed under its general conception. The point is that scientific problems are so defined within the scientific community as to be open to resolution in the sense that certain experimental results or theoretical hypotheses are satisfactory, at least for a certain period of time, to virtually everyone working in the area. Men of science work with presuppositions of fact as well as method in order that definiteness and determinacy be maximized. Duhem's claim that there can be no crucial experiment for a scientific hypothesis fails to reflect the pragmatic fact that there *are* crucial experiments—from the point of view of the working scientist, that is—though there can be no purely logical basis for them. Without experiments which can settle disputes, science could not be as compelling as it is.

For science is compelling, in a manner unique among interrogative methods. Art and philosophy never achieve the unanimity of successful scientific theories nor the equivalent of the sense that to object to the conclusions of science is to commit a vital error. Taste enters art; aesthetic values permeate philosophic systems; both render compulsion indeterminate and pluralistic. I submit, however, that the specific compulsion of science does not stem from its greater truth or higher cognitive status, but rather that science is compelling by choice and aim, not because the truth is so powerful. That is, science is the method devoted to maximizing certainty, minimizing ambiguity and doubt, and achieving the most determinate means of validation. The role of evidence in science, the constant testing and retesting of conclusions, the perpetual search for new data and explanatory theory, is the justification of a method that, by making certain fundamental assumptions, creates determinate and compelling solutions to its problems.

The compulsion of science is not a result of the greater success or value of science but is rather the source of its success and the key to its value. Beginning with Galileo and continuing through the positivism of

Comte and Mach and the social sciences today, science has distinguished itself from disciplines devoted to normative considerations and purely theoretical implications—in short, all the areas in which unanimity is impossible once controversy is permitted. Rather, science turned to areas remote from human concern in order that decisiveness and determinacy be maximized. Of course, the evidential reflection of scientific discoveries into ordinary affairs reveals how misguided the claim was that science (particularly the social sciences) could entirely escape normative considerations or philosophic scrutiny. By eliminating the eternally doubtful from its domain, science progressed rapidly and efficiently, for in the areas of physics and chemistry simple problems could be found which permit definite, if not final solutions. Everyone could agree that the passage of an electric current created a magnetic field. There are, in the lives of all of us who are willing to observe our surroundings intelligently and reason upon our observations, certain observations we all accept. Philosophical doubts such as Descartes' are dismissible as "mere" philosophizing. Psychological criticisms of perceptual errors are set aside for investigation at another time. The fund of data common to all men is large enough to permit the entrenchment of a method devoted to the use of such data to maximize determinacy and precision of solution, and to minimize divergence of point of view and ambiguity of thought.

The strength of science is that it presupposes within its search for order and determinacy the right to ask *any* question, provided a means can be found for answering it. The method of science is unending, since it constantly returns on itself to attack assumptions essential within previous investigations on the basis of newly discovered evidence. Not only is the universe large and the amount of possible knowledge virtually infinite, but science cannot ever possess all this knowledge at once and still be science. There are two reasons for this: first, that science moves from assumption to assumption, returning on itself to criticize older views, but never ceasing to question—it is a perpetually interrogative method, despite its determinacy; second, within the scientific enterprise, many vital questions are dismissed as unscientific—just as Galileo dismissed the search for "underlying causes" of falling bodies—which return to haunt the fundamental assumptions of science. Science seeks independence, but it cannot completely find it, for that would be to totally dismiss philosophic and aesthetic concerns, and the intervention of such enterprises is unavoidable in a rational life. A science without art and philosophy could exist, but it is questionable whether it would be "satisfying" to its adherents. The ideals of order and logical rigor to which science appeals to generate determinacy where observational evidence alone is not sufficient bring into science a residuum of indeterminacy that can never be eliminated, an indeterminacy which calls for a continual readjustment of theory to discovery. Simply consider the theory of relativity, whose great fascination was only partially its great *scientific* success. It captured the imaginations of men because of its transformation of the role of the observer within science itself, the place of man in the world as knower. It offered as fact what had been only philosophical speculation before.

If science is viewed as grounded in a method which compels the most determinate solutions possible, it ceases to be the only genuine candidate for rational method. It by no means guarantees assurance or complete determinacy of resolution. Determinacy of solution and compulsion of evidence are gained by rigid adherence to methodic canons of investigation and logical rigor. Questions that appear at first to be significant become devoid of significance either permanently or until new hypotheses and experimental techniques render them soluble. The questions that remain are often superficially far less interesting—except that they are manageable, and by being managed, lead to the solution of other more intrinsically important problems. No scientific solution can be thought to be completely definite or precise; new theories are constantly required; laws are constantly modified under the pressure of discoveries based on finer techniques of measurement; fundamental assumptions are constantly attacked and defended. The determinacy of science is both its great strength and its limitation. It gains clarity, order, and precision; but also ignores problems that do not permit such determinacy, yet which are, nevertheless, open to methodic investigation and appraisal, if not so determinately. That there are such problems, and that science cannot and should not deal with them, is what must now be shown.

Other Interrogative Methods

I have argued that there are modes of validation that are not scientific, that place no emphasis on the collection of evidence. I have also suggested that these may be construed as "solutions" to "problems" of an unscientific kind. Let me hasten to add that such an extended usage of the word "problem" is fraught with danger. An obvious example is

that of a painter, let us imagine presented with a commissioned work—
a portrait of a lady. He has his paints, his canvas, and the lady is seated
on his right. He has posed a question for himself—"How shall I paint
her?" "What kind of portrait would be appropriate?" He can begin
with any number of subquestions: "What kind of person is she?" "What
strikes me as most important about her?" "Shall I begin with her face
or her hair?" And so forth.

What is most important here is that none of these questions need be
answered in advance, no matter how explicitly the artist considers
them. He may respond to the lady by the feel of certain colors, excited
by certain facial lines, the carriage of her head, the crinkle of her smile.
The psychological question, "What kind of person is she?" may be sub-
ordinated to the question, "What strikes me as important about her?"
Here the artist may give an answer only by painting the portrait.
Whether or not he decides in words, on the basis of evidence, what the
lady's character is, is quite irrelevant to his work as a painter. Such
matters he must decide for himself as means to ends, and he may or
may not be articulate, or conscious of his decisions. The consciousness
that is manifested in the painting may be manifested only there, in its
results on the canvas.

Nevertheless, there is a rational method of great force and significance at work in situations of this sort; it is revealed as well as expressed in the work of art that results. Something vital about the subject
of the painting must be captured within it. The whole must express
within itself a definite, intelligible sense of a person, if not the one per-
ceived by everybody. The painting must also satisfy its audience as a
painting, in its colors, arrangement, order, and strength of line. The
skill, understanding, control, and capacity to criticize as well as execute
such a portrait are definite signs of rational capacities at work. The outcome of a method of painting, in the hands of an expert, is something
open to inspection and appraisal as to whether it is a success or valid.
The expression, "You have captured something about her mouth" is
vivid praise, while "The eyes are all wrong" is strong criticism. In general, we are well acquainted with successful and unsuccessful portraits,
and the differences among them. Not any painting is a valid portrait.
For this reason an artist who proposes to paint a portrait must seek to
find the painting which will prove valid. The results of his search can be
tested and validated. The project he undertakes, and the judgment of
the result, mark the employment of an interrogative method in which
questions are asked and answers given in the results displayed.

I hesitate, however, to call such a valid result a "solution to a problem," for what appear to me to be significant and compelling reasons. Most important of all, when we speak of problems and their solutions, we usually have in mind "*the* solution to the problem." That is, not only is a specific problem taken to exist, but it has one and only one solution. Consider an arithmetic example here: if we are given $3x = 9$, and asked $x = ?$, only one answer is valid. It is true that there are cases in mathematics where more than one solution is possible—for example, there are many ways to prove a theorem. The essential point is, however, that a valid proof is precisely and unambiguously that. The means of validation can be so clear and straightforward that disputes are minimized. This feature exists in the sciences as well; the validation of a hypothesis takes place in such a manner, and amidst sufficiently powerful presuppositions, as to minimize divergence of opinion as to whether it is valid or not. At the frontiers of science, controversy is common and welcomed, but always in the expectation and hope that the controversy can be resolved. Indeed, even in cosmological speculation, which might *a priori* be thought embroiled in perpetual controversy, community of assent is being reached today on very important matters. As science develops toward more elaborate systems of thought, and the volume of evidence grows, the proposal of alternatives which are capable of validation in terms of available evidence becomes more difficult. This too promotes community of assent within science.

In art, however, divergence of point of view is not only unavoidable, but is essential and even desirable. To introduce criteria of validation into art which would render every work of art clearly and universally valid or not would eliminate the indeterminate element in artistic creation and appraisal that is so essential to them. There is no "best" painting at a given time analogous to a "best" theory in science. The portrait painter does not have to paint "the" portrait of his subject to be successful. He must paint *his* portrait, leaving room for countless others to do the same, and equally well though very differently. Art seeks wealth of point of view and divergence of outlook. Every painting reveals some uniqueness which not only marks it as different, but which demands that it be looked at without limited preconceptions. Every artist seeks a new means of expression. The greater the fund of these, the wider and more exciting the work of art becomes. To limit art to but a few valid works by the imposition of narrow and restricted principles of appraisal would be to destroy it. Art would cease, and a mechanical routine would take its place. We could agree, if we so desired, to a narrow and precise set of criteria for the validation of works of art based on principles of symmetry, color arrangement, and the like. But art would cease being the promulgation of newness of vision coupled with force of presentation and would become a mixture of composition and draftsmanship.

Inherent in art, then, as art, is a sense of the wealth of human possibility, difference of point of view, and variation in taste and preference, as well as insight and vision. The principles of validation of art incorporate this within them. There is no "problem" that an artist proposes to himself when he begins other than that of creating a work of art. There is no solution to the question of how to do so except the work of art itself. There might have been many such works equally satisfactory as answers to the question posed. The wealth of possibility remains throughout art, so that there are thousands of "problems" at any stage but the last, while the "solution" is only one of countless alternatives. If so, it is no solution to a problem. It is, however, a valid product created by the artist in response to some need or purpose and can be appraised for its validity and success.

I mentioned the compulsion of science, its elimination of variation and controversy. Art by no means shares this property; divergence of judgment is essential to it. Yet powerful compulsions can be found in art based on its significant means of validation. Not everything is valid. On the most trivial level, a canvas with a splotch of green in its upper right-hand corner creates demands on a painter to balance it, to oppose or contrast it. A preconceived idea also creates demands of execution, which as they fall short of the idea, compel readjustment and reconception. Musical progressions and modulations compel both composer and audience to expect a particular resolution. These demands are the basis for any subsequent judgment of validity. And in the judgment of the value of some works of art, the compulsions of appraisal may bring virtual unanimity in fact—though it must be granted that the methods of analysis do not force such unanimity.

The difference between art and science is that the latter presupposes —and thereby institutes methods for achieving or approximating—an ideal of determinacy in its judgments of validity. It seeks an ideal of determinacy, though it can never quite attain it. A valid scientific conclusion is the only one valid. Thus we may say that evidence, when it can compel, does compel us to accept the conclusions we do. This is its compulsion. Of course, evidence cannot compel us to accept the methods of science. Nothing can do this. We adopt methods if we so choose. Or we can be causally or psychologically led to adopt a particular method, but that is another matter. The point I am making here is that evidence compels only after we have submitted to the method of science. Art cannot compel acquiescence, at least not so determinately. Even after having accepted the perspective of art, in seeking to validate artistic works a man is never compelled to accept but one work as most valid among all the competing possibilities—if works of art actually do compete. I may prefer one, but I must acknowledge divergence of taste: others may prefer another. Even more important, in comparing *Hamlet* and *The Brothers Karamazov*, I may find them both valid, in different respects. Perhaps I decide that works of art do not compete. What is essential is that I grant that there is no way of determinately ordering them in terms of their validity. Many can at once be valid, exciting, even great.

In other words, in science the ideal is maintained of having gathered sufficient evidence to order all possible theories in terms of the evidence and to determine the superiority of a particular theory; while in art great works of art coexist without competition. Only a very partial order is possible. We may study, explore, and reread the works of Sophocles, Chaucer, Dostoievski, Shakespeare, and Proust. Nothing therein, or in art altogether, compels us to choose among them. The coexistence of all these great authors and their works reveals the world to us through art. Single perspectives in art are shallow and limited. In a sense, we may say that science strives for the ideal of a single world-perspective, the maximization of determinacy. In art, the world is revealed through multiple and divergent perspectives, as many as possible, making determinacy impossible. In science, theories either coalesce into supervening theories, or conflict and exclude each other. In art, valid works coexist and reflect upon each other with reinforcement or diminution, but not inclusively or exclusively. Yet to deny that art is interrogative and compelling is to accept but one determinate method as definitive of interrogation and knowledge. The control, methodic interrogation, and validation of art renders it rational to the highest degree —purposeful, organized, and controlled.

A mundane example might also be illuminating. Consider two very different ways of driving an automobile, exemplified by two men, *A* and *B*, both of whom have just passed their driving tests. Both possess a method of driving, albeit hesitantly and awkwardly. *A* takes the position that he "knows" how to drive, which he has proved to himself and others. The proof is a validation of the method of driving an automobile. *A* is satisfied with his performance and does not interrogate his own skills. He has passed the test; he can drive; he worries no further. He acts straightforwardly, even consciously and articulately, according to the method he has learned. He signals when he should, becomes easier in his movements, reproduces his teacher's lessons more and more gracefully, and soon settles into a routine of habitual success. He may or may not be a good driver. Most likely he will not be, unless he had an excellent and onerously perfectionistic teacher who taught him excellent habits without exception. Even then, it is difficult to believe that he would always be successful without a considerable degree of self-examination.

B, on the other hand, has passed his test with the same success as *A* but is overwhelmed by the dangers of the road. He constantly worries about his driving and constantly tests himself to determine if his awareness, control, and routine habits of making turns and using his brakes are as perfect as they might be. He notes the capacity of his car—the kind of road that makes it difficult to control, how it behaves in sharp turns, and the like—tests his reflexes and habits, and constantly studies himself to see if he is lapsing into poor and dangerous habits. His attitude toward his driving examination is that it proves nothing about his genuine skills, so he continuously revalidates his performance. His constant scrutiny of himself is an interrogative attitude; driving is for him a questioning as well as a performance.

Both *A* and *B* may drive well or poorly, given these contrasting methods. Indeed, since interrogation need not produce answers, *A* may well be the better driver due to superior natural capacity or initial training. Both men "know how" to drive an automobile, proved by the examination. Yet the routine, habitual nature of *A*'s attitude, whatever his natural abilities, renders his driving less self-conscious and self-aware than *B*'s. There is distinctly a rational quality to the self-awareness and critical consciousness that *B* brings to bear upon his actions. We cannot say that *B* knows driving better than *A*, but he does know himself and his abilities far better than does *A*. We have here a degree of self-consciousness or self-knowledge that is contained in highly interrogative methods that is absent from ordinary cognition of an object thought to be totally external to the person involved. *A* simply gets behind the wheel and drives; he knows how to do so. But he doesn't know that he knows, or how much he knows, for he has no methodic interest in his own abilities. In the long run his performance is a matter of chance. It may get better; it may get worse. Since he does not examine it continually, criticize, appraise, and correct it, whatever happens is not within his control. *B* at least struggles to improve. His interrogative methods are likely to allow him to function at the peak of his natural ability. *A* may not do so. If he does, it will be entirely good fortune or superb training.

It is important to be quite clear that *B*'s self-examination and critical appraisal need not be a matter of articulate consciousness. He may never formulate to himself the results of his criticisms. Most intentional appraisal is facilitated by formulation; criticism and interrogation are founded on language. But language is in this instance a means of criticism; it is not inherent in criticism. *B*, for example, may seek an intuitive sense of a precise skill, measured by the ease with which he stays in lane, his solid control of his car through all conditions, and finally associate with this a particular muscular attitude. His ease and stance become for him good driving. He may obtain them through a critical appraisal that is only occasionally formulated and articulated.

Perhaps other examples of this may be more striking. Consider the portrait painter whose self-interrogation consists in following forms and colors by other forms and colors, tested by a completely visceral reaction: "No good!" or "Finally!" Articulate and verbal consciousness is not necessary for appraisal and continuous validation. Consider a young man studying singing. There are two methods he can employ. One is to take frequent lessons and, relying on his teacher's trained ear, to develop habits of vocal production of sounds his teacher indicates are good. He does this by repetition and practice. The second is by constant experimentation with different modes of production, to seek the feel, the placement, the muscular attitude, and the awareness of resonance and breath that are part of good singing, and by a complete and articulate consciousness of all of them become capable of producing a beautiful sound at will. This latter method is articulate and verbal, and perhaps may be more successful. But the former is the method utilized by most singers—that of reproducing a satisfactory tone and vocal line often enough to develop muscular habits upon which the singer can rely. This method is interrogative in that a particular skill is purposefully learned. Constant reappraisal is a necessity. But the articulate awareness of every step is not essential. Interrogative methods are only occasionally verbal and articulate.

Returning to my example of the different methods employed in automobile driving, I would like to suggest that although in both cases something is known—how to drive—there is a genuine and significant difference between the two methods, which I consider a difference in *rationality*. Regardless of whether *B* is articulate and outspoken, whether his knowledge is propositional or not, his method is critical, evaluative, interrogative, and rational, whereas *A* indulges in habitual response, routine awareness, and self-blinding. His is a nonrational possession of a skill. The analogy I suggest to defend this use of "rationality" is that of the breakdown of religious authority, either in the Greece of the Fifth Century, or during the Renaissance, when the essentially "irrational" acceptance of authority was replaced by overt questioning and the demand for *proof*. Rationality is here not to be construed narrowly as scientific proof, but as critical appraisal of any position rather than its acceptance on faith or authority. Rationality is marked here by the demand for the revalidation of accepted truths, by the refusal to accept a claim through habit and routine. Thus, although authoritarian methods have means of validation—the decrees of the authority—interrogative methods are based on continual reappraisal and revalidation. Of course, the mere demand for proof is only the inception of reason, which goes on to produce objects that pass the tests posed, devises new tests for critical examination, and so forth indefinitely. It is the indefinite progression of new appraisals, criticisms, and the production of new judgments to meet the new demands that is rationality.

Rationality is the perpetual methodic interrogation of one's world and one's actions. Every unexamined principle, rule of method, or unquestioned assumption is irrational. The sign of rationality is its willingness to confront every act or object with a question and to find some way of answering it. The termination of this endeavor, upon any grounds but those of practicality, is a termination of rational appraisal. The recognition that reason is perpetually interrogative leads to the mistaken view that ends must be intuited if they are genuine ends, that no rational foundation underlies normative judgment. The error consists in supposing that there are final ends which are not rational in being final.

4

The Method
of Moral Judgment

The examples chosen to indicate the character and purpose of interrogative methods have not so far been moral. Clearly moral behavior can be highly interrogative in its quest for the validation of moral actions as those which are "best"—either for the agent or in some more general sense. However, it is very important to be clear that morality need not be interrogative or rational any more than beliefs about the world we live in need be scientific (or "rational" in that sense of the word).

The particular mode of compulsion of evidence in science—once given its ideals—depends, as I have indicated, on adherence to presuppositions and principles of analysis that force the acceptance of specific conclusions as valid or true. The body of principles and criteria of method built into science are the source of its determinacy as well as its compulsion and are a mark of its sophistication and its strength. However, this very strength is also a liability. Methods of science are inappropriate to areas which permit no determinate solutions or empirically definite tests of validation. What seems to follow is that no rational methods at all are legitimate in such areas—if we identify the "rational" and the "scientific." Evidence, if it cannot be decisive, may be thought to be quite illegitimate.

The view that ethics is devoid of rational status is derived from such a conception of rationality; science, with its principles of evidence and reliance on empirical validation, is taken to be the sole rational interrogative method. Particularly, rationality is identified with determinability, which only science provides with empirical adequacy. Moral questions do not permit determinate resolution, and in this sense ethics is not compelling as is science. Not only may one refuse to be moral at all, as he may refuse to be scientific, but given his acceptance of the methods of ethics, he may not be led to conclusions that everyone else will agree to. This indeterminacy within the methods of ethics is fundamental to them.

On the surface, methods of moral judgment do not appear to be as thoroughly interrogative as the methods of science. Science seems to be the interrogative method *per se*, while men often make moral judgments without interrogation or analysis, without constant reevaluation—in other words, irrationally. Indeed, the good samaritan, the wise man, is often thought of as an unreflective, unquestioning person whose soul is simply and plainly good. The philosophic question of how we know that such a man's actions are good is often set aside as irrelevant to such moral issues.

Yet the same kind of question led to science as an interrogative method, and I suggest (the argument will follow shortly) that morality entails an even greater degree of self-criticism. It is quite true that men can be "good" without conscious deliberation concerning either the consequences of their actions or the paradoxes of moral judgment. But such intuitions carry no means of validation; and no act can be self-validating. Just as scientific judgments must be confirmed, ethical judgments must be tested, in further experience and consequences of action. Without some means of validation, habit and chance alone rule. Science became paradigmatic of rationality when it gained the sophistication of perpetual revalidation. If a man is a scientist, he is committed to continual criticism. A man either accepts the rules that define rationality in science, or he gives up the right to make any scientific claims at all. Why is not the same true in ethics? We may by luck or habit choose a good or advantageous act, but without means of validation it is not possible to be sure or even reasonably satisfied. Indeed, how even consider such an act intentional and rational? Interrogative methods are essential in order that we be able to claim that *principles* are at work rather than blind habits. The acceptance of formal restrictions upon one's search for right rules of conduct—such as the Generalization Principle—which parallel logical conditions in scientific theory construction, only circumscribes the context of validation. Such restrictions increase rather than decrease the requirements of validation. Not only may a scientific theory be tested for its empirical adequacy, but it must be consistent and rigorous in its form. Moral principles must both be adequate to experience, and also possess the form of principles as well. A maxim of conduct may satisfy the former condition, by arising within a narrow and distorted life, yet fail the second and be invalid as a moral principle for this reason. Acting rightly presupposes an interrogative method with rules of validation. Without sufficient self-analysis or appraisal, one can only act routinely or blindly. Without means of validation, one's actions are only actions. They become according to law, rule, or principle only when means of validation exist for testing them. It is the tests which are the mark of rationality in ethics.

Before going on to analyze these matters in detail, the consideration of a specific example will be useful. Consider a priest to whom is confessed a heinous crime, one sufficiently loathsome as to appall and shock him. The rules for his conduct are fairly clear: the act of confession is sufficient unto itself; the priest is only a mediator between the criminal and his God. On the other hand, the priest is also a moral person, with convictions and feelings as well as principles of conduct to which he subscribes. I hope here to set aside minor theoretical issues: a conflict between one's religious, professional, and moral principles is first of all a *moral* conflict—or so I shall view it. Principles to which the priest subscribes are in conflict. That is the source of moral adjudication and appraisal.

As Kierkegaard pointed out in one area of ethics, and Dewey in another, the absence of conflict marks the absence of moral judgment. And it does so just as clearly as does the absence of principles to serve as the ground of action. If the priest is "sure" of his religious and clerical duties to the point where no questions can arise concerning them and their application, his claim to make a moral *choice* is without significance. His freedom from conflict marks the existence of routine habits of judgment that reveal that his moral stance—his "attitude" toward things, his ways of reacting to them—is in relevant respects uninterrogative. It is quite true that in some sense of the word, his reaction in circumstances such as those I have described is "moral"—the sense that he uses moral terms of judgment, is aware of his obligations, and makes judgments of censure and praise. But he is not employing an interrogative *method;* rather, he reaches "moral" conclusions by other methods—as one can make judgments about the physical world through intuition or cosmological speculation, without utilizing methods of science. The priest acts morally in following his professional obligations above all else. But while it is legitimate to speak of his act as involving ethical reactions or principles, the absence of any means of validation of the priorities he accepts without thought or conflict makes it unjustifiable to speak of his act as a *choice* or an *appraisal.* For example, if he never dreams of questioning the principles of action he has adopted as a priest—that is, if his training as a cleric is total and completely without room for self-examination—only in a degenerate sense of the word does he "choose" to follow his professional obligations.

Obviously, there is a sense in which every act may be viewed as a "choice," but this is distinctly an extended use of the word. I suggest that whenever a person makes a *choice*, he may be asked if it was a *good* or worthy choice. These questions indicate that some validating method is presumed, according to which a further judgment may be given. For example, if a man says "I have a terrible headache; I must take some aspirin," we may realize the senselessness of asking him if it is good to take aspirin—unless we have another drug to offer, in which case we are making the validatable claim that our choice is better, perhaps more efficient or less dangerous. He may take the pain of the headache as sufficient in itself to require no further validation of the act of taking aspirin, to the point of disregarding the question of the effectiveness of aspirin for reducing the pain of headaches. A headache may "call for" aspirin, without reflection or analysis. Questions of the form, "Is aspirin good?" or "Is it right to take aspirin for a headache?" are without significance here insofar as the man acts without any interrogative attitude, without accepting the relevance of some means for validating his actions. A woman who took thalidomide when pregnant, and who took it only to relieve her emotional tension, may truthfully say, "The thought of consequences never occurred to me"—meaning that she was not interested in testing the goodness of her act except as it produced relief: and of course, thalidomide was wonderful for that. She may even mean implicitly that she is not responsible for her deformed child, for she never thought of asking questions of the physician who prescribed the drug. Without questions, one need make no definite responses for which one is responsible. The Greek assumption that every human action aims at some good presupposes an interrogative attitude. It is inadequate precisely in that it neglects the fact that most human beings often act without interrogation and without the willingness to consider consequences that are not obvious. It is in this sense that most men fail to choose what they do.

To say that one chooses is to make a claim that entails some method of validation, the asking of some questions, for which one is responsible. (I must point out that choices are often *implicit* in action or judgment. When a person acts without stating his explicit intentions, we do say that he chose to do what he did—meaning not so much that he weighed his action and its consequences in his mind, as that he *should have.* Here too is the claim that we should be rational in our moral behavior— meaning that we are expected to seek extended means of validation of our actions, even though we often do not.) If a man is asked why he lives in carefree poverty, he may reply "I choose to": such a reply always permits the further questions, "Why?" and "Is it really a good choice that you have made?" He may refuse to say, letting his reply be a pretense of arbitrary taste. But the very word "choose" suggests a basis for the action upon which a test may be performed.

Part of what I am getting at here is a reappraisal of the so-called Kantian doctrine that "ought implies can," though this will properly be postponed to the chapter on freedom. Here, however, I wish to recall that Kant argues quite specifically that responsibility entails freedom, in some sense of "freedom," and considerable analysis has been devoted to this relationship. The difficulty, though, is that however elaborately the analysis of "He could have acted differently" is presented, there are always equally legitimate, though different, contexts in which we may say correctly "He had to do that"—either because of the kind of person we are talking about, the events of his early childhood, the nature of his own commitments, or the like. Though the conflict here is more apparent than real, it has created great confusion, and entirely, I suggest, due to the erroneous nature of the original doctrine. "Can" must not be construed in a loose sense denoting some kind of freedom, especially a freedom related obscurely to necessity and determinism. Rather, a moral obligation entails the existence of a *choice*, and choice entails some means of validation whereby one's actions can be appraised and evaluated. If one is not in a position to utilize any means of validation, then one is not responsible either—though perhaps a man may be in a position to transform circumstances so that he may make significant choices in the future if he cannot at the moment do so.

Thus, in the classic case of a man who cannot swim faced with a man who is drowning, the former is often excused from the obligation for saving the drowning man's life because he cannot do so. On the other hand, an incorrigible thief, whose life is misery because he steals unceasingly and is caught often, may also claim that he cannot help himself. The difference between the two cases lies not so much with the ability to act as with the making of relevant choices. We can almost never prove that a man's inability to swim makes it *impossible* for him to save a man from drowning. We can only consider the risk and arduousness of the task too great. This consideration alone entirely undercuts the force of the "cannot" that is thought to relieve obligation. The first man may test his actions by their probable consequences, and weigh not only his conventional moral responsibilities, but his own definite attitude toward the importance of human life. Nevertheless, the probability of success in saving one life is low; the probability of losing two lives is high. He may, of course, *choose* neither course of action, by simply without thought or deliberation throwing himself in the water; or by complete paralysis of fear becoming immovable and inactive. But if he does judge and appraise his actions, he may discover that by conventional criteria of validation, as well as his own, his choice to try to save the drowning man will probably have unfortunate consequences, marking the invalidity of that act. On the basis of what he knows, he can only validly choose to try in a way that will increase the probability of beneficial consequences. The situation might be entirely different if the drowning man were his son, for his particular obligations as a father may require a reappraisal of the priorities controlling the rejection of the low probability of success. The point is that to validate an action is to judge its effects (or presumed effects, if one is making a prediction of validity) and the affective qualities they possess for the men involved. A man may choose not to try at the risk of his life to save another. The question is not whether he "could" have saved the drowning man, but whether his choice not to do so is valid. To say that, if one cannot do something, he is not obliged to do it substitutes a formula for a specific act of validation. In fact, choosing not to do something expected may be valid even where it is not impossible to do it, if the risk of failure is too great. Also, one may be obliged to try to prevent atrocities even where one cannot succeed, just because they are so horrible no excuse can be accepted for not fighting them—though one is not to be *blamed* if he fails. It is this aspect of blame that creates the confusion involved. The analysis I am giving clearly separates failing in one's obligations and being blamed for doing something wrong. This is very important, and is the ground for repudiating the doctrine that ought implies can.

The thief above is in a totally different situation. He has no ability at all to make a choice—at least that is what the claim that he could not help himself amounts to. He is overcome by habits beyond his control and cannot even begin to change them. In contrast, the nonswimmer may regret his inability to swim and seek other ways to save the drowning man. If he does not want to save him, and feels no obligation at all, but catches at his own inability to swim as justification for ignoring the whole problem, then he falls into the same category as the thief. Whether or not he is obligated to save the drowning man, he is obliged to try, to choose, to interrogate the situation in which he finds himself. If the thief is without the beginning of moral ability to choose, then he has no basis for appraisal and validation. He has asked no questions, given no answers. We may well consider him a kleptomaniac. The thief who unquestioningly takes small items from a department store does not *choose* to do so, unless he can explain why, at least to himself. Unless he is open to interrogation as to the validity of his actions, he is not an agent able to choose.

What is important here is the role of choice in moral responsibility, and the corresponding importance of validation in moral judgment. When a man chooses one alternative in a difficult situation, we may feel that he acted invalidly, but agree that his choice was not censurable by anyone else. We often accept the decisions of others when we feel they were chosen with concern and on the basis of principles of action and directed toward beneficial consequences. We often direct the strongest judgments of censure at men who do not make choices, and who seem not to recognize the need for them. A man is obligated to choose, whatever he decides. And we may condemn him for not choosing as well as for choosing wrongly. Without choosing, he does not weigh alternatives to determine which is most valid. He acts blindly and lacks the control over his actions that is given by validated choices. One may be determined by one's nature and the environing circumstances to make a specific choice; yet if one utilizes a method of validation for this choice, he becomes responsible for it. An unquestioning and thus unvalidated act is *irresponsible* in the sense of being thoughtless. We condemn men for being thoughtless, whether they can help themselves or not.

The upshot of this argument is to emphasize that moral judgments without means of validation are at best habitual and routine, and generally without moral significance. A method is implied in choosing and being held responsible for one's choices, a questioning, interrogative, and validatable method. The *methods of moral judgment*, at least where responsibility lies, are as rational and interrogative as science, though with quite different means of validation. But that is only to repeat what this section is intended to show. Let us return to the priest mentioned above.

I will assume here that the priest is faced with a moral problem, and is ready to examine the principles involved and to search for a resolution of the difficulties facing him. If he acts directly and without pain, conflict, or thought of validation, he is on the path of intuition and arbitrariness, which is no more to be desired in ethics than in science. He may not even have made a validatable choice to rely on intuition and habit. He can neither control his future reactions nor the results of his actions without rational examination and interrogation. Intuition may be correct, but as haphazardly and arbitrarily as in science.

The priest, then, must recognize the obligations of his calling, and feel also the heinousness of the crime confessed to him, as well as the desperate need for moral judgment. Shall he break his vow of silence, violating the sanctity of the confessional, or overlook human law and its moral foundation? If he personally despises the criminal, and acts accordingly, this is but an evasion of the problem, just as if he loves him and protects him. A man's feelings are always relevant to his moral decisions for they are part of his means of validation, though some of them may lead him away from the poignancy of moral indecision. The priest's feelings about the criminal enter into his judgment of the consequences of his actions. For example, his judgment may well be in conflict with a moral principle that demands generality beyond concern for any particular person. A father whose son has committed a crime, and who refuses even to consider protecting him out of unthinking respect for moral law, is no more to be admired for having made a choice than the priest whose vows are utterly sacrosanct. He too refuses to judge the principles he lives by, putting some principles forth as absolute, and therefore irrational. The blind and uncritical acceptance of a rule has no more essential moral value than an action performed unthinkingly. To refuse to subject a choice to methods of validation, and to run the risk of failure, is not to make a choice at all. All principles in ethics, even the principle of objectivity—that one ought to make moral judgments "impersonally"—can become automatic and devoid of rational analysis. "Are these circumstances like the others, or is there something special about them?" This question is essential to any validation of any particular act. No formula answer can be given to it.

The priest must then be assumed to be completely open to self-examination and criticism. He respects his office and its duties, but recognizes the demands of morality as well. He is personally fond of his confessee, yet sees also the need for his redemption through punishment. What then is *the* answer? The point is that there is not *one* answer. The conflict of moral principles and circumstances does not permit a perfect resolution; otherwise the conflict would not be a genuine one. And partial resolutions can be validated only according to choices made by individuals as they are involved. Just how important is the priest's office? How much does this man's soul mean to him or God? How important does he hold conventional moral laws to be? All of these must be put together into a conception of himself, what he is, and what he wishes to be, in the choice he makes. Such a choice is part of the unification of self we have been seeking as the ground of responsibility. The priest may simply assume he knows all the answers, and act uncritically; or he may struggle with unresolvable difficulties, testing and evaluating as best he can. Given the struggle, with means of validation, can he choose wrongly if he reaches what he considers a valid decision? Of course, in terms valid for someone else, or himself at a later time, and none of these takes precedence over the others. Given the quest for the resolution of a moral problem, the use of a method for the validation of that resolution, any valid decision is just that, a valid one, regardless of what others may think. There may be many equally satisfactory and valid choices possible. But not any or every choice is a valid one.

Let me emphasize, however, that although every appraisal implicitly involves the critical consideration of the principles appealed to in making valid judgments, it is not the case that one can suspend principles altogether in making moral judgments. The function of principles is to ground the judgment in a context that assures the judgment of the maximal likelihood of validity. One of the most obvious facts of moral life is that unprincipled judgments or judgments based on loosely-held principles are often destructive, and bring detrimental consequences to the agent and others. Tragic heroes are admirable precisely in the fact that they maintain their identity through adherence to principles which they will not abandon in the face of hardship. A corrupt man is one who abandons his principles easily. Firmly-held principles offer the greatest possible security in action, provided that they are not unquestioningly or dogmatically followed. Moral wisdom is the knowledge of those principles which ought to be followed in *most* cases to promote validity in action—although any particular case may be an exception.

It will be noticed that in all the choices mentioned in which validation is taken seriously, part of the process of validation in moral affairs is the study of oneself and one's particular characteristics. The man who cannot swim must know that fact and take it into account. Otherwise we wonder on what basis he made his choice. If he overlooks his own abilities, he does not choose to jump in despite his inability to swim: he just jumps in. The priest must judge his various inclinations and the scale of priorities he tends to employ, as well as his personal feelings about the confessor and his crime. The driver who chooses to adopt driving techniques markedly different from those generally advised must make the definite claim that *for him* special methods are more suitable—perhaps only on the basis of feeling, but on some definite basis. Self-knowledge is essential to moral judgment.

Some interrogative methods—art, science, and, I am arguing, ethics —are nonterminating in principle, and applicable to any and all subject matters. Ethics, science, and art all share in common a pervasiveness of concern that is absent from other methods and ways of dealing with things. They may be applied to any and every subject matter whatsoever. Anything may be studied scientifically; it may also be placed in an exhibitive context for the purpose of arousing aesthetic response; and it may also become part of one's moral frame of mind and stance in the world. Thus I may ask of anything at all: "What should I do about this?"—and view my answer as a moral one. The view that men are responsible for everything they do stems from the recognition that anything they do and come in contact with may be taken into their moral perspectives and dealt with accordingly. Any person I meet is either an object for my manipulation and use, or may be treated with respect and dignity. Everything I do may be thought about, evaluated, and judged for its place in the moral realm, either in that it promotes my true self-interest, or aids someone else in satisfying his needs. In fact, we do many things without moral reflection and interrogation; this does not, however, militate against the realization that we may at any time take up any of our acts as requiring reappraisal. Habitual actions may be uninterrogative, but everything done habitually—including the habit itself—may be interrogated for its moral aspects.

To the extent that anything may serve as the source of moral judgment, we may be judged by others for our lapses in awareness and absence of concern, as much as for choices wrongly made. If we refuse to choose—meaning that we act without interrogative concern and awareness of conflict, in an immediate and habitual pattern—that too is an act for which others may hold us to account. We are open to judgment for all that we do, and cannot escape the pervasiveness of moral concern. Refusing to choose, at least in the moral domain, is itself a moral judgment if not an interrogative one, and we can be condemned for our refusal. The driver who relies on his original training and automatic reactions may be condemned by a passenger in his car for being so poor

a driver as to risk the lives of others. There is nothing we do that is free
from the possibility of moral evaluation; it is this fact that is the source
of the anguish the existentialists find throughout life and consciousness.

Sartre claims that anguish so permeates human existence that it cannot be avoided, however we struggle with it; our denial of anguish only
places us in the state of bad faith. Sartre's fundamental example, indeed, is of a woman who spends an evening with a man refusing to accept the fact that she is a sexual object to him, and who gives up her
hand as hers when he presses it: "This is not mine, I am not responsible
for it." The attempt to flee from freedom and become a thing is in bad
faith. On the unreflective level, one is still free, and one is conscious
(unreflectively again) of anguish.

The problem Sartre has is that he wishes to claim that every human
being is not only free, but conscious of that freedom, and thus in anguish. But his necessary extension of this consciousness to unreflective
consciousness of anguish violates our sense of the ability of men to shut
themselves off from everything around them, including what is obviously true. Perhaps I am inevitably free, but I may not know it. The
proof Sartre offers that I must think of myself as free in order to consider myself an agent at all, though powerful in its implications for
would-be moral agents, has no force for men who blind themselves to
everything around them, and who therefore never experience anguish,
even unreflectively. Sartre's analysis unavoidably becomes intuitive and
almost mystical, with power only for those to whom felt anguish is common and significant.

The pervasiveness of moral judgment and evaluation, however, may
well be viewed as the source of anguish, which is the reflection of the
human inability to settle a moral question either by escaping from it or
by resolving it completely. To this extent, awareness of the inevitability
of conflict, and of the possibility of being called to account for every action one takes, can be accompanied by anguish and a sense of futility.
The apparent solution—of escape from life and its cares in order to
overcome the pain of anguish—is not a significant solution. To escape
from anguish here can only be to escape from the pervasiveness of
moral concern and the unbounded responsibilities we bear toward
events around us, what we do, and what is because we "allow" it to be.
We may seek to deny our guilt: guilt for our actions which resulted in
consequences we did not and could not foresee; guilt for having acted
habitually without thought of what might and then did occur; guilt in
the very necessity of acting when we cannot know the results, however
we struggle to control them; and finally guilt for having endured evil

without opposing it, either by turning away from fear, or by refusing to know that it existed. The man who "does not know" of his government's evil ways, in prisons, in war camps, or in manipulating public opinion, may be telling the truth, but he is not thereby free from guilt. He should have known; he should have refused to live in a world where there could be such enormities and he not know of them; he should have tried to know, yet he did not. When we take social conditions into account, and say that we understand his not knowing, we mean either the statistical fact that most of his countrymen act in the same way, or that most men would act the same way under the same circumstances. How then hold this particular man responsible and guilty? The point is that we can and often must make moral judgments about everything we do, sins of omission as well as commission. What we don't do or know can always be brought to our account as something we *should have* done or known. The pervasiveness of responsibility is the heart of moral judgment; nothing is free from it. It is the source of anguish. Whatever I do is and will remain partially unresolved, partially unvalidated, a risk of my moral character as well as of painful consequences. Yet doing nothing is acting also, so I cannot escape my fate—to be a moral agent when I wish not to be one. However I struggle to escape my moral being, it resides in my acts and withdrawals, and I am accountable for them. The condition of being a moral agent is that only by giving up one's moral being, thus becoming an object and denying that one has purposes, goals, even desires, and can be judged for them—in short, by giving up all evaluation of any sort—can one escape this anguish. Unlike Sartre, I can see the possibility of escaping anguish; but only at a price no one would be willing to pay. More important, others will not let us do so.

What then of the denial, "I could not help myself"? Sartre's very odd doctrine of freedom is developed to cope with the plausibility of this reply. I suggest that an elaborate notion of freedom is unnecessary, for being able to act differently is quite irrelevant to the fact that one is accountable for everything one does and does not do. If a temptation to sin is too great, a man may succumb to it. Sartre is fond of the example of the French Resistance fighter caught and tortured to divulge information. I think Sartre's view absurd that the man "may" *always* refuse to tell, that he is free to keep silent, and that this is the source of his guilt if he succumbs. Whether or not the man "can" keep silent, it is his actions and their consequences which are on trial, not his freedom. Perhaps he may claim to himself: "Someone else might have withstood the torture; I couldn't. I am particularly sensitive to pain." If this is true—

and well it may be—it is relevant to subsequent judgments of blame. But it is quite irrelevant to the fact that this man's actions are the cause of the deaths of many of his fellow countrymen. It is *his* divulging their names that has destroyed them, and he is accountable. Perhaps he will later be exempted from censure on the grounds that no one could have been expected to withstand that torture. But he cannot know that. Moreover, it is irrelevant to his state of mind, which is not only dismay at himself, but at the world which has forced him to act contrary to his principles. The constant pressure to act when we are not ready, or not even aware, results in anguish. The flight from anguish is a flight from judgment, a flight from test, a flight from moral awareness and the willingness to accept the necessity of facing every moment of life with judgment and appreciation. This permits me to repeat what I mentioned before—that the total absence of conflict in a moral situation marks the absence of choice and of significant moral attitude. The unavoidability of conflict, and the irresolvability of all moral decisions, is the agony of anguish.

We are constantly on test in our actions and refusals to act. Whether we explicitly make our decisions or not, we are nevertheless praiseworthy or culpable. Our futile attempts to deny guilt are just that—futile, for there is always a legitimate mode of appraisal according to which we are guilty: no one can say that he did *everything* he might have done to help others. Our moral universe is as large as our entire world; yet we can be and are efficacious only in a small part of it. We will be punished only for some of our transgressions. But punishable or not, we are not able to live without failing, even by our own modes of evaluation. Moral life is a continual pressure, accompanied by perpetual conflict. Our desire for complete escape can be fulfilled only at the expense of any moral attitude altogether. Anguish is not a necessary condition of human consciousness. But it is a necessary condition of the moral consciousness in which one sees the applicability of moral evaluation to everything and every deed.

The awareness of the pervasiveness of accountability need not produce greater interrogation or rationality in moral affairs. One may still act routinely or on rigid principles. To do so, however, is to close these principles themselves to moral judgment, which contradicts the realization that *everything* may be examined for its place in the moral realm. To take the latter principle seriously, and thus to face moral anguish seriously, entails a perpetual search for moral judgment and the validation of every moral claim. There is a definite hypothetical imperative to be found in moral consciousness: if one accepts the principle that life is a constant test of our moral being, in which every act or failure to act brings the possibility of being held to account, then explicit and methodic analysis is essential to determine the validity or invalidity of everything done. Refusal to consider the examination of even the most commonplace or conventional principles of moral judgment is to exempt them from the perpetual examination. A judge who takes the rule of law as absolute, and condones moral crimes in the name of national security and progress, is guilty of a closed method, and we condemn him for it. Given his level of awareness of the process of moral evaluation, he should consider the legal code with critical eyes and judge it on the basis of the moral principles inherent in his own civilization and his own consciousness. A judge is sometimes responsible for interpreting the law and even its conditions, given the moral ideals toward which he bears his ultimate loyalties.

The first condition of moral judgment, then, is the awareness that no subject matter is free from moral judgment, that every thing, deed, action, and event is subject to moral appraisal. This implies that methods be devised for such appraisal which, because their results may also be scrutinized morally and appraised as being good or base, right or wrong, are unending—or, more accurately, are only tentatively terminatable. That is, if we judge the worth of an action by its consequences as well as by principles whereby to evaluate the consequences, then both the consequences and the principles of evaluation are themselves open to further evaluation, and indefinitely. We terminate a judgment on the basis of convenience, or when it becomes impractical to continue further. But in principle we can go on, and often at another time find that we must.

The fact that everything can be morally evaluated implies that methods of moral judgment and action must be rational and validating, thus interrogative. The making of a moral judgment without questioning or validation is empty of moral significance. The fate of a moral being to be caught forever in unresolved moral concerns, never finding peace, never free from the possibility of his own failure or others' condemnation in whatever he does, small or large, principled or arbitrary, is the existential ground of anguish. Not to be in anguish is not to be interrogatively moral, to rely instead on settled rules of conduct, and thus to deny the perpetual interrogation of the moral life.

Given, then, constant moral awareness and evaluation, the perpetual need for judgment and moral validation, an ethical man must not only make decisions but act upon them. The other side of moral issues is that they demand something more than rational deliberation. They demand that we act in some way, do something about them. The failure of ethical issues to permit unanimity in decision, the existence of remote consequences which may be relevant to the judgments before us, the differences among men in their feelings toward such consequences, all tend to paralyze the deliberative man, for in knowing the issues, he also knows the indeterminacy of the considerations which ground his undertaking. As Hegel explicitly pointed out, there is a perpetual and unbridgeable gap between thought and action in the domain of ethics. This gap is the source of despair. All the rational consideration in the world may not render a man moral, if he does not act on the basis of it. Yet actions take place at a given time and under particular circumstances, while rational deliberation is unending. Hume turned to moral sentiments to bridge this gap; Kierkegaard to the leap of faith. But there is no solution to the inevitability of moral conduct being partially unjustified, to the fact that other, conflicting alternatives may be equally justifiable either to other men or even to the agent struggling to make a decision. We sometimes say, with utmost sincerity, that when the balance is so close, either action is equally valid. And so it may be theoretically, except for the fact that a decision in moral affairs is seldom trivial for anyone involved. A Dane, asked to hide a Jewish child from the Germans, had to weigh not only the life of the child, but the safety of his family. If he was unconcerned about one or the other, there was no interrogative moral problem posed, although lives were at stake. If he took both seriously, no resolution allowed unquestionable justification. If his moral convictions were so clear that the rightness of his protecting the child ruled out the consideration of all other matters, then one can admire him for rectitude and courage, but not for moral sensitivity and rationality. If he was torn because he saw the problem in its full magnitude, then he might have been able to reach a judgment within the total picture by weighing the various probable consequences, and making a judgment based on them. But nothing in the situation could have *proved* to him that he was *correct*. Such words as "prove" and "correct" fail to mean anything in such situations.

The urgency of moral action is unavoidable in human life, while the denial of the relevance of normative analysis to any particular act or event is a repudiation of one's moral being. The reasons for such a denial are often quite clear—as in science: by repudiating the eternal normative merry-go-round, one may gain the possibility of explicit and determinate solution to particular kinds of problems. Modern man extends his schizophrenic attitude throughout the domain of his existence, separating the scientific from the philosophical, and both from the ethical and the aesthetic. Perhaps the success of methods in each of these domains presupposes a partial isolation from the others. But when they are torn apart completely, it becomes virtually impossible to rejoin them and restore a sense of unity to human experience. Thus, a scientist not only develops bombs, but claims freedom from moral judgment while doing so. He becomes a man in bad faith—in my sense of the phrase: he repudiates the fact of his being a moral individual in everything he does, and claims that because or insofar as he is a scientist, he is free from moral criticism. Of course, he is not and cannot be; he has simply found a new way to flee from the anguish of accountability. The artist, who likewise denies *any* moral function to art, commits the same error. It is quite true that in artistic criticism we may and perhaps should refrain from moral judgment, but this is a far cry from the claim that we should refrain utterly from judging art in its moral role. Every work of art is in fact the result of human actions; these must be considered for their moral consequences, at least insofar as we are moral beings called upon to make such judgments. Our frequent refusal to judge art morally is either irresponsible, or based upon the tacit premise that art cannot be of much effect. The latter judgment is often quite true, but too often accepted without consideration or thoughtfulness. The role of novelists as social critics is one that must be attacked or defended on moral grounds, not on the basis of the freedom of art from all ethical and moral considerations.

I have spoken of the urgency of moral decision. However, many individual and social decisions in the moral realm are not urgent, so we postpone them until they become so. If they do not raise conflicts impossible of resolution, we tend to move along with them in a routine manner. Unfortunately, moral action cannot be postponed without serious danger. A man who refrains from opposition to his government's repressive policies may find subsequently that it has become far more repressive, to the point where even minor opposition brings a risk of jail or death. A man must sometimes stand up for his moral beliefs, or be held to have repudiated them. They may later become so urgent as to be unavoidable. One must act one way or another, make some decision, for the issues at stake may permit no escape from the necessity of choice, however much we hope to find one. Here is the other side of anguish— the despair at the urgency of one's moral actions, when coupled with the anguish of being forever unsure of the consequences of one's actions.

The indeterminacy of moral judgment, when linked with the necessity and urgency of action, produces the eternal gap between rational deliberation and moral conduct. Yet we cannot evade action. Does it then follow that if rational deliberation is incomplete and indecisive, any actions which are undertaken must at best be arbitrary—thus that the method of ethics is not rational?

What I have just called "moral deliberation" is the judgment of the consequences of proposed actions, and the appraisal of such consequences in terms of one's own attitudes and feelings relative to principles—for example, that one is a representative of *mankind.* The determination of the consequences is simply empirical investigation, based on the projection of probabilities. It, however, cannot complete a moral analysis. This analysis, if it is to be *validatable*, must reflect an adequate awareness of the agent's moral attitudes and sentiments, not only here and now, but in the future, whenever validation will take place, and on an ideal level so that he does not ignore the representative role of moral judgment—that in every action, one defines rules for all other men to follow, whether one wishes it or not. An action is valid insofar as it continues to represent truly what one as a man is, in the direction it provides to his future life. In effect, one completes oneself in one's ideal aspect in the action in question, and dismisses countertendencies and ambivalences as superficial and as not really part of oneself. The validation is the further judgment that one has indeed known oneself so fully as to have acted in accordance with one's true being as a man.

Here, scientific knowledge cannot alone be determinate, since the feeling of things, the quality of response to a given action, is of fundamental importance. My feelings about my child are above all the crucial factor in determining whether I should or should not try to save him from a burning house. An individual agent, something more than part of a statistical assemblage on which common generalizations are based, must react to and include himself in the moral judgments he makes. A psychologist may predict what I will do and how I will feel about it afterward. The point is that how I feel, now and then, is the basis on which I judge my actions—given all the general principles and predicted results. Moral validation is an individual act, by which I mean that it is finally made by an individual, taking his own feelings and ideals into account, for they are the final deciding factor upon which he relies, in which he projects himself as what he expects himself ideally to be. He represents himself as seeking an ideal of humanity in what he does. The validation takes place when his expectations are fulfilled, and fails when his expectations about his guilt and feelings of satisfaction, as well as his sense of the ideal in experience, are not preserved. An action of mine may change the face of the world in important and significant ways. But to some extent it is always *my* judgment about these changes, my feelings and responses, that are the data upon which the validation rests. The feelings of other people, of course, enter into and affect mine in important ways. Their condemnation may well make me feel guilty. They may even punish me. All of this is part of the validating process. I have in my actions to produce and sustain the "best" alternative. There is no way to judge if it is truly the best except by looking to see the results and then deciding. Validation continues indefinitely, with indefinite consequences. But at least partial judgments are always possible.

The indeterminability of moral validation does not imply that it is not rational, only that it is not completely decisive. The fact that men differ in their attitudes toward things is something each of us must consider in his own judgments; and yet he cannot fully and decisively incorporate this fact with his own attitudes to promote finality of judgment. When Agamemnon first agrees to sacrifice his daughter Iphigenia for the glory of the Greeks, he risks discovering not only that his feelings may change, but that others may despise him for what he did. If he were *very sure*, the moral sentiments of others would matter little. But in fact, most men are susceptible to influence, and often rightly, for moral feelings reside amidst contexts of social interaction. There is no way for a man to add up all the relevant information at a given time to reach a decision for everyone; nor even one he can be completely sure of for himself.

The method of validation of ethical judgments is not to be equated with scientific or empirical inquiry. A man may possess a set of implicit criteria in terms of which he can judge the worth of an action in terms of a finite and easily determinable class of its consequences. In this case, as Dewey pointed out, evaluation strongly resembles empirical inquiry. What is ascertained are the consequences of proposed actions, and the emotional quality of these consequences forms the basis on which the action is judged. The greater the felt value of the consequences, the more valuable is the alternative being considered. It is a matter for empirical investigation to determine just what consequences do follow. Yet seldom is it true that a given individual possesses so clear a sense of which consequences will prove most satisfactory; and when he does, he usually possesses so clear a set of values concerning the original alternatives that he need not look at consequences at all. That is, he is capable, under the assumption of a clear and definite set of values, of acting without any conflict or interrogation at all. At best, he may be rational on the first and simplest level, judging alternatives not only as they stand by themselves, but in terms of the consequences they engender.

He does not, however, consider the possibility that the principles by which he judges consequences must themselves be questioned. Thus a scientist may judge his work on weapons to be good because it is patriotic, and because he enjoys the demands imposed upon him. He gains some, but not necessarily great, sophistication by considering the immediate consequences of his actions, and utilizing his set of immediate values to judge them. Weapons bring death and destruction; they also can be used to further his country's aims and aspirations. He may settle for the latter good without ever raising the far more complex question of how his patriotic values contribute to a world open to warfare and hatred rather than to peaceful means of settling disputes. In other words, he may judge by the consequences of his proposed actions, testing the consequences by his feelings of patriotism, without ever questioning those feelings themselves, their origins and consequences. Dewey made much of the continuum of means and ends to point out the need for the test of such feelings. The problem is that the notion of a continuum leads to the view that testing is unending; yet it must end if action is to take place.

Actions which can bear the brunt of rational criticism after the fact, even years later when new facts have come to light, must implicitly involve deliberate analysis as far as it can be carried. They also depend upon the possession of great skills of choice and deliberation, initially on an intuitive level, though subsequently they are validated by their fruits. It must not be supposed that such actions are arbitrary in not being susceptible to rather definite test. It is just that such a test takes place at a future time, in terms of both the agent's and others' later feelings, as well as the other consequences. The world as it becomes because of a man's actions is the basis for the evaluation of what he has done.

Suppose a man discovers that his son has committed a theft. Let us further assume that he sincerely subscribes to the principle that a guilty person deserves punishment except under mitigating circumstances—circumstances which affect the nature of the act, not the agent or judge. On the other hand, he deeply loves his son. He must weigh his actions and determine what *to him* (for in a moral judgment, only he can make the determining judgments for his own actions) is the legitimate or valid thing to do: What is right? What ideal of mankind or fatherhood can he live by? He knows that social convention deems all men to be equal before the law; but here is a special case, for his son is involved. Fathers have special duties and responsibilities to their children, even to the point of protecting them from the consequences of their rash actions. However, what will be the consequences of his aiding his son and protecting him from punishment? Will his son take this opportunity to become a man at once, and face the world responsibly, or will he assume that he needs no responsibility since his father will always protect him? Further difficulties arise if the father considers the possibility of his son's being found out regardless of what he does to protect him. What will other people's reactions be to his attempts to save his son, both toward the father, and toward the son if they have to judge him? Will the father's protection hurt or benefit his son in the long run?

The answers to all these questions are embodied in the making of this moral judgment. Often we struggle to determine the answers; sometimes we guess at them or ignore them. For example, the father may refuse to face the problems of his son's reactions, assuming that as his son, he can do no wrong. The likelihood of a man's making a valid judgment under such circumstances is small, and depends primarily on the strength of his desire to protect anyone close to him—which if strong enough ceases to be a validatable principle, and becomes empty rule. The deeper his struggle, though, with the problem, and the more he discovers about himself and his son, the feelings of others and the nature of justice, the more likely are the father's reactions to be valid. The knowledge of what others may do, and the ability to act so that they and he will reach the most satisfactory resolution, is a great skill. It is what is called *moral wisdom.* Just as a fine mechanic can tell what is wrong with an engine by listening to it briefly—though he makes further tests to be sure—and a doctor diagnoses a common ailment by simply looking briefly at a patient's throat, so a morally adept man can feel or intuit his way through complex moral problems by a quick grasp of the motives and reactions of other men as well as his own. The mere facts of psychology do not themselves create a moral judgment, which is why ethics is not a science. But without the facts, no one is in a position to make valid judgments but by chance.

Any resolution of the above moral problem depends on the agent reaching what I have called a "valid" or satisfactory act, one which will now and subsequently prove to be the best action under the circumstances. What can such an action be? It is obviously difficult to spell out the details of validation, since they differ from case to case, and person to person. Essentially, however, a validating judgment depends on holding up rules of conduct along with present and projected feelings concerning the principles and circumstances involved, and determining that action which will be consonant with the agent's ideal sense of himself—a union of what he is and what he wishes to be. An act of mine must be valid for me—in that it is my feelings which matter—though my feelings about others' reactions should not be overlooked, nor should my quest for general rules which are applicable not only to me but to all men in like circumstances. I count the reactions of others because they affect me. I seek general rules of conduct in order to give grounds and reasons and to understand my own choices. I formulate ideals in order that my actions may have a representative role for all men. Although my feelings, attitudes, values, and priorities are determinate in my validating an ethical judgment, there is nothing arbitrary about this. Feelings and attitudes are not arbitrary; they are facts to be noted and employed.

If the father above chooses to turn his son over to the police, and by so doing destroys his son's life and his own as well, if the father is despised by all his friends and does not feel strongly enough about the principle of equality before the law to rest happily with it, then he has been untrue to himself and to his son, and betrays within himself the invalidity of his actions. The father's claim to have done right is testable only by taking all the facts and consequences of his action into account. It is an implicit prediction about his and others' later reactions, and their consequences. These reactions are the ultimate test of validity in normative judgment. If the father protects his son and feels remorse for having broken one of his own fundamental moral principles, that is not a valid action for him. On the other hand, if his son means everything to him, then regardless of others' feelings, the father did what was right by his own convictions, and these are what count. Note, however, that the latter convictions must not be understood as absolute and unquestioning—this would abandon both rationality and validation. The man's son means everything to him in that saving his life and making him happy is what he *truly* desires, not blind protection which can result in harming him. Though a crime may go unpunished—and society can bear this without disgrace or collapse—the boy's life may change and he may settle down to become a worthwhile person. To his father, that proves his actions right. If the boy continues stealing, however, the father must reappraise his decisions in the light of their failure to make his son into a decent person. Life is a perpetual test and validation of one's actions, and we stand before it without hope of flight from the necessity of judging and being judged.

I am arguing that if ethics is methodic—and it is difficult to see how it can avoid being so without degenerating into caprice—it is distinctly interrogative. Indeed, it may be the interrogative method *par excellence*, in that it seeks judgments of the goodness of actions of any sort. Fundamental to moral judgment is some form of questioning, and some method of appraising possible replies. On the basis of subject matter alone, most men make moral judgments without particularly questioning what they do. But this is no more justifiable than is the making of assertive judgments without questioning in science.

I am making a stronger point, however, than that ethical judgments necessarily entail some interrogation, and that is that it is always legitimate to ask, after a moral judgment has been made, for some form of justification or validation. I am also taking another form of Dewey's claim that evaluation takes place in a continuum of means and ends. My way of putting it is that every value judgment can in principle be validated; that it is always appropriate to seek such validation; and that whenever validation is denied, the judgment in question becomes arbitrary, capricious, and indefensible. In this respect, the method of moral judgment is like the method of science. They differ only in their means of validation.

It is a common error to equate the inevitable presence of diversity in value judgments with arbitrariness. Because the unavoidability of difference of opinion cannot be eliminated from value judgment, it is supposed that some component of arbitrariness exists; and once we admit arbitrariness or irrationality into normative judgment, it seems possible to bring it in to any stage of validation of that judgment, even at the very beginning. If upon rational analysis we are eventually led to a point where all that can be said with respect to a difference in the considered judgments of different people is, "That's just a matter of opinion," then it seems that at any other point one could have said the same thing. Thus one might be arbitrary in any moral affair, and we have one version of Protagoras' view that each man is the measure of all things. The problem with this view is that if one refuses to ask any questions, he is left with arbitrariness and caprice; while if one once begins to ask questions and seek answers, then he is committed to continuing the process of evaluation and validation indefinitely.

The point is to locate the apparently arbitrary element in evaluation properly. It is not arbitrariness; it is rather diversity. Different people, using considered and rational methods of evaluation, may be led to different conclusions on the same question. It does not follow that there is anything subjective, arbitrary, or capricious about this, except where these are equated with difference of opinion. Reason is to be equated with unanimity of judgment only in science. Ethical methods of evaluation leave room for divergence of opinion. Yet they still entail perpetual and unremitting search for validation. A number of arguments may be given to justify the claim that evaluation is a method which involves continual questioning, that in evaluation one is always committed to seeking some further justification for a judgment made. I consider these decisive—though I repeat that even when different people perpetually question and seek to validate their judgments, they may be led to different conclusions. Let me now try to give the arguments for the indefinitely interrogative character of moral judgment.

1. Nothing is self-validating. The search for self-evident principles has proven vain. First principles may exist in some logical sense, but they cannot be self-evidently or obviously true. We validate first principles by treating them as generalizations applicable to a wide range of cases, and test them by their applicability and range of satisfaction as in science. To validate a proposition or an act depends on the existence of a method of validation which must be applied to things. This necessarily takes one beyond the object of evaluation. As Dewey saw, there is a continuum of means and ends, where ends are deemed desirable by virtue of their capacity as means as well. They move on to other things.

An infinite regress or a vicious circle of validation is thus suggested. But these can easily be avoided in a manner suggested also by Dewey—by appealing to a context of validation. We justify a particular decision by appeal to some principle—e.g., the utilitarian principle of greatest happiness (in some sense), or some general principle of value. But we have validated the particular decision only if we can justify the principle used. If we are led on and on, we have an infinite regress. However, the principle itself may be thought to be tested by each particular decision it is applied to—does it produce satisfactory results? We seem to avoid the infinite regress by developing a vicious circle. However, the circle is not vicious, in that the criteria for the validation of the principle look outside the given case too—to conditions of general applicability, to consistency, to ideals of rationality, and so forth. Various contexts exist in which every principle may be tested. Because the contexts are different, no circle results. It is the continual reflection of all human judgments upon each other that is rationality.

2. Every act undertaken brings with it empirical consequences that are unavoidably bound to the original action. I never merely pull the trigger of a gun: I fire a gun aimed at something or someone—that is how I kill him. Actions are bound in a fundamental way to their consequences, and only a blind and arbitrary act of intentional method can separate them even in principle. At the very least, every act undertaken can be validated by the events which issue from it, and it is unintelligible to claim that the process can be interrupted at any particular point. An event with apparently auspicious consequences may bring deadly

results in the future. These may entail the rejection of an earlier value judgment. All value judgments inevitably look to an indefinite future in which they are in effect open to perpetual test. It does not follow that no value judgment is to be trusted, since it looks to the entire future; only that every value judgment is tentative and fallible.

3. The realization that scientific propositions are open to perpetual reexamination from the standpoint of reason has its counterpart in ethics. Where testing ends, rationality and justification end as well. It is arbitrary to cease collecting data, reevaluating principles, and seeking ways to qualify one's judgments. Just as in science, if one refuses to consider the possibility that a given principle, even a mathematical one, may be the wrong one to use in a given case, so in value judgments, where one declares a given principle unquestionable, he has abdicated the possibility of justification. Now one can abstain from all justification, though it is certainly arbitrary to do so. Even in science, one may refuse to investigate, and accept what Peirce called the "method of tenacity"—sticking to one's beliefs no matter what. Nothing can prove such a method wrong—the method disdains all proof. But the method disdains *all* proof; justification is impossible; sheer arbitrariness remains. Once one allows any questioning at all, then he is committed to the results of the interrogation, and the further investigation of the questions which underlay the initial investigation once they have come to light. In short, one either repudiates validation, or one evaluates what one does, and must continually interrogate and reinterrogate experience to maintain the validity of one's judgments. The only legitimate and rational method for interrogating the world propositionally is science. The only legitimate and rational method for interrogating the world actively and evaluatively is the method I have described of moral judgment.

4. Once one has asked one question, one is committed to an interrogative method which can provide answers to the question posed. But no method can be self-validating. One may continually reexamine the tools of the method, casting into doubt the answer to the original question. One may ask questions without interrogative methods; but interrogative methods are reflexive in that they allow themselves to be cast into question.

5. Put another way, in terms of levels of consciousness: there are modes of awareness that are not methodically interrogative, such as passive vision; there are also modes of self-consciousness which are not methodically interrogative, such as embarrassment or self-loathing; and there are modes of methodic self-consciousness in which interrogation

takes place. Only in the latter case is validation systematically possible
—that is, where a method exists for testing judgments. And whenever
there exists a method of validation, either it is itself arbitrary and without foundation, or one may seek to validate it also, and one has taken a
highly critical, self-conscious attitude. This level of critical self-awareness is the beginning of the development of rational methods, wherein
methods of interrogation are reflected onto themselves. Ethics is degraded without this element of self-consciousness. Of course, nothing
can compel a man to be highly self-critical and self-conscious if he
chooses not to be. But I am tempted to give Aristotle's casual dismissal
of those who identify pleasure with happiness—such men are too slavish
for us to take seriously. We are not addressing ourselves to men who
seek nothing and never question what surrounds them, who are obliv-
ious to the problems that confront them. We are concerned with men
who endeavor to be honorable and good men, and who ask how to do
so. They have clearly adopted reflexively interrogative methods of a
fairly high degree of self-consciousness. They are committed to a perpetual quest for further validation of their judgments. That is the source of
their despair.

Despair is the condition of moral agents who can never know assurance in their judgments, who make moral decisions with concern and
commitment, yet realize the irremediably fallible character of what
they do. They cannot escape into lack of concern, for their total being is
committed to ethical action. Yet they despair that their best efforts are
for naught. Despair is the quality of a finite being before an infinite future. Nothing can turn finiteness into infinitude; nothing can render
our judgments secure in that indefinite future which can bring anything. Every value judgment looks ahead to what will come. Despair is
the mixture of concern with a finitude that can abort every project,
every attempt of a man to identify himself with his projects. Every judgment risks my being if I am concerned enough to trust myself to my
deeds.

The proleptic quality of moral judgment constitutes not only a form
of knowledge of the world, but of oneself. A conception of a total self in
a wealth of relations to things around it and to the future as well is embodied in moral judgment. The less integrated and holistic is one's sense
of himself, either due to ignorance or out of ambivalence and a sense of
personal fragmentation, the less chance there is of validity in his judgments. To make a rational or valid moral judgment depends upon possession of knowledge about one's own reactions and feelings, as well as
one's priorities, ideals, and principles. If I implicitly and unadmittedly

despise my son, I may turn him in for punishment for that reason alone, not on the basis of moral principles I hold dear. Can I then escape the guilt that will follow such a blind act? If I pretend to weigh and deliberate before acting, but nevertheless will protect my son against *any* pain, even legitimate punishment, then I may unwittingly harm him. If I am to be in a position to act validly, I must know myself above all, to weigh my feelings against my principles. I must know what I believe and what I feel, my true aims and ideals. I must know who I am and what I am, to the extent that after I act, I must know if and how I will be different. The more consistent and integrated I am in my judgments and behavior, the better I know myself, then the better chance I have to make valid moral judgments.

If a man does not understand himself, then it is difficult to see how he can act validly except by chance. Of course, we always know something about ourselves, and it is on this basis that we make our moral judgments. Often, the moral heroes among us are the principled martyrs, who have become nothing more than the incarnation of an idea, and can know themselves as that idea. Antigone, in Anouilh's play, goes to her death because she must, because she is Antigone. She is born to the deed, and knows it. Heroes always have their deeds of heroism marked out for them by what they are. For this reason they avoid the hesitations and false starts the rest of us are prone to; but they are less human too. They are the less human as they are the more gullible. Their lack of moral conflict is the mark of their exile from mankind. For without conflict, they cannot be said fully to choose what they do. They pursue their destiny to its end. Hamlet is the human hero, with his feeble efforts and self-doubts. He lacks the skill of action following deliberation, and marks time long after the evidence is in. He fails to know himself and his hesitation; and this lack of self-knowledge paralyzes his will.

We always know something about ourselves, and attempt to act upon it. But often we do not know just what we know or how much; and sometimes we know relatively little, being prey to neurotic fancies and morbid habits of thought. The less we know, the less capable we are of valid action. And the less we know of our ignorance, the less capable we are of judging our own weaknesses. It follows that the less we know of ourselves, our motives and desires, goals and ideals, the less responsible we can be for our actions, unless we possess at least the knowledge of our own failings. Knowledge of ourselves is necessary to morality. Without knowing how little we know—that is, without a profound awareness of our own poor habits and weak tendencies—we cannot even begin to anticipate our own future being. Yet we do not know that we lack this knowledge; we feel that we know our principles and sentiments very well. How then can we be responsible agents? We try and fail. We had no awareness of what was lacking in the process of judgment. It is self-knowledge that makes men free.

5

Self-Knowledge

Preliminary Considerations

The Socratic dictum "know thyself" has not adequately been recognized to be the heart of moral wisdom. Perhaps this is due to inadequate conceptions of self-knowledge, but it is also a consequence of letting a theory of value predominate over the analysis of moral responsibility. (I must except Kant from this criticism; his mistake lies only in the attempt to discover moral knowledge *a priori* in the practical reason —a species of self-knowledge, if a rather peculiar one.) The quest for knowledge of what is good seems to be of much greater importance than the discovery of rules for implementing and being responsible for what one believes is good. And this knowledge of the good seems to be based on principles that are independent of the natures of particular agents who must follow such principles. What I want to show is that without a rather profound self-knowledge, a moral agent cannot adequately validate his claim to do what is right. Without self-knowledge, no one can know if he can or will pay the price necessary to follow his principles.

Ethics is fundamentally a mode of *practice,* acting upon things in ways that change and improve them. Therefore, it is susceptible to the same kind of development as can be found in most artistic production: the preconceived idea—in this case, a prior moral judgment—undergoes transformation as it is implemented and enacted. A splotch of color has its own constraints and exerts its own forces upon the brushstroke that follows. So the undertaking of a moral act exerts its own pressures on events and persons to transform the initial judgment. A man's family is held as hostage while he is asked to aid in espionage. He is first given very minor tasks to perform, tasks he cannot justify refusing to perform at the risk of his family's well-being. Gradually the magnitude of the demands placed upon him is increased, to the point where he is asked to do outright spying, even perhaps to perform murder. If he had initially been asked to do these things, he would have refused, no matter what happened to him or his family. His revulsion against such horrors was quite strong enough. But the gradual sapping of his moral will, and the erosion of his ability to endure harm in the name of principle, eventually permit him to degrade himself completely, with no more revulsion than to his initial indignity. He loses the ability to judge comparatively: all violations of principle become the same for him. The view that the deliberation upon and the articulation of moral ideals is what is critical in such situations is quite mistaken. What is essential is the quality of activities that erode moral capacity and conviction, and of methods which strengthen men in their convictions. To focus on *statements* of valuation, on articulated ethical judgments, is to distort the quality of the moral life, which is primarily the enactment of one's moral being. A man who utters moral claims without acting on them or being changed by them is not a full moral agent. His passivity and lack of conviction are far more indicative of his moral being than his utterances. A man may claim ideals without knowing how much they mean to him, nor how able he is to pursue them. Lack of such self-knowledge can render moral principles and values impotent if not incoherent.

Knowledge in ethical matters is less knowledge *about* anything—though it indeed often includes this—than knowledge of *how to act* in valid ways. What is important is making right choices, in the very literal sense of making and doing, not merely thinking them or uttering them. That is why we all experience the despair of our own inadequacy. We often know in times of crisis what we ought to do, at the price of our own and our loved ones' pain. But we try to evade our obligations by the claim that we are not heroes—our failure is one of will, not of conviction. The point is, however, that a moral belief is genuine only when acted upon. Ethical knowledge is a skill of choosing, evaluating, and acting. Without action, it is but the form of morals without the substance. One must be able to bring *oneself* to action, and one must know both that one can act, and that the act will prove worthy. One must know oneself doubly, then, one's strengths and weaknesses, and one's ability to accept the force of one's ideals.

A crucial failure in moral responsibility is not merely in lacking the courage of one's convictions, but is to be found in the submission of one's convictions to the transformation they undergo when acted upon. Many men, who in all good faith and moral sincerity hold a given social practice to be wrong, nevertheless consciously refuse to participate in open opposition of any sort, even at private attempts of persuasion. Usually they claim that they are too busy—which means, we may suppose, that they have "better" things to do. What they often imply is that they can entertain the moral principles involved at a distance, but that personal participation is unpleasant for them—*and they make this judgment without even trying participation to see*. What they do not know is the satisfaction moral action can bring; their claim that they would not like it may well be completely false. They lack the experience of action itself which carries its own constraints and influences as well as risks. There are many men who act according to their convictions because the experience of moral action is for them rich and rewarding. For such people, to believe is to act, and the test of validity is at least partially the heightening of their moral awareness through activity. Such people can act morally even when the general success of their deeds seems small, for they find in themselves the grounds of validity for their actions. The point is not that such self-warranting is the highest form of moral conduct—such moral feelings should be examined and tested for their success in concretely improving the conditions of life—but that the validity of moral judgment is to be found in action, not in the verbal expression of moral conviction. Ethical knowledge is knowledge of how and when to act in ways that will prove morally valid or right, not the mere verbal form that "such and such is the right thing to do." Verbal expression can aid in deliberation on how and when to act; but it can also stand in the way of action.

The value of verbal analysis—for example, in a sport such as tennis—is that it can enable quick learning and rapid communication, though only as a general rule and by no means always. Ultimately, the test of knowledge of tennis is to be found on the court *in play,* however well a person may talk about the game. So also, moral wisdom is found in the choices acted upon, not in the words that describe them. The separation of the soul of man into a rational or deliberative part and the enactor or will distorts the nature of willing as much as the separation of tennis knowledge into verbal and physical components. Tennis is often played by feel, sometimes even by acting correctly when everything feels wrong, and only occasionally when verbal approval or censure accompany a stroke. The body is not always run by the knowing mind in tennis; the will is not always directed by the judging mind in moral affairs. Deliberation is a process which *may* precede moral activity if circumstances warrant extended analysis prior to action. Such circumstances arise if consequences are unclear, or if moral sentiments are weak and indecisive, so that one cannot be sure of his "real" convictions. Investigation and study are called for. Deliberation may also *follow* action in the attempt to validate it in terms of subtle and hidden consequences. But deliberation itself is not moral judgment: it may precede, accompany, or follow it. Deliberation is the scrutiny of possible actions to determine if they are likely to prove valid. Skill in moral action rests in the act carried out skillfully, not simply in the deliberation upon it. In circumstances under which we would agree to an action as right—namely, to avoid telling a frightened old lady that she is dying—only some of us may possess the skill to tell her that everything is fine in a convincing and persuasive manner. This too is part of ethical knowledge insofar as morality is a form of action. If we cannot perform an action the way it ought to be performed, we probably ought not to perform it at all. We must know our concrete skills as well as our ultimate aims.

Ethical knowledge is knowledge of what to do and how to do it, and is fundamentally employed in consideration of the agent's own actions, not those of others. We do, of course, praise or condemn the actions of others, but only insofar as that praise or condemnation is an act itself, and open to its own tests of validity. Here is another facet of moral action which is often neglected: moral judgments addressed to others' behavior are themselves moral *actions*, and must be evaluated as such. They are not what they have often been taken to resemble, facts or beliefs about others' activities. Condemnation is itself an act—a spoken utterance, or even an inflicted punishment—to be judged as right or wrong as an action. All the difficulties of validating moral judgments enter here, which explains why complex motives and needs are often taken into account in such judgments, for they affect both consequences and the basis for validation.

Since ethical knowledge is the agent's, employed in *his* actions, it must contain, implicitly or explicitly, knowledge of himself as agent engaged in his actions. Otherwise it is difficult to understand the basis on which he can act validly. A given action is valid for a particular agent. I make the claim that "*I* should act" in such and such manner. It is then necessary for me to know the nature and qualities of the "I" involved, and the reasons for its particular obligations. Moreover, one cannot claim the rightness of the act in question unless he can validate it within his own priorities and values. One places him*self* on the line in each of his moral actions, for not only is it his judgment that he should act, but it is his own judgment of the validity of that obligation that is embodied in the act. When I have done something wrong, that I have thought right, I suffer a double failure: I have failed both in my act, and failed in my evaluation of the act. I have violated my own self in not paying it due heed. I may, for example, have followed the dictates of others in my action, denied my own deepest convictions in my judgment, and discover through subsequent misery and guilt that it was wrong to do so; or I may have followed my own precepts erroneously, which I also discover in the validation which follows. In both cases, I misjudge *myself* and what is and will be satisfactory for me. Here guilt is not always something from which to escape, for it may be the only mark of moral failure. It can be eliminated by the refusal to validate one's actions, but this is the refusal to be a moral agent. It can also be avoided by knowing oneself to the point that one can act in ways that enhance and conserve oneself, rather than violating it—that is, by acting validly. Only the latter is legitimate for a moral agent.

The double failure involved in performing an invalid act is of critical importance in moral responsibility. One may fail in one's *act,* and one may fail also in one's deliberate choice of the act. The point is that men continually undertake actions in which they may succeed or fail. But only occasionally do men fully *choose* what they do, with sufficient cognizance of the various possibilities before them, and the likely consequences for themselves, that risks a double failure as well. In this sense, an irresponsible man can fail in what he does; but a responsible man fails further in his *judgment* as to what he ought to do.

The claim that moral failures are always at least partly failures in self-knowledge requires further examination. Consider a number of Germans who participated in varying ways in Nazi activities during the reign of Hitler. Let us take first the simplest case—a perverted mind and a monstrous heart, a sadistic and cruel SS guard in a concentration camp. His inhuman and cruel actions, his lust for pain and bloodshed, brand him to be the monster he is. But they also reveal the emptiness of his moral convictions, and the meaninglessness of his conscience. It is a fact of great social significance that, given any moral code, however humane, some men will choose to violate it, or at least will desire to do so if it is feasible. To such men, only the barriers of law and the dangers of punishment serve to restrain unholy feelings. For them, the collapse of order is accompanied by the release of violence and accumulated passions. On the Day of Judgment, some men will loot, rape, and kill, if only to express their desperation and deprivation, moral or otherwise. Social psychologists trace such deviate behavior to different types of deprivation, to educational, parental, or economic hiatuses in the constitution of personality. The appeal for social reform, even that embodied in Freud's *Civilization and Its Discontents*, is founded on either the misery or the destructiveness of men in normal social relations. If conditions are ripe, some men will exhibit, not their primitiveness, but the pent-up violence hidden in their hearts.

The immorality and violence so close to the surface in modern society, which is restrained only by fear and external discipline, does not raise fundamental moral issues. Society must protect itself from disruption through efficient measures and the encouragement of beneficent social attitudes, which can restrain as effectively as formal rules of law. The danger here is of men without moral scruples. In the name of security, society can enact means of restraint and protection. Other men must be protected; men must be protected from themselves and their destructive impulses. The more clear the danger, the less the issue is morally problematic. The maniac, fanatic, and the person in the mob, are so clearly despicable that we condemn them almost without moral concern. We fear and despise the monsters among men; but we often do not care about *condemning* them. If we do condemn them, it is for the complete inhumanity they reveal, rather than their moral judgments. They are bereft of virtually all the moral capacities necessary to responsible moral judgment. The lost souls among us, however destructive, can only be pitied. They never had a chance. If Iago is but the incarnation of evil, we admire the forcefulness of his machinations, but ignore him as a human being faced with moral difficulties. Othello bears all the weight of our moral reactions—though his helplessness mitigates our censure. The domination of destructiveness in men marks their lack of alternatives to what they do. They are destructive and can be nothing else. We pity them for their lack. They fail to possess any semblance of moral feeling. They lack ideals. They are not worthy of being considered men.

The SS guard, then, is simply a failure as a human being, a cripple. He is judged by men of conscience to be despicable and monstrous, not to have acted responsibly but to have acted wrongly. How could he have acted responsibly, having so little understanding of general moral principles, and so little feeling for common notions of right and wrong? A man-eating tiger is only an instrument of death. He is not a moral agent. So also with men whose moral sensibilities are sterile and withered, and whose violent passions are insurmountable. The greater their evil, the less we take them to account for their irresponsibility. We recognize *our* obligations to them insofar as they are men and we are responsible moral agents. But that is quite another matter. We can evaluate our actions toward wild animals also, but we take into account their wildness and danger.

Contrast the violent and pure reaction of the sadistic guard with the bureaucrat—such as Adolph Eichmann—who accepts the responsibilities of his *position* though they involve murder and destruction. Such men can justify themselves in two ways: first, to refuse justification altogether in the name of duty—to one's country or to superior authority; second, a genuinely moral one, to weigh the needs of the country against the harm caused to some few Jews and political opponents, and decide that the latter price is worth paying for the salvation of the nation. The first rationale reveals a moral bankruptcy similar to the guard's. Both reflect sterility of moral existence: one the emptiness of all principle; the other the absence of sufficient integrity to face a moral problem as such and make a risky but considered judgment. Eichmann is the soulless man, no more to be valued or morally condemned than the beast in human flesh. Neither can participate in human society insofar as it is a moral one, for neither grasps the principles and methods of moral judgment. Neither, that is, possesses either moral skill or the knowledge of their lack. At least, if I fail to grasp the moral dangers of my present course of action, but recognize the risk of failure, I can refuse to act until I can understand, or at least throw the responsibilities onto someone else's shoulders. Our condemnation of Eichmann is for his lack of humanity and manhood. He was not evil; he simply lacked common human feelings. This is a judgment as devoid of moral depth as is the recognition that deprivation can lead to destructiveness. The latter fact is not a moral claim. The only moral judgment of relevance concerns how we ought to treat such men.

The final case mentioned above, however, of the man who recognizes the moral import of his own actions, but who makes the choice to sacrifice some persons in the name of the state, is very different from the other two. For one thing, this man's attitudes, his skills and reactions, are appropriately moral; he acted in ways which could be and were intended to be validated. He chose to work with the Nazi state to save Germany at the expense of some (it became, to his dismay, a great many) of its extremists. He discovered, in a gradual unfolding, the enormous price paid for Germany's evanescent success, in numbers killed and mutilated, in the nature of acts beyond his dreams. The "Germany" he loved became an abstraction empty of meaning; the German people he loved were corrupted, bestialized, even destroyed. This man made the *wrong* choice. Events as well as his own sense of moral evaluation proved him wrong. A proof of his failure is his own sense of guilt—without it he too would be devoid of moral capacity—which follows from his facing without pride his having failed. He did not know enough. He may have acted from cowardice to save his reputation, and gone along with the new government out of self-interest. His sense of guilt would mark the discovery that he was more vulnerable to temptation than he thought. He may genuinely have decided to set his own moral ideals aside in the interests of social order. His sense of guilt here would mark his discovery that one is intimately part of one's moral ideals, and that one can sacrifice them only at enormous risk and with profound justification. If he had known himself better—either his weaknesses, or the strength of his true convictions which he denied, he would have saved himself and acted rightly. The first crime he committed in the name of the German state risked himself upon an altar of moral action. His failure is embodied in the experience of remorse he undergoes *because* he is a genuine moral agent to whom moral convictions are significant. His case is the tragically moral one. However, his tragedy should not lead us to the conclusion that we should seek to eliminate the pain of remorse upon having failed morally, but rather that in this kind of tragedy is to be found the heart of moral action, and the anguish of moral being.

A moral agent who has failed, has failed to understand *who he is* in his relations to the things around him. He has failed to understand the extent to which his own being is implicated in the actions of other men in his society, and how he can be brought to failure by developments outside his immediate personal life. Moral failure is a failure in knowing oneself in its ties to the rest of the world. It arises from a mistaken conception of how one's being is part of the actions of other men.

The question of punishment I shall leave aside now, for it is a separate question facing a judge as moral agent, considering action to be undertaken by him. In the last of the three cases, perhaps the experience of remorse and the admission of failure may produce a form of moral salvation, requiring no other punishment. Men are often restored to moral dignity by the undergoing of nothing more than the experience of failure. Perhaps, on the other hand, moral failure may be thought to necessitate some form of punishment proportional to the extent of the failure, as Dostoievski implies in *Crime and Punishment*. The issues involved in decisions concerning punishment are no more than and no less than those involved in any moral decision. They are irrelevant to the success or failure of the moral actions they are directed toward. Some failures may legitimately be treated without punishment. Some successes may be condemned if they risked too much.

Moral praise and condemnation are addressed not only to an agent's actions, but to the agent's attitudes and self-knowledge. The greater his knowledge of himself, of the ways in which his own nature is intimately part of a world larger than himself, the greater the probability that his interpretations of his present course of action will be legitimate. His failure to know himself, his ideals and his intentions, risks his failure in what he does. It is worth looking at a number of somewhat peripheral aspects of self-knowledge, as well as one or two alternative conceptions of knowledge of oneself, before returning to the subject and showing how it is the foundation of moral responsibility.

Psychoanalysis and Self-knowledge

The twentieth century has marked the advent of an important view of man, and a fairly complex sense of what is meant by the exhortation, "know thyself." In psychoanalysis, the patient tells of himself, and gradually and painfully comes to a discovery of what and who he is. At the same time, his discoveries produce a transformation within him. If successful, the psychoanalysis results both in the patient's awareness of himself and in his ability to control his actions and desires in valuable ways. What the patient discovers in himself he did not originally know, and yet it was part of himself. The classical psychoanalytic view of man is pluralistic—he is not an integral unity, but subdivided into parts, with separate functions and roles. A man comes to know himself when part of him becomes aware of other aspects of himself, almost as if they were internal selves. Finally, when the various parts are restored to equilibrium, if not harmony, a patient may consider himself a complete and healthy person.

According to the pleasure principle, men seek the maximization of pleasure. The pleasure principle cannot, then, but conflict with the moral dimension of human experience. This insight led Freud to the permanent conflict between Eros and Thanatos. Unfortunately, the permanence of conflict within the self in no way alleviates our moral problems. Polarity of forces suggests either extremity or equilibrium, neither of which brings genuine moral resolution. The open questions remain. We can always ask if an appeal to feeling is itself right, or if the restrictions of conscience are themselves good. The determination of answers to such questions can appeal to fixed laws and immediate feelings only in a capricious and circular fashion. "I appeal to my feelings because it is right to do so" is no explanation, if it is right to do so because I feel it is. What I must discover is what my deed, which I performed quickly and with great passion comes to mean to me, and what its consequences entail. My failure rests in myself and in my relation to things. I do not bear up under the consequences. I come to recognize the unforeseen eventualities, and recognize that if I had foreseen them, I would not have done what I did. I come to feel guilt for my own shortcomings, as revealed in my own actions and judgments.

The incoherence within the self of Freudian psychoanalytic theory permits one to absent himself from the force of such self-criticism, at least in a global fashion. Perhaps "I" told a lie to avoid being found out, but this "I" was really a combination of various psychic components of my personality that altogether constitute my being. Perhaps the instinctive part of me resisted prospective anxiety so strongly that "I" could not do as I wished to do. Such an explanation resembles very closely claims such as "I wished to jump into the water to save his life, but the crowd restrained me." The claim that the control of a part of a man over the others may be so great as to eliminate all conscious awareness of the possibility of telling the truth seems utterly specious as an explanation of moral misconduct. Sartre, indeed, criticizes psychoanalytic theory for attempting to replace the *I* with an *Other*. This criticism has considerable force. Unfortunately, Sartre appeals to the notion of a pre- or unreflective consciousness to explain the phenomenon of self-deception and unrecognized patterns of human action, and this notion does not appear to be very different from unconscious personality factors—both are out of awareness. Sartre's point, however, is that we can understand human actions as purposeful in a full sense only if they are *conscious*, reflective or not. Psychoanalytic theory makes human purpose unintelligible.

The difficulty Sartre captures is that if a man is not a unity, but is instead a multiplicity of psychic elements, each part of which can perform moral functions such as choosing, willing, desiring, and having goals, then the process of moral evaluation becomes inexplicable in the same way that two people can dispute over a moral difficulty without resolving their differences. The demands of moral responsibility are that we are required to make decisions and to act upon them. This means that whatever internal strife exists, whether between moral principles and inclinations or faculties of the mind, it must be resolved in an act of the agent if the right thing is to be done, in any sense of that word "right" at all. Insofar as I plead that *part* of me is too strong to be overcome by another part, I am making a claim that is quite incoherent from a moral or purposive point of view. We are all aware that moral conflicts exist—they are the very stuff of ethical evaluation. An anthromorphic rendering of such conflict does not change the force of the moral imperative—which is that decisions and actions must be undertaken by an individual as such, in resolving the conflicts which arise. To give in to an internal conflict, by claiming that one part of the self "wanted" to do what was right while the other did not, is to abdicate the requirement that decisions ultimately be made by the person involved. If I claim that a part of me made a decision to do what was right, but that another part refused, I render incoherent my own actions and intentions. It is myself that I must deal with most explicitly in seeking moral activity, not a part of myself. If I am tempted to lie to evade an embarrassing situation, it is intrinsic to my decision that *I* am tempted, not someone else or only a part of me. So a conflict between oneself and an *Other* within, if a fact, is irrelevant to appraisal of an action as moral or not. If I am to validate my own actions, I must take my feelings as well as my ideals and principles into account, or else I sunder myself into parts. The whole meaning of validation depends upon the fact that conflicts can reach at least temporary resolution under the passing of time. This is not possible when the self is conceived in a nonholistic manner, or as an arbitrary part of the person.

Psychoanalytic theory is at least partly an attempt to deal with man's moral being and problems of responsibility. Its essential incoherence is not due to its being a scientific theory passing as relevant to moral questions. The concepts of anxiety and guilt are central to psychoanalysis in their moral dimensions. The attempt to understand oneself through psychoanalysis is an attempt to understand the patterns and structure of one's behavior insofar as they reflect on one's sense of guilt and failure. Yet the discovery of underlying motives seems to excuse one from responsibility and therefore from guilt. The complex self, with its attendant components of shame, guilt, despair, and responsibility, is reduced to a sum of parts, in none of which does responsibility lie.

The incoherence of psychoanalysis is even greater in that, although it seems to eliminate an individual's responsibility for his actions by basing them on events relatively remote from the moment in which he acts, it also presents a much wider conception of self in its plurality than as will and desire. A man's being extends widely in time and space; what at any moment affects his moral being is difficult to bound and delineate clearly. Psychoanalysis reveals how one's being forms an extended and structured order throughout a wide range of existence.

When one establishes a conception of the human self of indefinite spatio–temporal range, one affirms as well an extended conception of moral responsibility. Whatever a man does, whatever its consequences for him, is relevant to his moral being. Does this imply, then, that he is responsible for everything that happens around him? In one sense, quite unmistakably. If I stand idly by and watch the commission of an act of violence, I am guilty for not having tried to stop it. If I plead that I am too weak to have succeeded, and would have only been hurt myself, I am guilty unless this claim is a fully validated one, in terms of my general moral awareness. And there may well exist cases in which, though I could not have succeeded, I would have been wrong not to have tried.

However, if a person is but a composite of conflicting forces, how can a man be an agent at all? The compartmentalized and divided self is empty of moral significance, for there is no longer a *person* of moral capacity. If the three musketeers, inseparable as they were, divided on a moral issue, *each* would have had the responsibility of acting according to what he felt was right. It would be no excuse to say: "Separately we do not act, but as a triad we are divided; thus we are incapable of moral decision, and also without responsibility for it." The obligation for an individual to decide and act on the basis of his decision is inescapable. We may find excuses for his not doing so, but these are never reasons. They are at best reasons for others to withhold censure. The division of the musketeers on a moral question should promote separation and individuality, not paralysis. But when the division is internal, there is no individuality to be preserved. The various parts of the psyche cannot literally oppose each other; they cannot have different motives, desires, or goals. In fact, no psychic part of the personality has responsibility. How then derive responsibility from the sum of the parts?

What I am arguing against is the view that moral self-knowledge is to be equated in any but a metaphorical sense with knowledge of a person's parts, in the sense that such parts are not he (in that their resist-ance frees him from responsibility in any way). Rather, if there is a moral significance to self-knowledge, it is the discovery of the unity within a man's being, and how unbounded is his obligation to be aware of who and what he is. A claim that something is none of a man's busi-ness can be a denial of himself. Suppose I claim that I "could have" saved a drowning man's life, but did not for he was nothing to me. Such a claim is seldom accepted simply on the basis that the responsibility was someone else's and not mine. We usually condemn failure to act to prevent harm to others except where the risk to oneself is too great. We cannot easily determine where our responsibilities end, and may fail to act on them only when opposing reasons outweigh our obligations to act. Thus I, seeing an adult smoking cigarettes, do have a responsibility to him insofar as I recognize the potential harm in his actions. But I weigh against this my responsibility to respect him and his own de-cisions in such personal or inessential matters, insofar as they constitute him as a responsible adult—without respect one cannot be or become capable of responsibility—and decide that I should not interfere. Be-sides, he probably wouldn't listen to me, and would only become angry. The excuse that I am not responsible for the choice I have made is difficult to understand. "This is not *my* task" is never completely satis-factory. Even on a ship where duties are divided among the crew, the captain is responsible for everything that takes place. Life in general is like this. In much of our lives we are the only captain.

What a man knows about himself constitutes the basis upon which he judges, of all the things he should do, which he cannot escape doing, be-cause not to do them is to act wrongly or invalidly. Here psychoanalytic theory touches on some very important points, despite its theoretical difficulties. The causal base for psychoanalytic explanations contains information that is very important to an individual's appraisal of his moral being. For example, a man may discover that his unconscious guilt at loving his mother and wishing his father dead makes him seek out ways of hurting himself—such as failing his school examinations, driving his friends away, even suffering frequent accidents. The issue is not whether the phrase "unconscious guilt" is felicitous, but whether the individual in question does or does not act self-destructively *because* (in a causally determinate if not quite necessary sense) he did desire his father's death just before his father actually died. Given a causal push toward self-destruction, the name of the cause, or even its precise con-comitants, are not of vital importance.

What is of great importance is that this man is actually influenced to act in unfavorable ways, and is not aware of it. Should he then not study hard? Should he stop alienating his friends? Without doubt: but his lack of knowledge as well as will (which are interrelated, if psychoanalysis has any truth at all) make his doing so very difficult for him. In fact, without knowing that he is so affected by events he is not conscious of, he cannot even observe the nature of his own actions and the pattern of self-destruction therein. He is simply unable to do what he "wants" consciously to do, and thinks he ought to do. He is guilty, for no "reason" that he can perceive, of being immoral and irresponsible. He is not only guilty for his failures in action, but for the inability to control himself to the point where the probability of continuing these actions is at least slightly diminished. His expectation of failure is legitimate, for since no control is available for him to break the causal pattern, he will continue acting as he has been all along.

His discovery that he is burdened not only with the guilt of his known failures, but by past events which influence his behavior and dominate his actions, improves his moral position immensely. First of all, his increased knowledge may strengthen his resistance to failure, for he may now resist his primary feelings of self-loathing in addition to the symptoms of his continual failures. That is, he may seek to reach a more adequate appraisal of his faults and virtues, putting aside many of his failures as the result of a basic tendency toward self-hatred, and correct his failures by dismissing them—not as wrong, but as without moral foundation. Second, he may judge the price necessary for him to do as he apparently should (five years of psychotherapy, the pain and anguish of abortively struggling to study and perform well, constant failure in his social contacts), and decide that it is not worth it. He may instead throw the whole thing up, and leave school or withdraw from intimate social relations. What he *should* do is tempered and conditioned by what he is and what he knows about himself. He may even decide explicitly that the anger expressed toward people he meets is a necessary and unavoidable condition of his learning to deal with them kindly and sensibly in the future. It is for him right *under these circumstances* to act angrily and even cruelly. He has no choice of those available to him that is better. Such a decision presupposes a firm foundation in his own self-knowledge.

The question that arises in psychotherapy is whether a person truly can on the basis of self-knowledge make valid decisions, or whether, however much he knows, he may still be incapable of valid action and even of right decision. Let us hypothesize a man in terminal stages of psychotherapy, who has explained his entire history and found its pattern and order, yet who finds that in his relationship to his wife he continually repeats the same actions that have promoted difficulties and anger. Not only does he recognize while so responding that he is doing so (or if not concurrently, a moment later), but he finds that preparation in advance only postpones his troublesome reactions a short while. He simply cannot avoid the destructive and often cruel words and actions that have weakened his marriage. However much he sets himself to act differently, the same pattern recurs.

Here we see the second component of self-knowledge: it is not alone an articulate verbal account of a person's causal antecedents and effects—that is, knowledge *about,* or psychological knowledge—but is also knowledge on an active level. One knows himself only insofar as he possesses certain skills—in particular, the skill of so responding to situations and circumstances as to change them in intended ways. When the attempt is made to analyze moral actions, as in psychoanalysis or in courts of law, articulation is a great virtue, and the analysis of the person involved is likewise articulate and discursive. But often moral consciousness is nonverbal; the agent recognizes the problem posed and the conflicting inclinations and moral principles present, yet finds the solution obvious in terms of himself. He possesses an ease of movement and a quality of decisiveness. He can weigh, discard, and accept factors as presented, partly intuiting, partly feeling the need for action and the tendencies within his own being. Often such a skill is the result of years of training and experience in making such decisions; sometimes it comes easily and early. In either case it is essential to moral action. And in either case it manifests self-knowledge—the self-knowledge of self-preservation. An individual with this skill is so aware of his moral standpoint in the world that he finds it easy to move and act while preserving himself consistently, insofar as he does not violate his own needs and principles.

Psychoanalysis stresses ease as a factor in morality also, but not ease of decision amidst conflict: rather, ease as an accommodation to circumstances to avoid conflict. The elimination of psychic conflict is for early Freudian psychoanalysis the heart of the pleasure principle. The achievement of a state of mind wherein moral conflicts are minimized is a genuine goal. The view that the nature of the world is such as to render conflict perpetual and unresolvable, that anxiety is a necessity of life, and at best to be minimized, is to psychoanalytic theory the height of pessimism, rather than the source of goodness. Yet any legitimate analysis of moral validation must come to terms with the realization that pain and even death may be the only possibilities whereby one can remain in congruence with his needs and values.

The antithesis between psychoanalysis and moral responsibility is often more implied than real, in that however important adjustment is, it simply cannot be achieved in the face of intransigent conditions. The view that conflict and pain are but symptoms of mental illness is simply on a moral par with Stoicism and Epicureanism in aiming without justification at the minimization of pain in life. The possibility that conflict is unavoidable is faced by Freud directly in the bitter view of *Civilization and its Discontents*, wherein he recognizes that the force of moral obligation necessitates that individual needs to some extent will always fail to reach accommodation with the needs of others, and that some "frustration" of desire is a necessary quality of human life. But even minimization of conflict is itself a moral value—almost without any but immediate or unreflective foundation—one which is rejected by Sartre and other existentialists as an inferior goal for man. Perhaps we should abdicate the entire dispute as without any but arbitrary and personal foundation. But it seems to me that the process of validation can be found evidenced here in a very illuminating form, precisely insofar as the dispute is unsettleable in any logical or even consensual fashion.

The view that men should seek gratification and to minimize pain is ancient but still popular, and can be found in Epicureanism, Stoicism, Christian monasticism, as well as varieties of Eastern philosophy. This view should not be confused with the empirical generalization that in fact all men *do* seek such gratification, which in any but a trivial sense is quite false. Sacrifices and risk are common throughout history, and are admired not only when they are offered in a good cause, but as an example of genuine self-denial in the face of one's duties and obligations. The view that men *ought* to avoid pain, however, is a strictly moral one, for which only moral justification can be offered. Let us then imagine two men to whom this message is addressed. *A* is a classic case of the obsessive neurotic, whose ability to act is rendered impotent by his inability to choose. He experiences moral obligation as a terrible conflict against which he balances his needs and desires, as well as his counterobligations, in a highly obsessive and uncontrolled way. His resulting passivity and immovability—to the point where he never decisively acts in the events of his life, but only awaits their completion—does not eliminate his sense of guilt; he is utterly miserable, without defense, and cannot act to make his life as he chooses. He cannot take refuge in the view that he is evil and glad of it, for he cannot even take credit for his own lapses.

If he now is offered the moral claims that gratification and ease of life are the highest goods, that pain is strictly an evil to be eliminated, that moral obligations insofar as they produce pain are without justification, he will be quite receptive. It is indeed true in his experience that moral obligations are but a source of torment without even the gratification of having observed them, for he is not able to observe them. And truth *within his experience* is all that counts here. The truth or falsity of the general rule that moral obligations always create more pain than pleasure is irrelevant. As the moral agent involved, he is the one who must act on his duties and responsibilities. He cannot achieve what is right. So he seeks instead the alternative of rejecting the obligations and the pain of failure with them. He experiences torture and self-doubt without the compensating and justifying resolution in action. It is legitimate for him, since no anguish he feels enables him to act rightly, to try to eliminate the anguish. In this manner, coming to the realization of his own incapacities and obsessions, he can justify his acceptance of adjustment and lack of concern at the price of his moral principles by his incapacity to act rightly in any case.

Contrast here *B,* who has lived a relatively calm, peaceful life, with its pleasures and occasional problems, its virtues and richness. He is faced with a rising political party which advocates the extermination of a minority group of which he is not a member nor does he know any of its members personally. Plainly and simply, this is wrong, and he sits down to write a protest to the local newspaper. To the claim presented to him that it is none of his business, that he will only harm himself by getting involved, that men should live only for their own pleasures and try to escape conflict, he responds with revulsion: a life of ease without opposition to evil is not a life worth living. (I will not consider here the further point that his temporary isolation and lack of concern for what takes place around him at an early stage may lead to considerably greater horrors later, when his sons are conscripted into the army and his property is taken over by the state.) To the argument that nothing he will do can help, he replies that that may be true, but he can only try. His convictions—particularly on the level on which he acts—are uncompromisable as such; though he is willing to reflect on and modify his convictions, he will not agree to ignore them, partially or temporarily. To him, to know what is right is to do it. The gap between deliberation and action is easily bridged by his conviction. This ability to act is the most important form of ethical knowledge, far more so than the ability to reflect on the principles of what is right, for it reflects a unity of self that is necessary to the validation of one's moral judgments.

Note that both *A* and *B* may agree that the impending destruction of the minority group mentioned is wrong, and that they should both oppose it with vigor and strength. *A*, however, cannot and does not act, thus repudiating the very character of his judgment. He is even afraid to speak to his friends about it, since no one can be trusted. No wonder, then, that he may well decide that pain without consequence is unjustifiable, and that the elimination of internal conflict and anxiety is the goal of life. *B*, however, finds the justification of his actions in doing them, in the achievement of his own protests and resistance, small or large. The "rightness" of the act *means* for him that he must undertake it; while the "rightness" for *A* means only that it will cause him pain and suffering.

A, moreover, is faced with a further problem, in that his own choices will eventually be judged right or wrong by himself and others. *B* has already affirmed his judgment in action, and if proved wrong is ready to suffer for it. He will not be brought to regret his judgment of his obligation. This he believes; and he is likely to be correct about it precisely because of the strength of his convictions. He knows himself enough to assure him security, at least within the range of human error. His decision preserves and reaffirms his unity as a moral person. His sense of himself and his requirements in this situation virtually validate his action in themselves. Though he must in fact wait for the future, the unity of his being and the strength of his convictions go a long way toward determining that future. His action is likely to prove to be valid regardless of the rest of the world's reactions to it, for he has shown both the strength and courage of convictions necessary to make it so. *A*, however, has already manifested his weakness and paralysis in both his failure to act from conviction and his choice to seek respite from pain. He has also refused to make any further moral judgments or evaluations, and has withdrawn from moral analysis. When the opinions of others fall upon him, he will be completely vulnerable to them, to the return of the guilt from which he never really escaped, and to both external and self-condemnation. In this lies most of all the invalidity of his decisions. Only if he could decide with conviction and as a moral affirmation to choose his gratification over the demands of moral obligation would he be able to defend his position as "right," in which case he would have had the strength originally to have chosen to pursue his moral obligations, and acted upon them. That is, he would have possessed precisely the skill he lacks, of making choices and carrying them through. Weakness and self-denial are psychologically understandable; but they never justify the rejection of responsibility.

The claim that men ought to seek gratification and to minimize conflict is not generally defensible, not even to men who suffer internal conflict most. But its appeal is directed to the latter, obscuring the consideration of relatively remote consequences by immediate relief from pain. It is true that an effective moral agent acts with an ease and self-acceptance that a man paralyzed by obsessive self-doubt lacks. The internal conflict of obsessive doubt ought to be eliminated in a good life. But this general thesis makes an appeal to self-gratification and avoidance of internal conflict that can be quite self-defeating.

Therefore, the pleasure principle in psychoanalysis does not solve the problem of moral responsibility, and indeed advocates an indefensible moral position with respect to it. No escape from moral obligation is possible based on weakness, neurosis, or inadequacy. One may only refuse a given obligation by affirming another opposed to it. If a psychoanalyst wishes to recommend on *moral* grounds that obligations need not be observed, he implicitly destroys every means of controlling unconscious impulses to provide individual well being, and furthermore repudiates the role of principle and rule in human life, rendering it but a mechanical process of the satisfaction of needs, which is impossible and intolerable. In the name of *pleasure,* chaos, turmoil and conflict are offered.

What follows from this is that the psychoanalytic view of man must be reinterpreted so as to provide knowledge of man on a moral basis. The ethical implications of psychoanalytic theory are ineliminable, and the arguments for it are necessarily moral. Even more important, the logical difficulties of psychoanalysis, which arise when it is viewed as a science, become clearer when we see values other than prediction and control which are inherent in its foundations. Most of all, however, the role of psychoanalysis in transforming the active capabilities of men makes it fundamentally a domain of moral judgment, not a scientific discipline. The patient, in successful therapy, discovers new ways of acting and abilities he never had before. He develops the kind of knowledge essential to moral action. The content of the actions undertaken by psychoanalytic patients are almost always moral in character.

There is considerable discussion among contemporary clinical psychologists and psychotherapists on the role of the therapist's values in guiding a patient's moral outlook in successful therapy. Sometimes it is claimed that it is possible for the therapist to withhold his own values and to discover what the patient "really" wishes, when he desires two incompatible goals. On the other hand, the determination of what is good for the patient is jointly determined by both therapist and patient, and it is foolhardy to suppose that the therapist's moral stand can be absented entirely from such determination. A psychoanalyst who despises sexual relations outside marriage will explore all alternatives to this before accepting it as necessary for a given patient. No doubt there are patients who are so committed to sexual freedom as to make it necessary for a psychoanalyst to accept it if he is to treat them. But the majority of relatively uncommitted patients are not so able to withstand his very subtle moral manipulation, which is often not entirely at his conscious control. In fact, perhaps they put themselves in his hands so that he can in some sense tell them what to do.

Putting the problem in terms of the intrusion of the therapist's *values* upon the patients' seems to me to mistake it. It is quite possible for a particular therapist to avoid articulating moral praise and censure, and be justified in then claiming that he altogether avoids affecting his patients' values directly. It is true that he implicitly accepts goals of successful therapy which may be called "moral"—of adjustment, self-realization, peace of mind, even the enrichment of capacity to make moral decisions—but he may well view his task as one of removing obstacles in the path of the patient's own realization of these goals, without intrusion of more specific moral values of his own. The problem of values in psychotherapy is complicated by considerations of ultimate or proximate goals without clearly distinguishing them. Mental health itself is unavoidably a normative concept, but it can be relatively free from the encumbrance of particular values directed toward the means to be used in achieving it. The values the therapist lives by may not be brought into the therapeutic situation—though he cannot perform therapy at all without norms applicable to his own therapeutic practice.

The latter norms, which are not to be confused with the values men live by outside therapy, would seem to exert an unavoidable influence on the course of psychotherapy. Many psychotherapists believe, sometimes implicitly, that therapy can be successful only when based on a departure from pre-established and harmful patterns of behavior. They encourage patients to leave their marriages and begin anew. Others take the opposite approach—that too much and too rapid change puts too great demands on the patient's ability to respond. Few patients are capable of withstanding the hidden pressures a therapist can exert, particularly if the patients are dependent on the therapist for their precarious stability.

If we realize, however, that psychotherapy is not intended primarily to be an experimental procedure whereby information is gathered about the patient and his life, tested and evaluated by its predictive consequences, but is instead a process whereby the patient's attitudes, patterns of behavior, feelings, and goals are transformed, it becomes clear that it is virtually a paradigm case of the method of moral judgment. First of all, almost trivially, therapy is a form of action, engaged in by both therapist and patient, and of significant moral import. Second, it involves the constant scrutiny, test and validation, of the patient's actions and decisions. Furthermore, the active dimension of psychotherapy renders it open to moral judgment as are all human actions, for in nothing we do can we escape the possibility of moral praise or blame. Any therapy is an object of moral judgment. It is a continual process of judgment which is itself evaluatable as successful or not. It is necessarily a perpetually self-interrogative method. Every pattern discerned in therapy has moral consequences of far greater import than the causal relationships discovered. For example, the discovery that a patient regularly enters into sexual relations with men who are not willing to marry or capable of marrying her is more than interesting in an empirical or scientific sense. It reflects on many of her most fundamental moral beliefs—perhaps that love should be a precondition of sexual relations, or that the goal of sexual intercourse is to promote intimacy as a prelude to permanence. When the pattern of her behavior is unknown to her, she may never realize the sterility of her everyday actions from the point of view of her own values, and thus never have to face the conflict between her deeds and her conscious beliefs. Every new man is a new possibility, wherein she may discover intimacy and love. Each experience is a failure, producing degradation and pain, but without greater meaning. Even the relationship of her degradation to her self-denial and self-flagellation is unrecognized by her. Upon the uncovering of this pattern—pointed out to her by her therapist, and only gradually accepted by her—she is thrown into a moral conflict at once, since her desire for intimacy is as great as for security. The resolution of the conflict—either by abdicating her belief in the connection of sexuality and love, or by her willingness and strength to wait until she is capable of finding men who will love her—does not merely have moral consequences: it is a moral decision. Her actions are performed with moral intentions and desires, and they can be evaluated as valid or not by the new facets of her life they promote.

In psychotherapy, then, action is undertaken which is itself in response to other actions in and out of the therapeutic relationship. This action is almost never purely a sequential and unreflective response to other actions, but is both a revelation of and a consequence of reflection on the patient's life. It manifests self-consciousness on the level of awareness at first, as conversation about the patient's life, and then on the higher level of methodic transformation of self in response to this primary self-awareness. Psychoanalysis is highly methodic as an evaluation of the character of a patient's life and value of his acts. Such a method can set aside specific or proximate goals of life in the interest of global achievements, such as consistency, peace, or strength of mind; but even this kind of choice is a moral one, not merely because it involves moral values, but because the decision is a response to actions as right or wrong, to be accepted or rejected, and is itself under perpetual reexamination. Furthermore, the treatment reveals the extent to which and the ways in which the patient's very being is bound up with and part of a wider world. How events threaten him and change his patterns of behavior is brought to light. The very process of therapy defines the character of the patient to him, and determines what he will become in the future.

Even when concerned with issues of no apparent moral quality, therapy reflects moral considerations. For example, suppose that a patient is a student who comes for help because he finds it impossible to study for examinations, and does far worse than other students who appear to be quite inferior to him in native ability. Perhaps it is logically possible that this student might improve in school and be affected in no other way. However, in fact—and this is probably the fundamental claim of psychoanalytic theories—his improvement is a function of his attitudes toward his parents, brothers and sisters, and his peers. In changing his performance in school, he may discover—either as a prior condition, or as a consequence of his change—that his father feels highly competitive toward him, and does not wish him to do well. The outcome of his therapy—either improvement and confrontation of his father's unacknowledged feelings at the risk of alienating him, or acceptance of his father's needs and conforming to his desires in order to remain in his good wishes—is fully a moral judgment, in which the student must consider the consequences of his actions and his attendant feelings. Any major change in his school performance will both reflect and create changes of a sweeping and all-encompassing character. The lack of conventional moral prescriptions is not of great importance, partly because some conventional attitude can always be found which bears on the issues, such as the importance of self-improvement or obligations toward one's parents. It is the force of evaluation, judgment, and validation that reveals the moral nature of the decision. If the patient discovers that his need for his father's approval outshines all else, and can affirm this with the awareness of the dangerous and stifling consequences for himself, as well as the reactions of others to him, then he has made a moral decision, with its attendant risks.

Through all this, the therapist plays the role of agent actively involved in the entire process of decision. He cannot be a therapist and merely observe; nor can he escape responsibility for his own deeds. A suicide is a definite failure for him, and he can be held morally accountable. He cannot even plead having followed the rules faithfully. He may be accused of having failed to see that this particular patient required departure from general principles. A poor therapist is despised far more than a poor mechanic, precisely because of the moral significance of his actions. Partly this is due to his dealing with men; but it is even more a recognition that the substance of his deeds is permeated by moral judgments and principles, conventional and otherwise, because of the method at work.

The role of a therapist as agent reveals the necessity of moral analysis to psychotherapy. The problem lies not with his values intruding inadvertently and unconsciously upon the patient's decisions, but with the impossibility of his treating his patient without making decisions and facing attendant consequences. What is most striking among the therapist's responsibilities is that his style of treatment is itself a moral judgment, in which his own values must be laid against his desire to help the patient. He may decide that as a moral agent, he can only view "helping" a patient in the narrow sense of making him a (morally) better person, at the risk of being able to treat only a very few people, of a very particular disposition. He may, on the other hand, partly as a consequence of a liberal and tolerant attitude, decide to abstain as much as possible from particular judgments and condemnations, to promote the widest possible divergence of life-styles in his patients. Perhaps he may succeed with a great number of patients. Perhaps not, if they require a more definite sense of what is right and wrong. This is but another of the factors he must take into account. The moral agency of a psychotherapist creates for him very special responsibilities: he bears the responsibility in his own person and actions for another's life. Thus the moral exhortations found in some psychoanalytic writings are quite legitimate, for they reflect necessary attitudes in psychoanalysis. A responsible psychoanalyst may well proclaim to the world and to his patients that he views therapy as a moral act, and even lay out his general principles for them to consider.

It is now possible to return to the concept of self-knowledge. Psychoanalysis is on the one hand the embodiment of what many people consider psychological knowledge, and in the therapeutic relationship may well be thought to lead to self-knowledge and self-awareness. This view is partly justified, but not where self-knowledge is thought to parallel scientific or empirical knowledge of others. Even the psychoanalyst fails to "know" his patient in the empirical sense corresponding to articulate and verbal prediction and description. His assertions are often without sufficient evidential support, and raise many theoretical and logical difficulties.

But if we recognize the moral character of the therapeutic situation, and its ultimate commitment to creating and implementing moral decision, to the point where it virtually crystallizes the process of moral judgment by stabilizing and delaying it, the scientific inadequacies of psychoanalysis may be viewed as a direct consequence of its moral function. The patient seeks to understand himself in order to become a more successful agent. He thus learns first of all what he is and how to act in accordance with his "true nature," for this strengthens the possibility of valid action. Not acting, or acting in ways that produce anxiety, are always due to something denied or sacrificed in oneself. The patient must learn this. Some articulation of who and what he is is necessary, but not in the mode of empirical science. The role of concepts such as unconscious motives and desires, sublimation and displacement, is to reach the patient on an active rather than a theoretical level. The theoretical inadequacy of a claim such as, "The patient unconsciously wanted to kill himself; that is why he tore his clothing," in that it is neither a plausible reason for his action nor a causal account based on accumulated evidence, is no liability in therapy itself. The manipulative force embodied in the sentence, "You want to kill yourself," in both pointing up self-destructive patterns in the patient's life, and in compelling attention directed to actions which are very risky, is most important. The patient is forced to make some decision respecting his actions, for he has been confronted directly and forcefully. He is put on the spot by the therapist, on an unavoidably moral level, concerning his virtual suicide. This is an example of how a therapist may deviate from empirical explanations to create moral agency.

Perhaps it may be thought remarkable that psychoanalysis, which implicitly aims at the fulfillment of the powers of men as full agents, should so methodically direct the destinies of its patients as if they were objects and not human beings. How can men under the direct control of a therapist, subject to his direct influence, come to be full moral agents subject only to themselves? Once therapy is viewed as a form of manip-

ulation of an *Other* within, how can that Other be transformed to endow
the agent with responsibility? If men are creatures subject to the control
of others, how can they become in control of themselves?

In the next chapter, I shall discuss the specific goals of psychotherapy, to show that they are not expressible in terms of the theoretical
foundations of psychoanalysis. The multiplicity of self-existence makes
neurosis intelligible, but at the expense of rendering the self-unity of responsibility absurd. Psychoanalysis is indeed committed to a view of
men as things, subject to external control. What I wish to show is that
such a view is not incompatible with a view of men as responsible
agents.

The source of the difficulty lies in Kant's second version of the categorical imperative: *Act so as to treat all men as ends withal, never as means
only.* More specifically, it lies in the attempt by post-Kantian philosophers to have that principle while relinquishing Kant's own foundation
in reason *a priori,* which is a bit like wishing to have their cake and eat it
as well. Men are ends for Kant in being the source as well as the object
of the moral law. Moral principles are legislated in the practical reason.
By virtue of possessing that reason, men transcend their limitations as
objects in a causal order. If we reject reason *a priori,* then it follows that
men do indeed inhabit a causal order which cannot be transcended in a
clear and decisive fashion. Sartre's analysis of freedom is an obstinate
attempt to preserve the duality of Kant's view without rational foundation.

The metaphysical issues at stake here are of critical importance, and
will be taken up later in the discussion of freedom. Here I shall anticipate the later discussion by making the point that it is an error to suppose that causal and moral determination are ontologically incompatible. Psychoanalytic theory suffers from a categorial dependence on neurotic states, to such an extent as to render self-realization unintelligible.
But its thesis that responsibility can grow out of causal determination is
a reflection of a fundamental metaphysical insight.

The fundamental principle is that men are never *entirely* self-contained, *entirely* free from the influences of others, *wholly* ends in themselves. In Spinoza's words: "A man is necessarily always subject to
passions, . . . he follows and obeys the common order of Nature, ac-
commodating himself to it as far as the nature of things requires."
Nothing in the world is self-contained, including human beings. Freedom in the sense of eliminating influence is absurd as much as impossible. Men as experiencers act upon things and are acted upon. All that
can be done is to strengthen their powers, to make them aware of being

influenced, and to bring as much control to the influences they admit as possible. Psychoanalysis reflects the primary metaphysical principle that agency and responsiveness are joint concepts, and that moral agents with effective purposes are people most sensitive to what is around them. They are more powerful, but by virtue of their responsiveness and their consistency of action, not by virtue of their independence.

The critical point is that we come to realize that men cannot be ends *instead* of means, for they cannot be ends alone. (I am dubious as to whether anything can be wholly a means either.) In choosing for himself, a man leaves a trace of vital importance to others. The issue in psychoanalytic theory is not whether men treated as means are being mistreated, but whether the forms of control psychoanalysis affords can bring psychoanalytic patients to a sufficient degree of self-controlled activity. This, it seems to me, is precisely the empirical test that pervades all forms of psychotherapy. Does the patient become more dependent on the therapist, or does he come to sufficient self-awareness as to set the therapist's efforts aside eventually as irrelevant to what the patient wishes to accomplish? Are the techniques of psychotherapy efficacious so far as the patient's independent choices are concerned, or do they provide an artificial hindrance to the exercise of his intelligence? It still seems to me that the practice of psychotherapy is notable, not in its accomplishments or professional techniques, but in being a method of active judgment that can never be freed from examination and self-interrogation. It is a microcosm of the moral life. That is its major worth, at least to the thinking person who would learn something from it for himself.

The patient in psychoanalysis discovers himself, sometimes articulately and consciously, sometimes in the torment of his actions and the guilt he bears, sometimes in metaphorical descriptions of his unconscious motives, and in unfounded yet highly manipulative interpretations of his dreams. In successful therapy, he not only "knows" himself in that he can utter technical and colorful descriptions of his needs and tendencies, but he gains the ability to move freely and make decisions which minimize his guilt and anguish, and maximize the possibility that they will prove valid. Gross patterns of behavior and implicit tendencies of thought and action are "known" to him, often on but a level of feeling, so that he can react to his world appropriately and validly. The results of successful therapy are a person who is a more successful moral agent, who has become so through the judgments and actions of the therapist. "More successful" here is a judgment which can be made by anyone. Often the patient is given privilege; but any observer can judge as well, for in his terms a therapy successful to the patient may be a failure for others (i.e., a patient's wife who is divorced in a therapy successful in the patient's eyes). What is gained in therapy is the self-knowledge that enables one to act validly, which is the self-knowledge necessary to morality.

Self-knowledge and Self-fulfillment

The vital importance of failure to the moral person is the heart of moral understanding. A moral agent lives with the continual awareness that his most carefully planned actions may prove inadequate, his moral principles dogmatic, restrictive, and worthless, his rational deliberation a waste of time and effort. The future brings with it a continuous and unavoidable test of himself and his choices, even aspects of behavior he has not intentionally chosen. Anguish and despair are the consequence of the omnipresence of moral choice amidst dire uncertainty, and the omnipresence of failure, however carefully one tries to avoid it.

The possibility of failure entails the importance of two kinds of knowledge: knowledge relating means to ends to minimize the risk of failure in planning; and knowledge of oneself as the agent in order to control the felt qualities of choice and to bring one's intentions and feelings into line with one another. I shall assume that knowledge of circumstances and facts about the world, which enables the rational control of means in their relation to ends, is a clear notion and obviously necessary to valid conduct. I wish to examine the relation of knowledge of oneself to valid conduct and the problem of failure. I shall take the self-knowledge provided by psychoanalysis as my point of departure.

As discussed in the last section, the self-knowledge provided by psychoanalysis is a problematic notion. Difficult problems exist for the view that psychoanalysis provides causal knowledge about the patient undergoing therapy. The explanation of feelings and behavior in terms of unconscious motives and intentions is virtually indefensible, either scientifically or morally. The predictive force of psychoanalytic explanations is almost nonexistent, particularly in the context of therapy. The patterns of behavior and feeling which are discovered and related analytically to early events in the patient's life provide little predictive control of his behavior, except in an *ad hoc* fashion. It is not past events which provide predictive control, which underlie regularities in the patient's experience, but the patterns of behavior themselves which are discerned. Psychoanalytic explanations are generally retrospective; and their value depends on that fact. As for the moral implications of psychoanalysis, I have already shown how psychoanalysis, by assuming a theoretical conception of a self fundamentally divided, fails to provide a sufficiently coherent conception of the human person to leave room for moral responsibility. Sartre's criticisms of psychoanalysis are based on the realization that when a person is viewed as a creature subject to determinative unconscious influences, he cannot be held also to be a moral agent who makes genuine choices. All in all, psychoanalytic theory appears to be theoretically committed to the view that the intentions of men are always suspect, and that the unconscious forces which are at work in determining behavior make the apparent goals and intentions of agents not the agent's *true* or *real* intentions. The free and responsible agent seems to be but a fictional notion that cannot be defended from the standpoint of more adequate self-knowledge provided by psychoanalysis.

What is neglected in the above views of psychoanalysis is a conception of the force and nature of psychoanalytic *therapy*, as opposed to the theoretical foundations upon which that therapy is based. The theory's central incoherence, which renders the moral being of men unintelligible, in therapeutic practice is used to gain moral control by the patient. The basis for this is that the neurotic patient comes to psychoanalysis already possessing a sense of a divided self—otherwise he would not need treatment. Either he neurotically suffers anxiety at the disintegration of his self-unity—in being unable to make decisions, in failing to carry out his explicit plans, and so forth; or he acts in ways that jar severely with his surroundings. A patient in psychoanalysis can arrive there only through severe anxiety which marks the disintegration of some psychic unity, or by aberrant behavior that reveals the same divided self in its relationship to other things without accompanying anxiety on the conscious level. In both cases, the real self—of indefinite scope and ramification in its being in the world, subject to hidden and remote influences and creator of unseen and distant products—is sundered from itself. Compulsive behavior is, according to Freud's latest views, a way of avoiding consciousness of anxiety, a displacement of psychic energy from its deepest sources, and a sundering of ego control from efficient realization—in short, the disintegration of the ego. The compulsive behavior reveals personal disunity in its failure to relate means and ends in a coherent fashion in the patient's behavior. The psychoanalytic patient fails to act validly in terms of his most obvious needs and desires, with or without direct consciousness of his psychic condition that produces such disunity. He is unaware of the ways in which his being is bound up with other things. His aberrant behavior marks either his ignorance of himself as he is inextricably caught up in things, or his willful repudiation of that aspect of himself.

The function of therapy is to promote a unified self from the disunity of the patient's original state. The absence of anxiety in a healthy person can be understood only in terms of a unified conception of self arrived at through therapy. The incoherence of the psychoanalytic self is to be understood, from the point of view of the patient, not as a theoretical incoherence so much as an expression of his own divided self. His therapy is successful when he has succeeded in establishing from the incoherent elements of his life a unity of his person. He becomes an autonomous moral agent in the process of therapy. This is so important that the theoretical foundations of psychoanalysis become relatively unimportant by comparison. What is critical here is what psychoanalysis accomplishes, not its theoretical form. The latter must be understood in terms of the goal of therapy—the achievement of an integrated personality.

How, though, is this accomplished? Apparently, by the discovery and analysis of recurrent patterns in the patient's life. The theoretical structure of psychoanalytic theory provides a systematic way of viewing the events in a man's life that provides meaning both to the conception of his divided self—as subject to unrecognized influences and feelings—and to the possibility of integrating his personality into a unity reminiscent of Plato's just soul—by the elimination of undesired and destructive feelings. The divided self becomes a unity by the elimination of those aspects of his personality which are not "really" part of him. Of course, since the patient's behavior manifested such elements, they *were* part of him. But through therapy, he becomes a new person, free from the emotions that determined his behavior, and over which he had no control. He gains control of himself through knowledge of himself.

This latter form of self-knowledge is knowledge *about* oneself. Without knowing about himself, at least in the sense of discerning patterns in his behavior that make sense of his feelings of being a divided self, a person cannot overcome the division. Psychoanalysis provides a theoretical conception of the self that is fundamentally incoherent, reflecting the incoherence in the patient's sense of himself. Unity, unfortunately, has no theoretical counterpart; yet certainly something akin to the reintegration of the self is at the heart of the goals of psychoanalytic therapy. It is this I wish to analyze.

Let me first, however, link this up with the notion of moral wisdom. I shall assume that knowledge of oneself is essential to moral wisdom in that when one's behavior is subject to forces that he cannot control because he does not know they exist, then he is in some form of bondage. I accept Spinoza's view that passions enslave, and that only knowledge makes one free. A neurotic may well try to act rightly, to form his intentions and make his decisions according to quite valid moral principles; but insofar as his behavior is neurotic, it is the causal consequence of aspects of his life over which he has no control, for he does not know them. Self-knowledge provides the kind of freedom found in Spinoza— the ability to choose in accordance with things as they truly are, rather than on the basis of their apparent nature. The divided self which fails to know itself consciously is left to the capricious result of internal conflict. Knowledge about oneself and its divided nature brings the possibility of self-control, at least to the extent that the person's self-knowledge provides tools for making decisions.

The goal of psychoanalysis is not merely the achievement of knowledge about oneself, but the transformation of the person as the result of such knowledge; likewise, the ideal of moral wisdom is something more than the possession of sufficient knowledge about oneself and the world to allow for valid moral judgment. The history of man is filled with tales of *wise men*—wise not in science, but in goodness. It is sometimes thought that such men are pure and simple. But the unthinking exercise of moral habits, however praiseworthy, is not of moral value. If we suppose that in some sense wise men do face moral conflict, in what then lies their wisdom? In nothing, it would seem, other than their ability to make wise decisions—decisions proved valid by subsequent events. Can it be that such a skill is merely arbitrary caprice, or is it not obvious that the wise man acts in a way that is genuinely right—because he genuinely possesses ethical knowledge?

What then is the nature of a morally good man? Problematically, it would seem that all attempts to articulate this nature are doomed to failure by the very nature of what is involved. At least, those who have attempted to analyze wisdom or enlightenment agree on its ineffable character, its paradoxical nature. To Kierkegaard, the knight of faith is absurd. He has passed through despair and faced infinite resignation, yet he is not in despair nor resigned. He has faced the infinite and returned to the finite. He is a knight of faith, yet lives like a simple man. "In the evening he smokes his pipe; to look at him one would swear that it was the grocer over the way vegetating in the twilight. He lives as carefree as a ne'er-do-well, and yet he buys up the acceptable time at the dearest price, for he does not do the least thing except by virtue of the absurd." Consider also Nietzsche's description of saintliness, which he views as a form of hypocrisy: he asks, "How is negation of the will possible?" The answer he gives, paradoxically in terms of the humility of the saint, is that it is not possible. "Behind the question mark, as it were, of his fragile and miserable appearance [is] the superior power that was testing and proving itself with . . . self-control, . . . strength of will." "The inclination to lower himself, to let himself be stolen from, lied to, and exploited, could be the modesty of a god who walks among men." Christ let himself be crucified as an act of superior will. And in Zen we find: "Zen is your 'ordinary mind,' " and, "Desire flows into the mind of the seer but he is never disturbed." Yet it is desire that is the source of disturbance.

In order to get at this notion of self-fulfillment, I shall refer to the notion of the psychoanalytically healthy or mature person. In the literature, we find that such a person is marked by "the absence of anxiety, of irrational doubt, and of the inhibitions and restrictions which paralyze both choice and action." Mature individuals have achieved a harmonious integration of the various facets of their personality—the self-unity I mentioned above. They also feel quite free in what they do, though they often act as they feel they must.

The theoretical conceptions of psychoanalysis make such psychic health difficult to grasp. Surely it is not the goal of psychoanalysis to eliminate feelings—the repression of emotion is quite unhealthy. A healthy man is aware of his deepest feelings, and can reveal them to others. Yet the man who displays hatred or uncontrolled emotions to others is highly neurotic. Thus, a healthy person is aware of his feelings, capable of expressing them in direct ways, and yet does not possess the kinds of emotions or the attitudes to them that foster guilt in him or hurt others unnecessarily. Such a person will be angry; but he lacks the anger that leads the average person to destructive action. On the other hand, he becomes angry quite readily, and will show it easily; he is not afraid of the reactions of others. Perhaps he appears to be more controlled than the average person, but control is a form of repression and he is not repressed. The important point here is that in terms of the basic tenets of psychoanalysis itself, only a paradoxical description fits the healthy man. For he is both a man with deep and strong emotions, yet one who lacks the pathological aspects of such emotions. Within the theoretical apparatus of psychoanalysis, he may only suffer his feelings

or repress them. The person who has sublimated deep desires into socially acceptable forms both does and does not feel his true feelings. He
does in that if he did not, he would not be fully in touch with himself.
He does not in the sense that he completely lacks the guilt and shame
that usually accompany them.

One way to approach the notion of self-fulfillment involved here is
through an analysis of that peculiar concept of "selflessness." One
fulfills oneself by losing oneself! The saintly notion of selflessness is quite
enlightening if properly understood. Surely the saint is not selfless in
being without a sense of himself. His ego is not particularly weak. But
he is humble, self-effacing, and free from egoistic desires. He finds it
possible to love others in the ideal Christian sense that is free from pos-
sessiveness. Dostoievski captures some of this in *The Brothers Karamazov*
in the characters of Alyosha and Father Zossima. In contrast to Dmitri's possessive love for Grushenka and Katerina's self-sacrificing love
for Dmitri that threatens to engulf him, Alyosha loves unpossessively yet
without sacrificing himself in the ways that demand even greater sacrifices from his beloved. His love for Lise and the boys is selfless in that he
needs and expects relatively little in return; yet he does not appear
weaker or less decisive in his character for having less forceful passions.
The strong passions—such as lust—generally stand in the way of other
needs of the self. This is what Plato considered true bondage—to one's
worst part. The selfless lover does not love in the self-sacrificing way
that inhibits either his own satisfaction or that of his beloved. Rather,
he gains a quality of self-sufficiency and stability by virtue of his love.
The love of wisdom that is philosophy is a genuine passion for Plato; yet
it is cooler, more relaxed, and provides a sense of ease and self-sufficiency that is lacking from more ordinary modes of love. To Plato, the
philosopher is the happiest of men in his freedom from control by his
appetites. The replacement of the destructive passions by "selflessness"
strengthens rather than weakens the soul.

Nietzsche's insight mentioned above is inescapable—the selflessness
of the saint is in fact a significant form of the will to power. Selflessness
is not self-sacrifice or self-destruction. It is a way of realizing oneself by
abolishing the kinds of emotions that cripple one in dealing with others.
It is a way of ceasing to be what one has been. If "selflessness" means
anything, it refers to the absence of the phenomenological awareness of
oneself as divided, as a barrier to oneself. The neurotic continuously
feels the impediments of one or another facet of himself. He is always
standing in his own way. Fear, anxiety, or compulsiveness continually
intrude upon his awareness. A divided self is felt continually *as* divided.

But the mature person who is a unity of elements fails to be aware of himself *as a self* precisely because he does not stand in his own way. A man who is literally self-conscious—that is, embarrassed and awkward —is aware of himself as an impediment to his own goals, and aware of his divided being. A harmonious and integrated personality is not likely to be conscious of impediments within his own awareness. He feels selfless or egoless. But his phenomenological awareness of ease is the mark of a powerful and secure ego. That is one aspect of the paradoxical character of self-fulfillment.

What is suggested here is a distinction between the felt awareness of the self, which frequently seems to be negative or problematic, and some other sense of selfhood. If in making a decision one stops to consider oneself as agent, it is because he has failed to come to the decision without strain. Where the decision can be made easily, without internal conflict, then one is conscious only of the alternatives and the choices to be made among them. The selfless individual here is not so much a martyr, sacrificing himself to others, as he is unaware of being internally divided, in that the problems of a divided self do not arise for him. It is a strengthening or integrating of the person that is at the heart of the loss of awareness of one's divided being.

The integration achieved by psychoanalytic therapy is akin to the self-realization of the wise man. Psychoanalysis moves from the divided self at war with itself to a unity of the various facets of the personality. This unity is, however, not susceptible to analysis in terms of the theoretical components of psychoanalysis, which provide room only for a divided self. Here is one explanation of the paradoxical aspects of self-realization: the latter may be understood only in terms of a comparison with more ordinary states of consciousness, which involve a fragmented and anxious self. It rarely makes the felt qualities of self-fulfillment unavailable to those who seek to understand them. To describe psychic health to a neurotic, obsessively concerned with selfish and egoistic needs, tormented by self-doubt and a sense of his own lack of identity, is virtually impossible. The theoretical structure of psychoanalysis reflects this fact in allowing no room for the understanding of a person not divided internally, even as an ideal. Yet that unification of the elements of the self is the goal of successful therapy.

What seems to me most interesting here is that the self-unity involved in wisdom is not so much a unity of separate factors within the person, as a unity created by a self-awareness of a certain sort. It is not that the therapist brings into existence a unity within the patient's psyche that has as its result the ease of decision and sense of freedom found in the healthy individual. Rather, the knowledge the patient gains about the divided and inessential elements of himself brings to pass a new project or goal—of unifying himself in his feelings, behavior, and understanding. Part of this is accomplished by eliminating divisive feelings. Partly it is a matter of making explicit choices where none were recognized to exist before. The patient uses the knowledge about himself he gains through therapy as a tool for carrying out the goal he has always had—to build a unity out of the elements of his life. The unity is something created out of discordant and disconnected elements. The ideal of eliminating the anxiety of a fragmented personality is approached through the acquisition of sufficient self-knowledge as to make the project of unity realizable.

The ideal here is not in fact of a unity of disconnected elements; it is rather the elimination of the disunity of anxiety. Put most simply, there is nothing to unify; there is only the division within the self to eliminate. The consciousness of anxiety, of standing in one's way, of not knowing what one wants to do, vanishes. What is left is the absence of most ordinary ways of being aware of oneself, a negation of self in this regard. The integration of personality involved here is nothing but the absence of most kinds of self-consciousness. The utter conviction of being oneself holistically and undividedly is therefore also the negation of self-awareness. Put in Hegelian terms, a healthy person overcomes the alienation of the self from things found in the unhappy consciousness of being continually divided from them, and comes to realize himself through things as they become objects of his will. Self-awareness as a mode of consciousness of oneself *in opposition* to the environment that forms the wider context of one's being is given over to the self-assertion of one's being *through* the environment that comprises oneself. The integration of personality in psychoanalysis is thus a negative goal, yet one which manifests both the greatest strength of character (a character not working against itself), and the greatest degree of self-knowledge—*of*, not *about*, oneself.

The divided self fails to know itself in being ignorant of the pattern or order amidst the events of its life. The feeling of being at war with oneself, and a sense of ignorance of how or why, is the mark of complete ignorance *about* oneself. Knowledge about oneself provided by psychoanalysis at least reflects a coherent pattern of events and choices in the life of the patient. But it alone cannot bring with it a unity of self in feeling or awareness. It reveals the person's life to be intelligible as a unity, amidst the prevailing sense of disorder, or as a radically different unity from that of which the patient is conscious. What therapy seeks is the unity of self in feeling and behavior that is the mark of certainty of self, particularly in what one *will do,* and how one *will act.* What is involved is a transition from knowledge about oneself to knowledge in having a sense of oneself as part of a wider world. Spinoza represents this as a transition from the second to the third kind of knowledge, from adequate ideas to intuitive science. One comes to a sense of how one stands within a world, affecting it and being affected by it. The healthy person knows himself to be a unity insofar as he lives that unity in what he does. Here we have self-knowledge as the carrying out of a plan to be integrated and whole. Let me pursue this notion.

The healthy person knows himself and his true feelings or motives. He grasps the thread of unity in the history of his being, and is willing to stand by the things he does insofar as he has chosen to do them in full awareness of what he was doing. He possesses self-knowledge as awareness of himself and what he feels, though his feelings are radically different from what they were before. He possesses self-knowledge in the awareness of what he wishes to become and how he wishes to be as created in his deeds, though this is manifested only in how he lives. And he is self-knowledgeable in the thread of continuity in his behavior that preserves his being as orderly and peaceful. A harmonious or ordered personality, undivided by conflicting desires and acts of will, manifests itself continuously in what it does. It preserves itself and its ordered relation to things. Its integrity is never threatened. A healthy person thus knows, at least on an active level, what he is and how to preserve himself. He is in a sense untouched and untouchable by what is outside him. Yet he is highly responsive to things as well.

More accurately, he recognizes that his being is part of other things, as they are part of him, and abandons the sense of things *outside* of him. He incorporates them into himself, and ceases to be threatened by them—there is no longer an enemy, only a world to be defined and created. Above all, the healthy person lacks the sense of working against himself. In a genuine sense he is what he wants to be, and does what he wants to do, in an unambivalent and coherent fashion. He thus projects a unification of purpose, wish, and action in everything he does. He fashions a coherent and unified self in the choices and decisions he makes.

I am trying to analyze the conception of self-knowledge which underlies both psychic health and the self-fulfillment of the "wise man." I must return to the earlier notions of moral failure and valid action to bring psychic health and self-realization together. Valid action depends on the implicit or explicit realization of the risk of the self that takes place in an act and its consequences. In choosing to undertake a particular course of action, we are bound to it to the utmost depths of our being, insofar as our self is at test both in the deed itself and in the future that may vitiate both our intentions and our ability to persevere. The fundamental risk of failure in action can be mitigated partly by knowledge of the world in which such actions take place, but also by knowledge of oneself as the agent that stems from the realization that one is *unable to do anything else*, the sense of living as one must, of knowing how one's being and character are necessarily bound to the events which surround him. However well one may foresee the future consequences of one's deeds in their external dimensions and in the results of what one does, the final test of the validity of an action depends on the coherence of the self which has undertaken the action in question. Ultimately, a valid action is what one can best live with in the future. Hume's understanding of the limitations of reason alone in moral judgment may be recast as the recognition that knowledge of the external conditions and consequences of moral judgment is not sufficient to validate a particular judgment; that knowledge of the agent's person—his compulsions and passions—is implicit in the character of any valid moral judgment. To make a valid moral judgment is to represent oneself as standing upon it in the face of the unavoidable risk of failure.

In order to fail in moral action, one must in the deepest sense fail *oneself*. A valid action is one that is best in the deepest human sense. As Aristotle saw, to do the right thing is to affirm some human ideal rooted in the depths of one's being as a man, to realize oneself to the fullest in some particular manner. The principles that one lives by, the particular circumstances in which one finds oneself, the indefinite and risky future, are all brought into an individual synthesis expressed loosely by the words: "Here I stand; I can do no other." To fail is to fail to realize where one stands, what one is such that one cannot do anything else. To fail is to fail to be committed strongly enough to something to stand by it securely. The hesitancy of deliberation, the paralysis of will before conflicting alternatives, reveals that one's being is torn and dual. Decision may bring the self into a unity created out of its history and being. I am what I choose, not only in that I am responsible for my actions, but in that my actions reveal my being insofar as they bring a unity into my formerly divided self. Insofar as I fail to be sufficiently unified, in that what I become is out of step with what I will be, I fail. Failure is the result of one's future self being unable to share the value of a present choice. In the action, one engages one's total being into an indefinite and risky future. Failure is the splitting of oneself through time, the widening of the gap between the present and the future. To act validly, one must know oneself through time, and possess a sense of what one will be, sufficient to avoid failure. Self-realization is the performance of actions that are sufficiently in accord with oneself as one knows one to be as to preserve or even enhance the coherence within one's being and acting.

The deliberative and rational decision amidst the precariousness of one's existence marks the fullest achievement of predictive control over, and knowledge about, oneself. To know a great deal about oneself, the influences and habits that are part of oneself, the kinds of responses and actions that can be anticipated, is to be able to control the future in its influence on the self. One makes a decision having taken all that can be taken into account, in the most intelligent and rational way. The ideal here is of alertness to one's being, and the conscious control of the entire world and its future from the point of view of the self, viewed most widely. Here is the rational man who acts from the deepest sense of what he truly wishes and holds ideal. The complete understanding of himself and the influences upon him enable him to know fairly well just what he can or cannot live with. The changing adventures of the self are thus controlled by the greatest degree of knowledge about oneself.

The self-realized man, however, without such complete knowledge *about* himself, controls his being rather more from the other side. He knows himself in the sense that he is at ease to the point where he can stand by himself with complete conviction. He possesses a simplicity of being that renders his future self completely known, in that he will be what he is; or he will change only as he so desires. He passes the tests of action by virtue of an internal purity of soul that does not withstand vicissitudes of fortune so much as it fails to be changed by them against his will. The ability to be content with oneself may be illusory, so far as one is a smug, self-satisfied, and self-denying person. Self-satisfaction is an ephemeral condition that can be broken by fortune. The rich man who is self-satisfied can be destroyed by the loss of his wealth. The great lover can be rebuffed. The tyrant can be overthrown. Only the man at peace with himself, who has rejected external fortune as not essential to his true being, can be free from enslavement to circumstance. The Greek ideal of the freedom from fortune is also a freedom from failure; for failure is in a future filled with unforeseen circumstances. Insofar as one prevails before such circumstances and through them, one does not fail. One may come to define oneself so coherently before and in the world that every part of it enters an order of being so defined by that self as not to threaten it. One fails insofar as one discovers what one cannot live with. One minimizes the risk of failure by defining oneself so coherently and so widely as to assure oneself that he has done what he most deeply wishes.

This ideal of freedom has been manifested in many forms, theoretically differentiated, but strangely alike in their experiential qualities. The Epicurean saint achieves a quiet in his life of pleasure that is free from bondage to the transitory and sweeping passions. He seeks freedom from pain, and finds it in a peace of mind where what can cause pain is eliminated from life. It is not so much that he withdraws from life to *find* peace, as that his peace of mind brings him to an understanding that only simple joys are good—joys that cannot be taken from him, like sunshine, rain, and freshly-cut grass. The Stoic, who seeks to grasp what is or is not in his power, endeavors not to strangle his feelings so much as to make them independent of the possibility of failure. He seeks the freedom of mind that is acceptance but not resignation. His participation in the most risky of affairs, political activity, is made possible by an attitude of mind that makes him immune out of his realization that failure is so likely. The Buddhist, who comes to understand that all is one and that the antagonistic forces of life are only apparently at odds with each other, comes to a living union of peace of mind and goodness that prevails through the tensions of life. Christian saints, who commit themselves completely to the holy, find themselves in their devotion. By giving up oneself, one finds oneself.

All of these are ways of living with oneself that are the deepest manifestations of knowing oneself—knowing what one is so deeply, and with such utter conviction, that one prevails as one is through any vicissitudes of life. It is not quite true that one feels less intensely; rather, his feelings are transformed by a profound realization of what is important to him, and that what is so important will not be overcome by future circumstances. One seeks to live to the utmost, realizing everything human about oneself. As one struggles to do so, one finds one's struggles bring paralysis and despair. To achieve the ideal for which one is struggling, one must move from despair to peace; one must cease the struggle, yet preserve the ideal. One changes in oneself in order to know oneself; one changes through knowledge of oneself to come closer to fulfillment. This is the deepest realization of every saintly view in the history of man.

The question may be raised as to just why I call such self-fulfillment a state of self-knowledge. Why not simply hold that it is a personal form of being, quite independent of any kind of knowledge? If it is a form of knowledge, it should be classifiable as one of the common types. It is

not, however, knowledge *about* oneself. Although the healthy person
may come to health through knowledge about himself, a transformation
within him takes place above and beyond that knowledge. On the other
hand, self-realization is not a form of knowledge by acquaintance—that
would certainly not provide peace to a tortured life. Nor would it seem
to be a form of knowledge of how to do anything, particularly not of
how to act validly, since the rational and deliberative man possesses
that knowledge also. Does it make any sense to describe self-fulfillment
as the *knowledge of how to be oneself*, which is the only fitting way to describe it?

Before explaining what might be meant by this notion, let me point
out certain important cognitive properties of moral goodness in the
terms I have described it. First, just as knowledge of a skill would seem
to entail knowledge about *something*, so moral wisdom entails the existence of knowledge about the agent, if only implicitly. A golfer can always make some true statements about golf. And a wise man can always make some true statements about himself and his true or
undivided intentions, as well as about valuable principles of life. A neurotic person does not know what he "really" feels or wants. The undivided nature of the good man certainly allows him to tell us just what
he really is after when he makes a decision, however casually or undeli-
beratingly. His claim that "He must do this" reveals that he possesses a
sense of what goals he must live by. Second, just as knowledge of a skill
can be tested, moral wisdom can also, by presenting the agent with a
moral situation and asking him to resolve it, either verbally or by acting
within it. The test of his decision depends on some fundamental sense of
consistency with his conception of himself which is entailed by the decision; otherwise he would either be hesitant, or not be sure thereafter.
A person divided against himself fails because his inner conflicts cannot
be resolved in his active decisions. The wise man, who acts as he must,
cannot be undermined by evidence that he "really" wants something
other than provided by his actions. The claim that he didn't really want
what he brought to pass can always be raised, to be refuted, however,
by the thorough consistency in his life and behavior. The wise man thus
implicitly knows what he really wishes. This self-knowledge is central to
all valid moral action.

The self-realized man knows how to be himself, where the human self
is viewed as a consistent and patterned unity of feeling, intention, and
action. Here the human person is to be understood not simply as an internal or mental system, but as a complex interaction of feeling,
thought, behavior, and submission to circumstance. Such a multiplicity

cannot be unified completely; all we can do is specify the ideal. The self-fulfilled man possesses a sense of himself that allows him to organize the diverse elements of his experience into the kind of unity provided by the diverse elements of a work of art. Dewey saw deeply into the relation between the good life and a work of art. Divisions within the self are the foundation of failure in action. One is torn apart by varying goals and desires, by one's actions being incompatible with some fundamental self-image. The neurotic cannot simply be; he reacts with some degree of blindness to every situation. The psychoanalytic conception of the neurotic person views him as torn by conflicting elements of his psyche. He cannot then be himself in a consistent and undivided fashion. He must learn the skill of how to act in ways that continually preserve some unity of himself amidst change. I grant that it is not unimaginable that everyone might possess this skill without painfully learning it, as men learn the skill of walking. The fact that most men lack it, however, reveals their ignorance of how to be in a consistent sense, and of what a man's integrated self would be if he were to come to it.

The Socratic maxim "know thyself" is the ground of valid action and of moral wisdom as well. Yet would the wise man be able to answer Socratic questions put to him? Could he defend himself analytically as Socrates asks that Euthyphro do? Could he analyze justice or piety? Probably not! But he would know in every case what he had to do in order to be himself. He would not be flustered and shaken as is Euthyphro at the end of the dialogue. Rather, he would smile at Socrates at the first question of the nature of piety, and indicate that he knows how absurd it seems to prosecute his father for murder under such circumstances, but that his aversion to the taking of life under any circumstances makes it necessary for him to accuse his own father. He is weighed in the balance, and if he chose anything else would be found wanting. He knows not piety—that is, the wishes of the gods—but himself, and how he must face life regardless of the thoughts or actions of others, though he has in effect taken them into account. The good man has in effect come to the realization of his own ultimate commitments, what he *must* act and live by. Certainly this is self-knowledge.

The further question may be asked as to whether the possession of such self-knowledge guarantees moral goodness. Does the man who "knows how to be" necessarily act virtuously? It would not seem necessary that a man who knows himself to the utmost consider the happiness of men in general, and it seems highly unlikely that he would necessarily observe conventional moral standards of any sort. Can we not imagine a man whose self-knowledge reveals him to be a sadistic murderer who is constrained only by fear of punishment? May not a personality be integrated in destructive and socially aberrant ways?

A priori, it would seem so. Let us, however, not overlook the empirical components of moral judgment. If men are social beings, then the discovery of how one can be a fairly consistent person may well empirically involve the consideration of others as members of his society, and as moral agents. Just as everyone in Western society, however much he would like to forget it, must come to terms with his parents and incorporate them into his personality and life, either by a definite acceptance or rejection, so the wise man must know of his dependence upon others, the extent to which his own being and character are the consequence of social aspects of his life. Will a man really be better off for hurting others? Can he really break the moral standards of others and be fulfilled in doing so? Is the ideal aspect of the wise man's character to be satisfied by actions that others consider wrong? It is doubtful, particularly if we realize that the wise man seeks to preserve himself and his integrity, and to avoid failure. Violent actions are dangerous and generally to be avoided. I suspect that this is the basis for the quietude and peacefulness of the lives of saints. Men who make war and wreak destruction in the name of some ideal continually risk discovering they have failed themselves terribly. The wise man grasps, probably intuitively, just when and where his own integrity is at stake, and that others are part of it.

If we knew enough about human nature and the sources of satisfaction, we might well come to see that we are the kinds of beings who depend on others, and who are pleased when we can be kind and helpful to others. The *superego* of psychoanalytic theory represents the fundamental way in which other men become part of our own being, representing conditions that we must take into account in whatever we do. If we could, *without fear of embarrassment or harm*, we might all choose to be noble and generous. As we gain in self-knowledge, we may come to act more and more consistently according to our ideals.

But if a self-knowledgeable man were to persist in actions destructive to others, all we could do would be to put him away with the kinds of people we consider unfit to live in society. Personally, I tend to accept Dostoievski's view that self-doubt and self-loathing are the source of all destructiveness in men. The healthy man, freed from such doubts and self-hatred, will tend to grasp directly that his true being is eminently moral. Plato certainly held that view. But if it can be shown that there exist completely evil men, undivided in their wish to maim and hurt others, and who know themselves as such, then they must be caught quickly and put away. The conflict between society and moral heroism is a recurrent and unavoidable one, not only because society is conservative and repressive, but because the self-assertive hero, who does "what he must do" *may* be completely wrong in his judgments from any other standpoint than his own. In the last analysis, individual men may well differ in their fundamental ideals. If a self-knowledgeable man, who fully understands his dependence on other men, holds it valid to act to destroy them—perhaps at God's command—all we can do is stop him. It would not do to psychoanalyze him, for he knows himself. We can only accept his judgments as valid for him, and make our own judgments, valid for us, to prevent him from doing harm. I would like to repeat, however, that there is little evidence that such men exist.

Few men will ever approach the complete certainty about themselves that is the ideal of self-fulfillment. Self-doubt is at the heart of despair and the sense of being alone before the awesome peril of one's decisions. The wise man stands before despair and the likelihood of failure by so complete an acceptance of himself as to minimize the possibility of that failure to the greatest extent. The man who doesn't care risks nothing also; and if there are truly men who care about nothing, even their own being, then we cannot reach them on any moral level. Morality for most men is a continual struggle of their divided natures, part seeking the ideal, part continually failing. The wise man cares most profoundly about everything; but unlike most men, his love for the good also enables him to find it with conviction. Unfortunately, the peace that is goodness is not an ideal to strive for, although one can come to it through striving for the good in its other aspects. It comes as if by grace, as one passes through the desperate pain of despair, the torment of one's ideal nature vitiated by imperfect life. One awakens to the peace of no longer caring the same way about suffering, yet gaining the strength to care more than ever. If one's love must be realized or possessed, one can love only so much without return, for the pain is too great, and the risk of one's being inescapable. But when one loves *selflessly*—that is, without the need for any return at all—then one can love infinitely, and one can find oneself through that love as well, for one has no need to hide oneself.

The ideal of moral wisdom is of a state of being—an activity, I might add, in the Aristotelian sense—which permits only paradoxical realization in the terms of ordinary moral discourse. The good man at one and the same time cares infinitely about what is good and right, yet hesitates not at all before the peril of failure. He knows most deeply what he risks in his decisions, for he is utterly committed to the ideal in his life; yet he

never doubts the possibility of failure. He knows that the danger of failure is great, and cares immensely; yet when he fails—and all men
sometimes fail—he goes on without looking backward. He is supremely
self-confident; yet he realizes that no one can be certain in moral matters.

The apparent paradoxes here are the consequence of the rarity of this
special mode of experience. There is nothing absurd about self-realization, any more than the experience of a Martian would be absurd.
Probably everyone occasionally finds himself able to make an important decision easily and yet rightly, with great conviction. If only we
could remember such cases when we are tortured by indecision and
driven by despair. Unfortunately, when we do we only despise ourselves
the more for failing the ideal so completely. That is the most vicious
paradox of self-fulfillment: knowledge of the ideal makes men fall further from it if they have not realized it yet, for they hate themselves all
the more for failing.

Reasons and Causes

Our discussion of psychoanalysis must be extended to the consideration of a further point—the complex interrelationship of reasons and
causes. Although many philosophers argue that giving causes of behavior and justifying it by giving reasons are conceptually independent activities, psychoanalysis seems to confuse them, in a way essential to its
very conception. Not only do psychoanalysts speak of unconscious feelings and motives as purposive, though they seem only to be causes, but
psychoanalysts seem also to hold that behavior may be *excused* on the
basis of information about the agent's past, though only reasons seem to
have a place in excuses. The distinction between reasons and causes is
based on a logical distinction between causal and rational explanation.
It has been thought to solve the problem of freedom and moral responsibility by justifying the denial that causal explanation in any way com-
petes with rational justification. Although a man's behavior may be ex-
plainable causally, he must nevertheless, in the different context of
reasons, be open to judgments about his responsibilities and obligations.
In short, the claim that determinism and moral responsibility are incompatible is said to be the result of a confusion of reasons and causes.

The basis for this view is an unassailable logical point: actions offered as rational and justified are in fact and ought to be appraised very differently from behavior merely undertaken. To explain a rationally justifiable choice is to give the justification. Only where there is no justification available may we turn to causal explanation, which is very different, to very different purposes. An analogue may be drawn with deductive logic: where a mathematician offers a proof as valid, there exist two separate and exclusive ways of responding to it. Generally, we are meant to appraise the argument and judge if it is valid or not. We may also, bizarre as it seems, ask for a causal explanation of the mathematician's behavior. If this makes any sense at all, it must be as an explanation of mathematical creativity. The reason a request for a causal explanation is so strange in such a case is that where rational explanations can be given which are obviously valid, we seldom also seek causal explanations, even in cases where the latter are available to us. This is the substance of the Kantian claim that men inhabit both a noumenal and a phenomenal world at once—both rational and causal explanations may be given of anything they do. When a man is rational, he may be thought to be completely a noumenal being and thus free—not so much free from the possibility of causal explanation, but free in that causal explanations are inappropriate for a rational creature.

In Kant's ethics, the parallel between reason in mathematics and reason in ethics is virtually complete. Both are reason *a priori*, which provides a complete and unquestionable ground for the judgment offered. With such a conception of reason, we can admit great force to the claim that where reason is at work, causal explanation is illegitimate. Reason *a priori* brings with it a conception of a human capacity independent of causal antecedents. Perhaps in the case of any particular individual, of whom we may ask why he does or does not utilize his reason in certain ways, a causal analysis would be interesting. But as Kant showed, that is far more an explanation of why his will is not subject to his reason than an explanation of reason itself. The nature of reason *a priori* does not seem susceptible to causal explanation. Reason simply is—a capacity of men. Perhaps it is one of the elements of which no understanding can be given, though reason does attempt to complete itself by leaving the world of experience and seeking a more fundamental explanation in terms of God.

To relinquish the conception of reason *a priori*, and yet to preserve the exclusiveness of rational and causal explanation is, it seems to me, to take a rather incoherent position. The point is by no means that one cannot preserve the conceptual independence of the two, but that the basis for treating them exclusively rested originally upon a conception

of reason that no longer can be maintained. The parallel between justification in ethics and deduction in mathematics must be abandoned.
With it, I suggest, must go the view that where a rational explanation
can be offered, a causal explanation is inappropriate. Both rational justification and causal explanation can be given of the same events at the
same time. It is more than plausible, then, to wonder at their interrelationship. If we do not, then we lapse into the two completely arbitrary
positions: (1) where behavior can be rationally justified it is totally free
from deterministic influences and thus free—a species of the argument
from choice to freedom of the will; (2) as social scientists claim, where
causal explanations can be given, rational justifications are only rationalizations—they have no genuine explanatory force.

When it is recognized that both forms of explanation are legitimate,
in their own spheres, that all human behavior is open to both causal
and rational analysis, then either we find a coherent relationship between the two of them, or our ethical theory is at bottom unintelligible
and arbitrary. This, it seems to me, is the substance of the deterministic
argument against free will—it is a request for coherence. In seeking that
coherence, we may wonder as well if there is not some truth to the
Kantian view that *under special conditions*, causal explanation is inappropriate, although such conditions can no longer be identified with the
operations of reason *a priori;* and we may seek to define those conditions
as the seat of moral responsibility.

Consider a simple example: a man slaps a child across the face. We
ask him for the reason for his action, and he explains that the child lied
to him, and had to be punished. Here we have a very simple case of a
justifiable act, with its justification. A causal explanation would no
doubt have to refer to early events in the man's life that brought him to
have the feelings he has about lying—let me oversimplify and suppose
that he was brutally punished himself for lying when a child, and becomes uncontrolled whenever he is lied to. Here we have, then, a rational and causal explanation of a particular action. Is it not clear that
they are separate and distinct modes of explanation? In the first case,
the man has a definite goal in mind, and his behavior can be interpreted and appraised in the respect that it is an adequate means to its
stipulated goal—preventing the child from lying in the future. The
mode of analysis brought to bear in such cases looks to the legitimacy of
the principles involved, the relations between means and ends, and the
like. In the case of a causal explanation, we seek scientific proof, and
the "correctness" of the explanation. The actual relationship of means
and ends, the validity of the principles appealed to in rational justifica-

tion, are irrelevant. The two modes of explanation seem entirely exclusive.

I simply do not see the force of this position, despite the argument I have given for it. I am struck more forcefully by the social scientists' and psychologists' view that the rational account may be nothing but a *rationalization* in the worse sense—meaning an account invented for the sole purpose of avoiding condemnation by others of the man's furious and uncontrolled behavior. In particular, certain causal explanations are capable of casting an agent's *purported* justifications into doubt, as specious because they are not his *true* reasons for his actions.

The notion that the reasons offered by a person to explain his actions may be suspect, not only in the sense that the person is lying, but even where he believes that he has given the correct reason, is of such critical importance that even philosophers who reject the psychoanalytic conception of unconscious motives try to present it in some other fashion. Sartre, for example, introduces it through the notion of bad faith. The difficult part is to make sense of the notion of lying to oneself. Psychoanalysis and existentialism offer different analyses, but both accept that notion as critical to the analysis of moral responsibility, precisely because it undercuts the whole context of rational justification. It is difficult enough to appraise reasons given for moral decisions. It is doubly difficult when we have grounds to suspect that the agent may be lying about his real reasons, both to us and to himself. In the case where a father has punished his son severely for a minor case of lying, we may suspect that he is angry with his son for other things as well, and only using this example as an excuse for punishing him. In courts of law, the testimony of accused men is always suspect. They seek to justify their behavior by the best arguments they can devise, whether or not these were the reasons they had in mind at the time of their deed. In such cases, it is necessary to collect evidence in addition, which reflects on the plausibility of the reasons offered.

The notions of bad faith and repression both endeavor to make sense of the concept of rationalization as a species of self-deception. This notion—of lying to oneself—is a difficult one to defend. In psychoanalysis, self-deception arises from a plurality of inner selves in conflict with one another. Sartre assumes a metaphysical ground of freedom against which all excuses are in bad faith. The view I will defend in no way assumes the existence of self-deception. Rather, I consider Plato correct that the inability to know one's true reasons is sheer ignorance. Both Sartre and Freud assume the existence of covert purposes, and thus must explain how purposes can fail in their realization. The simple de-

nial of any but open intentions can be dangerous in suggesting that a
purposeful agent always knows what he is doing. My claim is that only
intentions based rather definitely on sophisticated and profound knowledge are "real" intentions. Otherwise our ignorance defeats our goals
and even our first steps toward those goals.

Note that although the notion that causal explanations may sometimes be given which discredit rational justifications appears to be nothing more than a species of skepticism, and a rather weak one, it has considerably more force than that. The point is that when moral judgments
are treated as they are in textbooks, the genuine and concrete difficulties of the problems which arise in real situations are obscured. Only in
the classroom can one give a reason not open to question. Every real situation in which a question of responsibility arises raises with it the possibility that the rational explanation given by the agent may be suspect.
A lover who has fought with his beloved over her dress may claim that
he is concerned about her beauty. An observer wonders what else is motivating him—is it fear that others will judge him by his woman? or is
this clothing symbolic of something disgusting to him? A man's conscious self is too small a part of him for us to accept his own accounts of
the reasons for his behavior without additional evidence. We are virtually always, except in cases where we don't care, led to the very real
question of what an agent's true reasons were for his actions. Only
knowledge of the causal patterns of his life can help us in determining
them.

The notion that justification may be suspect in moral cases clearly
breaks down even the tentative parallel suggested above between mathematics and rational moral judgment. A mathematician offers a theorem with a proof. It would not occur to us to question whether that was
his "real" proof: the proof stands on its own. We do not *accuse* a mathematician of having devised a theorem. We do not even praise him for
his ingenuity without the proof. In most cases of rational justification,
the justification is of greater importance than the action itself. Even in
experimental science, where we are given a law with the experiments
which confirm it, we do not question the motives of the scientist who
makes the claim. We simply look to the experiment and determine
whether it provides sufficient evidence to support the claims made.
Only in very extreme cases, when the conclusion of the experiment and
the evidence offered were wholly incompatible, would we wonder about
the psychic causes of such bizarre reasoning. And we would be casting
grave suspicion on the competence of the scientist in question by doing
so.

In science, mathematics, even philosophy, the primary concern is for truth, and truth is recognized by arguments offered to support it. There are many cases where justification fails, but these are not accompanied by the further judgment that it was morally *wrong* to make such inferences and draw such conclusions. No questions of punishment and blame arise with false claims unless there is deliberate malice involved —which is not usually the case in science. We are content with mathematical demonstrations because where they fail, we are willing to shrug and look for another proof. The prevailing rules of justification we accept in science and mathematics in effect either suspend value judgments of the moral worth of the conclusions reached, or implicitly take the position that such conclusions are of little moral relevance. Borderline cases—such as research into weapons of death and destruction—we feel do justify both consideration of the truth of claims made and causal analysis into the characters of scientists who would engage in such research. But we do not confuse the two modes of analysis. The morally corrupt character of a scientist would not cast suspicion on his work, which stands on its own.

In the case of moral judgments, however, no precise parallel can be found to the intimate relationship of the truth of a scientific claim and evidence offered to support it. In ethics, no rational arguments can be definitive as they can be in mathematics or science. We are almost exclusively concerned with the decisions made and actions performed. These are what we condemn and praise. We seek rational explanation only to help guide us in our judgments. Rational considerations in morals can never be decisive for everyone to the degree that they are in scientific confirmation. What are good reasons for one man may not be good enough for another. Very good reasons may be completely worthless if the results of action on the basis of them are destructive. We are doubtful about reasoning in ethics to begin with, and legitimately, since good reasoning can often lead to damaging results. What we are primarily concerned with are deeds, not justifications. Where a scientist engaged in war research devises new weapons, although the *truth* of his scientific discoveries cannot be impugned by attacking his motives, the worth of his work, in producing death and destruction, may very well be. He may be accused of wishing for destruction, and lending himself to the study of ways to produce it. His motives, irrelevant in science, are of paramount importance in moral affairs.

One of the primary differences between science and morals, then, is that science addresses itself to statements, and only incidentally to what may be done with them; while in morals it is what is done that counts, with justifications and analyses subordinate to the deeds. Science is a mode of saying, with an emphasis on what is said; ethics is a mode of acting, with statements understood as actions themselves. We do not accuse men for what they *say*—that is, for the content of their statements —but for what they *do,* where even speaking is viewed as doing.

Because we cannot determinately ground moral judgments by rational means, it is essential that we look to motives if we are to judge acts or agents we consider reprehensible. Where rational argument is not decisive, we seek to determine if the agent had good intentions. But the determination of good intentions is not alone a matter of believing what a man says his intentions were. There are behavioral manifestations of intentions that we consider. We seek to appraise motives, for they are part of the substance of our moral judgments directed toward others. It is critical to determine what an agent's *real* motives were. The reasons offered by the agent may have been invented after his act to justify it. Or he may simply not know his true reasons. In science, this would not matter, for there is no moral blame attachable to claims made, at least in normal circumstances. It is precisely the possibility of moral censure of an act that takes us beyond it and its purported justification to consider the true motives underlying it.

Once we begin to seek further than the outright reasons offered as justification, and ask ourselves for the "true" reasons under the supposition that we may be lied to, then the further possibility arises that not only may the agent be lying, but he may not know what his real intentions were at the time of his decision. If we can look to causal evidence to support a claim that a man may be lying about his real reasons, we may discover that the evidence we unearth reveals the agent himself was not aware of his real reasons.

Psychoanalysis handles this notion of a person not knowing his own true reasons by introducing various components of the self, one of which acts as censor and keeps the true motives from awareness. Such a mode of analysis does make sense of the notion of lying to oneself—but only by sacrificing the holistic self under consideration. A person deceives himself only if one part of him deceives another. This view is simply incoherent, at least from a moral point of view, in its abdication of the notion of a person deceived.

Sartre, through the notion of bad faith, presents a consciousness which *pretends,* which adopts various attitudes toward itself which are impossible, and finds itself play-acting. The conscious self assumes an attitude which cannot be true; that is how one can recognize the bad faith involved. A man does not really lie to himself, at least not on the level of awareness. But he sets himself, through certain conscious attitudes, to deny certain facets of his being.

In both cases, causal and behavioral factors in any agent's past reveal not merely themselves, but the presence of motives, intentions, and reasons that are not those offered by the agent in his own defense, yet which he does not know of. Now one may theoretically attack the concepts of unconscious motives and reasons, but in this case that would be a serious misinterpretation of psychoanalytic theory. The point here is that causal patterns are discovered which both render the motives the agent is aware of suspect, and point to the existence of other motives. We no longer can treat motives as purely internal states of mind; behavioral aspects of personality reveal intentions out of awareness. This both Sartre and Freud recognize, although it is not clear that their theoretical analyses make complete sense of this critical notion.

A man who punishes his son severely for lying may be told by his psychoanalyst that he "really" wished to punish himself. What sense can be made of this notion of a "real" intention out of awareness? The implicit claim by the psychoanalyst is that the person will be able to understand himself and his behavior more consistently, holistically, and intelligibly under the supposition that a hidden motive was at work. This retains almost a perfect analogy with the argument that the reasons a person has given for his behavior are lies—in showing that other behavior of his falls into a pattern incompatible with his own claim. By simple extension, one can turn to "unconscious" motives as well. A critical point in both types of argument is the argument from causes to motives of the form: people who have undergone certain types of experience come to possess certain desires, wishes, and goals—conscious or not. Every human action is at least partly a determinate inheritance from past events, in a causal order. No doubt it is equally true that every action receives its determination in part from the present and the future as well. The point is that a particular event becomes determinately what it is only as a unification of a multiplicity of determining factors. It is by virtue of the mutual informing of a single event by this multiplicity that it is possible to grasp the nature of actions. Causal knowledge of influences upon men can bear considerable weight in our determining what reasons are actually to be taken as intended. Reasons are given force by causal determination; causal determinants may be revealed by rational methods. The judgment of whether a given set of reasons does or does not justify a particular deed may not make reference to causal factors, but the latter are critical in our determination of the agent's true motives.

The whole analysis given above is one example of the continual need for reevaluation essential to moral judgment. We may be content with the reasons a man gives for his actions and seek no further. But implicit in going no further is the judgment that the reasons given are not suspect, and reveal the agent's true intentions. Once we begin to question these, however, and we theoretically are committed to doing so if we seek validation of the action in question, then we can turn only to causal analysis for our further information.

Although I feel that the above analysis sufficiently demonstrates the legitimacy of applying information as to causes in contexts of rational justification, I would like to make even a stronger claim—that embodied in the very notion of rational justification is some appeal to causal knowledge. The very idea that one can justify one's actions depends on a conception of a self constituted by causally related elements. This is what I take to be the substance of Hume's argument that without determinism there can be no judgment of responsibility.

Let us return again to the father who severely beats his son for lying, with the explanation that lying is wrong and he wanted to make sure his son would never lie again. Now, some causal relations are essential to the means-end aspect of the judgment that such punishment would have the intended effect. Rational deliberation depends on all sorts of causal connections, and would not be intelligible without them. This, however, is another aspect of causality than we have been considering. We are more concerned with causal influences upon the agent. Does not bringing these in commit the genetic fallacy?

It is fairly clear that on the level of simple justification, causal explanation is out of place. The genetic fallacy points to the fact that where we wish no more than to offer grounds for a judgment, a causal explanation cannot replace a rational justification. But we reach another level of analysis directly when we have a rational defense given for an action, and wish to attack or defend *it*, rather than the action itself. Here causal knowledge can render certain rational defenses suspect, not insofar as they do or do not support the act in question, but by casting the whole defense into doubt. "Those were not his real reasons."

Once we understand this, however, further questions arise. Notably, what enables a particular man to use a particular set of reasons as defense of his behavior, given that an abstract and rational relation of support does hold?—only some claim relating the abstract relation to himself as effective agent acting on the basis of those reasons. The principle that lying is bad and should be punished is meaningless unless the agent is capable of being causally effective in preventing further lying;

and if, moreover, that principle carries effective weight in motivating him to act on the basis of it. If a father cannot punish his son, his thoughts are trivial. A moral agent must be *causally* capable of weighing reasons responsibly and acting on the basis of them. If he is so deeply biased that a rational argument of the most persuasive sort cannot produce actions on his part in accord with it, then certain reasons, however legitimate, can never be "his." Only causal knowledge can tell us whether proffered reasons are truly the agent's. Reasons cannot carry determining force apart from a context of causal determination.

Reasons can fail to belong to an agent in a number of senses. In the sense given above, a reason may be held not mine if, although I give it and even thought of it in advance, sufficient knowledge exists about my character to reveal much more likely reasons. My whole self reveals what my reasons are. Unless I know myself, I do not know my true reasons for doing anything. In a more fundamental sense, however, a reason is not mine if the abstract relationship of either the principles involved or means to ends has no causal weight upon my actions and will —in other words, if the abstract relationship of justification fails to be part of my sphere of action in any concrete causal way. A justification relates premises and conclusions. If I am incapable of bringing these together, as revealed in my continual behavior, then the justification remains abstract and alien to me, even if I can articulate it. Let me explain this further.

What I am claiming is that in ethics, rational justification requires anchoring to the agent if it is to count as legitimate. Where in science and mathematics, perhaps in philosophy, the agent simply says, "This is *the* justification for *this* claim," in moral judgments he implicitly declares that "This is *my* reason for *my* act." The emphasis here is on the possession of an act by an agent, and of his justification as well. Having good reasons is not enough—they must be the true reasons for the act. Kant realized this when in his *Grundlegung* he not only made the good will the source of all moral worth, but pointed out that one could never be *sure* of the true motives of the will in any particular case. A good act may well be performed for some hidden motives, and this lessens its moral worth. Motives are critical in moral judgments, and we must look to the genuineness of the motives offered, however valid they may be abstractly.

What then justifies the claim by an agent that a set of motives are in fact his? Exactly what justifies his claim that an action is his action? It is precisely this that this essay on moral responsibility is written to explain, for only under conditions such that I can claim an act to be *mine*, and give *my* reasons for doing it, can I be held responsible for it. Now, it is often maintained that the existence of a causal order in effect enables me to deny any action to be mine—it is but the cumulative effect of a causal history of which I am a part, but not especially mine. This claim will be dealt with in the chapter on freedom. Here I wish only to antici- pate, by reference to Hume's classic argument, that without that causal order, I could not make my claim legitimate either. The only bonds linking my actions to myself are causal, both in execution and in antici- pation. Unless there is a coherent pattern to my decisions and expecta- tions, my actions are fragmentary and arbitrary. I may claim them as mine only insofar as they reveal a coherent person whose character is not only compatible with them, but the very source of them. The great strength of psychoanalysis is that it reflects this understanding pro- foundly. The realization that amidst bizarre and apparently inexplica- ble behavior is a coherent pattern of feelings and motives, that an inte- gral and intelligible self remains amidst the most chaotic behavior, permeates and is the very foundation of psychoanalytic theory. (The cases where no unity of self can be found are set aside as the conse- quence of nonpsychic mechanisms at work, like damage to the central nervous system.)

Another way of putting this can be found in an application of Dew- ey's conception of the interrelationship of means and ends. The claim that a man pursues particular goals can be attacked—and I might say can *only* be attacked—by looking to his actions over a period of time, and determining whether they are compatible with his professed aims. Such a procedure makes sense only if we presuppose a considerable in- terpenetration of means and ends, and in two respects. First, we can ap- praise goals as held only if the agent utilizes fairly efficacious means for achieving them, at least within the bounds of reason. If we find that he professes goals that he continually aborts, we may wonder if he is not lying to us about them, or hypothesize further, if he convinces us of his sincerity, that he is ignorant or mistaken. More important, the assump- tion we are committed to is that goals aimed at are to be found in some potential sense *within* means utilized, throughout the agent's life or at least over a period of time. Reasons are not merely final goals, but aimed at throughout one's actions and decisions. Reasons are effective for a particular agent only if the means he uses form a coherent order toward the goals defined. In this sense, reasons harness means, and cre- ate a causal order connecting past and future actions. A man with the goal of becoming president will act compatibly with that goal in every- thing he does, forming a causal order in his life, one which may even allow definite prediction. If we detect severe anomalies, either within the order of his life, or even in the events that preceded his ambition— for example, evidence that he was deprived of love when young, from which we conclude that he is really seeking a form of revenge—then we deny his professed goals to be genuine. It is our knowledge of causal patterns in human life that forms a ground for the criticism of the characters of agents.

In conclusion, the separation of reasons and causes has a solid foundation on the initial level of justification for an agent's actions. But in ethics we are committed to a continued analysis of reasons given, since men are often deceptive to others and even to themselves. In casting suspicion onto reasons proffered as perhaps not genuine, as not the agent's actual reasons, we raise the critical question of the possession of purported reasons. Just as we have to determine when an agent has indeed committed an act for which he is held responsible, so we must raise the question as to when his reasons are indeed his. Exactly the same considerations apply in the two cases. Ultimately, what is involved is whether the individual acted on the basis of self-knowledge, whether he knew what he was about, whether he knows himself well enough to know his true reasons. This kind of self-knowledge is not just causal, but it necessarily includes knowledge of the causal order within the agent's life.

Further Considerations

Moral judgment is the knowledge of how to act validly in given circumstances. It includes a recognition of the significant factors of the situation in which action is called for, particularly those which pertain to the individual involved, which form the self in its adventures through time. In fact, the so-called "objective" elements of a situation are irrelevant to moral action except as they are related causally, imaginatively, or in principle to the person in that situation or as he will become in the future. What I must consider in making a moral decision is what is and will be of effect to me and by me in the world surrounding me. I must come to understand how my own being is not enclosed within my skin, but extends into an environmental context of action and consequences. Although I must consider everything that can have a bearing on my moral being in order to make a valid judgment—at least negatively by

ignoring it as of no importance—it is always in terms of myself, my inclinations and attitudes. I can be responsible only when I face the necessity of action amidst insecurity, and seek validity in my deeds. To
this extent, my actions are the only record of what I take myself to be,
for they are the attempts I make to preserve myself in action and
thought. If I fail to know myself to any great degree, I will almost certainly fail to realize myself in my actions, and will exhaust myself in regret or self-torment. Here Sartre is completely wrong in taking a man's
actions as himself. They are so only when they are valid. Invalid actions
constitute a man's *attempt* to manifest himself consistently in the world.
They fail to be satisfactory when they are incoherent, when they reveal
and constitute a person divided against himself, or sundered from the
world around him. As Socrates puts it: "I do believe that it would be
better for me that my lyre or a chorus I directed should be out of tune
and loud with discord, and that multitudes of men should disagree with
me rather than that my single self should be out of harmony with myself
and contradict me." A man's continual attempts to make valid decisions, which produce untold harm to others and remorse in him, are
far more a revelation of his lack of self-knowledge and ignorance than
of himself as an immoral or evil man. He fails to grasp his own being as
it is manifested in valid actions. He remains divided from what he does.

What a man must know in order to be in a position to make valid or
morally right decisions is the importance of things, and if they are important, their causal antecedents and consequences. Persons and things
exist in a connected order, wherein their identities are manifested
through interrelations, antecedents, and consequences. A man who
chooses to accept his government's proclamations, though they violate
his own moral code, must, if he is to act rightly in the long run, be in a
position to forecast correctly what the consequences will be of his passivity, and how he will feel about them. In moral decisions, the self is projected into an open future, and knowledge of the consequences of a
present course of action, and their bearing on that self, is essential to
valid judgment. Unfortunately, the empirical consequences of action
can never be fully controlled, which makes moral action the precarious
thing it is. The practical burden of moral responsibility, insofar as it
promotes valid action, is therefore thrown partly onto the first condition, whereby a man may know the importance of things sufficiently so
that sometimes or often, depending on his strength of mind and will, he
can act according to his own self-awareness and be assured that no consequences will make him repudiate himself and regret what he did.
When things fail to matter to him, a man may well find it impossible to

act or choose. He thus may fail to possess the skill of moral action. He may claim that he can be confident of his choices only when he is sure of what the future will bring, and remain paralyzed. The only way to surmount the inevitable precariousness of the future and the danger of unknown consequences is by reacting to things here and now, letting them matter sufficiently to render actions on the basis of them valid. In short, moral wisdom rests upon the creation within oneself of moral conviction, and the awareness that such conviction is both essential to oneself and also definite and enduring. Only when a man fully grasps the ways in which his own being creates an ordered scale of priorities in an undivided way is he in a position to make secure and valid moral choices when faced with conflicts among his principles and desires.

Knowing what is important, however, involves far more than the articulation of a scale of values or a set of moral rules. Often the strictest and most rigidly enforced social canons are those which will be most often breached, precisely because they do not matter to their violators as much as the latter wish to pursue the forbidden activity. What I must know in myself, in order to evaluate my decisions, is the strength of my desires and principles, the price I will pay in refusing to act on them, what the price means to me, and just how, given my readiness to move into action here and hesitate there, I can most effectively realize my need to constitute myself with pride and avoid failure. To this extent, I must know where my tendencies push me, where I often try to act but fail, where I tend only too often to make mistakes. I must especially know my own tendencies to make invalid moral decisions—those which make me regret what I have done—and avoid them in the future. I must also be in readiness to act; a failure of readiness is the greatest moral lapse of all, whether I am in a position actually to accomplish something or not.

There are many forms of propositional knowledge that are relevant to moral decisions, and which may be taken into account in determining the validity of moral action. Knowledge of the probable consequences of my actions, as well as the course of action necessary to achieve proposed goals, is vital to the appraisal of conflicting alternatives. In respecting my own tendencies of thought and action, and judging what is of importance to me, I may often find psychological generalizations highly significant—though I may also refuse to accept the application of any generalization to me if I can justify doing so.

For example, the recognition that men in general tend to be corrupted by the pursuit of wealth is of great importance to me in determining my own actions. I may refuse to accept a position in advertising because of the danger to my integrity. On the other hand, I may also accept the position with the firm determination not to be corrupted— and if I know myself well, the determination may be altogether sufficient. However, refusal even to consider the application of the general rule to oneself is irresponsible, risking the danger of succumbing to temptation with no defenses at all. Knowledge of patterns of human conduct, general relations between inclination and action, and the general sources of guilt in men, are of great relevance in moral evaluation. If any of them are disregarded, some justification may be requested—either in refutation of the truth of the generalization, or in finding some circumstances which modify the situation before us.

The primary source of information which can counter popular generalizations and maxims of conduct is explicit knowledge of oneself on an articulate and conscious level. For example, if a man knows that he literally despises wealth, is easily frugal and careful with expenses, and seeks a large income only to retire early and be completely free of the need to work, he may deny that an increase in income always brings an increase in expenditure. It must be emphasized that what he must know is not alone his articulated values or thoughts, but the general pattern of his own responses which deviate from the generalization being considered. He may then justifiably act in ways that he should not if the generalization applied to him. It is this kind of knowledge—the discovery of both the application and irrelevance of psychological truths to a particular individual—that is available in psychoanalysis. The articulation of truths about oneself, even when garbed in poetic and metaphorical language, is of great power in permitting the transformation of habits and the modification of behavior. When it fails to modify an individual's behavior, it at least may provide him with forewarning, thus forearming him not to attempt what is not likely to be in his power.

Articulated forms of knowledge are only peripheral to moral wisdom insofar as the latter marks the transition from deliberation to action. All too often the alternatives at hand point to unfavorable consequences no matter what is chosen. Moreover, the relationship of psychological generalizations to one's particular capacities is often blurred by inadequate evidence to determine what is true for a particular man. Yet moral action is still demanded, and the capacity to make valid choices instead of blind ones is a genuine one. After one has weighed the evidence, considered the consequences, and scrutinized himself to determine what are his dispositions, he must act whatever the balance. Perhaps we might wish to say that when such a balance is reached, it simply doesn't matter which alternative is selected, or if it does, the choice is not a rational one. But the ability which some men possess of choosing rightly, amidst the limitations of articulated reasons, is not to be so cavalierly dismissed. It marks far more than capriciousness, for it is indeed testable. It is the same kind of ability a surgeon possesses, of making momentary decisions on the basis of a look or feel, and of doing so *correctly*, without being able to say just why or of laying down principles for someone else to follow rigidly. The difference between them is only that the ultimate test of a surgeon's success is reasonably clear—the patient gets well— while the test of a moral action is complexly interwoven with the character and feelings of the individuals involved, as well as with a future of indefinite range. Both kinds of judgment can be appraised as valid or not. Moreover, whenever actions are thought to be arbitrary, and a choice between alternatives thought not to matter, failure is very likely. An agent must work through any given balance of conflicting principles and inclinations in terms of himself, or he leaves himself wide open to failure, in discovering that he really did not know himself and his relation to others as well as he thought. Only by deep and reliable self-knowledge of one's own undivided convictions can one act with assurance of validity.

There is the further facet to moral action that an act undertaken itself reflects back upon the agent, transforming him. A man's decision to join the French Underground during the Second World War placed him in constant jeopardy, faced him with danger and hardship, and also gave him the moral satisfaction of such allegiance. Living with death and danger, in constant risk of exposure, was an experience of enormous impact upon anyone so involved. To this extent, self-knowledge as moral action is more than a manifestation of self: it is the remaking of oneself, and its very discovery. In the grip of a moral conflict, I must find within myself, as well as in the events surrounding me, what I am and what I will be; I must find in my act a new self which conserves the earlier decision, or else I will experience only guilt or regret. Here is the Hegelian sense that self-knowledge is the union of both the object and the subject as knower, as a valid moral act is both the reflection of a sense of oneself and the preservation of that self in the validity of the act undertaken.

What then of the man who fails in moral action? He obviously has failed in himself somehow, somewhere. The ways in which he may fail are manifold. He may, for example, fail to act as he should, only to discover to his dismay and remorse that he has become party to monstrous and unspeakable crimes. Such passivity and inaction have their roots in various possibilities. A man may refuse to act because he is afraid to risk

what he is and owns in the name of abstract and relatively remote principles (or for "others"), only to discover that the crimes are his though
he did not know it, for he cannot in the end accept himself and his silence, though it has become too late. He has failed in not knowing exactly what his own self-respect is dependent upon. Though he failed to
realize it at first, he is not a man solely interested in himself and his
family's well-being, though he even may wish to be, but is unavoidably
committed to moral confrontation of the evil in his world. His failure is
in not knowing what the apparently external events around him mean
to him, and how they in fact have or will become a part of him in his
values and duties. Here Freud's sense of the superego as *internalization*
contains a fundamental insight: moral beliefs and attitudes are never
completely external to a person. They inhabit and permeate the self in
its most fundamental priorities, and its capacity to conserve or enhance
itself.

Passivity may also be a moral failure in promoting unintended and
horrible consequences. Again, the moral lapse is above all a lack of understanding, of the world and other men in their motives, intentions,
and utilization of means, of himself as dependent on these external factors, and of the enormous risk a man bears in repudiating one's moral
duties in the interests of other goals. Another way of putting this is that
pride in one's deeds, if justified, is the fruit of moral validity, while self-
contempt is but the revelation of one's failures. Guilt, self-loathing, and
shame are the manifestation of a self ignorant of its own nature, and
signs of a lack of moral wisdom. They are almost always rooted in an
unwillingness or inability to know oneself to the extent that guilt,
shame, and self-contempt can be escaped. Even failure due to nothing
but a lack of empirical information is based on a lack of self-knowledge
—knowledge of the nature of the real risks run by a person in the unforeseen and dangerous future. As Whitehead observes, "It is the busi- •
ness of the future to be dangerous"—to the very being of individuals
who act within it. To fail because of lack of knowledge is, in the last
analysis, not to know how one's own being is at stake in the actual
events of the world.

If the view that guilt and self-contempt mark a moral failure which is
simultaneously a failure in self-knowledge is to be plausible, there remains a further case to consider: the man who explicitly chooses, with
all due awareness and self-knowledge, a destructive and vicious path. I
would not like to rest my case on the assumption that destructiveness is
always a manifestation of self-denial or "neurosis." A man's fundamental priorities may render him wanton and savage, vicious to others with-

out compunction or guilt. Can we not (*must* we not?) condemn his actions as reprehensible and immoral? Yet they may be valid for him. Is this not too relativistic a theory of moral validity?

Part of the reply—though only part—can be found in the recognition that moral action is not arbitrary or self-satisfying, but reflects the weight of the genuine relationships of an individual to his world. Men must consider the risk to themselves in ignoring, opposing, or deviating from accepted social opinions in making moral choices, and may make valid decisions only if justifiable in terms of consequences for them and their own principles. Here there is a further appeal to self-knowledge. In a society which condones and supports murder, the only grounds on which an individual can oppose social norms are to be found within himself. If he finds in himself a great desire to kill and maim without social disapproval, where are the grounds for calling his action wrong?

The reactions of others to what we do are therefore an essential factor to consider in our moral judgments, and in judging what is valid for ourselves and what we must do. Man is a social animal, as Aristotle saw, in the very nature of his being, in his dependence on the approval of others. A man who lacks all sense whatsoever of the needs and possible feelings of others—as does Meursault in Camus' *L'Etranger*—is an alien indeed among men. He lacks even a rudimentary awareness of the stuff of which moral judgments are made—the interdependence of men, and the commonality of their emotional responses. It is in the common world of other men, and the genuinely similar world we live in, that we find the roots of principles which affect us all in similar ways. Individual differences are blunted by the reactions of others. Each of us lives in a world filled with many men, and in considering them in judging what we must do, as well as our reactions to them, we find a common basis of action. Thus, their willingness to reveal their feelings in punishment is of critical importance.

Moreover, our commonality of social life is ruled also by a quest for ideals and principles, which strengthens the power of rules over us. Here we may turn to the insight provided by Kant that moral principles inherently embody a universal obligation, making no exceptions for circumstances or persons. One may argue that it is a necessary (though not sufficient) condition of moral judgment that the principles espoused be unrestricted in form. This demand is intimately related to the universality and unavoidability of responsibility for one's actions. Nothing one does is without moral relevance and free from moral appraisal; this is the source of anguish. Moreover, no person plays a privileged or special role; everyone is identical before the moral law.

Thus, the appropriate reply to a man who condones theft and murder when they are in his own self-interest is that he has failed to accept the minimal conditions for moral action. If asked, would he be willing to accept criticism for having without justification made an exception of himself, or does he feel it right for someone else to kill and steal from him? If he denies the latter, he has repudiated the universality at the heart of morality; if the former, he has repudiated rational judgment altogether. Acceptance of a certain body of rules is a necessary condition of moral judgment, though one may choose one or another if he has faced the appropriate risks. Even the rebel, who breaks all of society's rules, can be said to be acting morally only if the risk is one he takes seriously, holds as a principle, and weighs with alternatives as he determines his course of action. Conventional rules define the framework of moral action and reaction, though not actually what is right and wrong. They represent accumulated wisdom, gathered over thousands of years, of how men can live well together. What a moral individual must do is to consider those principles which represent the wisdom of life, take to himself those which are relevant to him and the situations in which he finds himself, and appraise them in terms of himself and what he knows is essential to his being. The latter appraisal depends on adequate and even profound self-knowledge. In the case where a man decides that in the name of justice he must rid the world of evil, we restrain him from committing severe acts of violence, but it is useless to make our condemnation forceful to him—that condemnation would mean nothing. We condemn him only as an example for others to learn from. Such a case must be contrasted with that of the man who places his self-interest first, for we normally take him not to have chosen an alternative set of moral principles in his own terms, but to have none at all.

The main point to keep in mind is that conventional or external moral judgments are important only when they are themselves acts of judgment—condemnation or praise. The view that appraisal is the making of statements is an error: appraisal is action with consequences in the world. The self-interested violator of conventional rules of conduct is condemned by us because of the cruelty of his actions, and we punish him as an act on our part which we on the whole consider right. Here it may be said that the extent to which others are willing to act in response to a man's moral judgments forms an essential part of the situations he must consider in making decisions concerning his own obligations. They define part of the risk of failure he undertakes in his decisions. On the other hand, society as a collective body may well decide that decreasing the need for and frequency of such moral decisions is good, and worth implementing by promoting tolerance among different points of view. This is itself a moral decision, justifiable only on moral grounds, however collective the act in question. Men who must risk their lives to criticize their government are forced into moral conflicts more often and more painfully than in societies where outspoken opposition is tolerated. In the latter case, there is less need for moral risk of self in criticism of official policies.

And so we might proceed in other cases to develop social institutions which minimize the need for moral heroism and confrontation. Such social accommodations may well be justified on the grounds that they promote peace and eliminate some of the pain of moral conflict—and it is quite unmistakably painful! However, conflict is never wholly to be eliminated, nor is its elimination clearly a desirable achievement. Too tolerant a society, like a too-conforming one where everyone agrees, may sap the moral fibre of men by exposing them to test too infrequently for them to amass moral wisdom. The danger of utopianism is that it may emasculate the willingness to risk oneself before the world, and thereby to gain and enhance oneself. This, it seems to me, is Nietzsche's primary concern: the inability to gain and strengthen oneself through moral action in modern societies due to the promulgation of the view that weakness is good, and that peace is the highest goal. The spread of agreement and the minimization of condemnation, confrontation, and conflict may devitalize the moral capacity of men to solve such conflicts when they cannot be avoided.

I have suggested that tolerance may be the source of inadequate moral skill, but I must reconsider that notion. Like other skills, moral strength of will is gained through use, test, and criticism. A restrictive society is one which minimizes the willingness of men to expose themselves to and to resolve conflicts, for the price for doing so is too high. The open, tolerant, and individualistic society faces men with the need for daily and quick decision, if usually on trivial, sometimes on significant matters. In this frequent exercise of capabilities is to be found the widest use of moral skills and self-knowledge. Moreover, the open democratic society is saved from degeneration into meaninglessness by the fact that life always does matter, and risks must be taken—at least by most people. Even having children is a fearful and sometimes devastating risk. In a society open only in principle, but in fact economically closed to most men, the everyday routine and mindlessness of life destroy men as agents, and turn them into virtually empty, mechanical beings. Alienation, in even a politically open society, can be generated by poor economic conditions. The risk that men will become devoid of moral capacity is a very real one, though its cause is not always easily determined or eliminated. On the other hand, an affluent society, rich enough to make few decisions of great moment, can wither the capacity to choose with attention to consequences, and numb the judgments of its members. There is no escape from the fact that moral judgment resides in contexts where consequences are important. Where importance fades, or where no means obtain for acquiring what is important, the ability to make moral judgments suffers attrition as well.

Tolerance

A few more thoughts on the subject of tolerance may be worth considering. In our time the conception of tolerating the actions of others has become virtually a moral principle: "Let him who is without guilt throw the first stone"; "Judge not lest ye be judged." I wish to show that, from the standpoint of moral agency, the latter version of tolerance cannot be considered legitimate.

Tolerance is, of course, a great boon to modern society. Surely it is far better to live and let live than to fight long religious wars of attrition, or to seek to convert the heretic to the true path at the expense of his worldly body. Is not the right to freedom of speech a right achieved through tolerance—of other beliefs and political views however atrociously misled? Do we not *tolerate* the weaknesses of others in the interest of a harmonious and secure society? Precisely because the punishment of others brings with it the potential mistreatment of ourselves, do we not abstain from judgment and condemnation?

John Stuart Mill never thought so. In his celebrated defense of freedom of speech, *On Liberty*, he offers no argument even faintly resembling such a compromise. We do not protect ourselves against retaliation in protecting freedom of speech, but against the suppression of views whose promulgation would be of benefit to us. Mill not only rejects the abstention from judgment; he praises the dissemination of any and all views, however misguided, in that they aid in deliberative judgment, particularly when met with rational thought. In short, he advocates the increase of rational judgment directed toward the views under consideration, and speaks against the performance of any retaliatory action directed toward the person holding them. His argument is that a balanced moral judgment is most properly directed, when theoretical views are under consideration, toward the views and not toward the individuals holding them. He rejects both the self-interest view implicit in "Judge not lest ye be judged" and also the equating of judgment and punishment. Rather, he proposes a principle something like: "Do not punish a man for expressing theoretical views, for the truth and society will both suffer for it."

The argument I wish to present, however, is to the effect that the command "Judge not" is impossible to maintain as a moral principle. This is true precisely because moral principles *demand* judgment. Abstention from judgment marks nothing but a lack of awareness that moral decisions are involved. The promulgation of the view that judgment should, under any conditions whatsoever, be avoided, or even that every form of punishment be refrained from, is impossible to follow in the name of what is right. Every principle calls for a decision to accept or reject it, and this decision is itself a moral judgment. If I decide to permit men to speak their minds as they wish without fear of reprisal, then I am making the moral judgment that *it is right to do so*—I am judging this case to demand these acts. I cannot avoid judgment; and implicitly, I cannot avoid deciding my view of the relevance of punishment here: that retaliation would be wrong. In short, an act of tolerance is the acceptance of a given act by another as right or good, in respects relevant to appropriate sanctions. (Not in all—his views are *false*, but his utterance of them is not "wrong.") The holding of religious views contrary to mine may be stupid, misguided, and dangerous to man's eternal soul; but it is not wrong to hold such views—at least, it is not punishable to do so.

The only way in which a moral judgment can in fact fail to be made is where the individual fails to recognize the existence of a choice or decision. Yet what is remarkable about cases of tolerance is that they are all cases where it is most apparent that some moral decision must be made. This shows that tolerance cannot be the omission of judgment. Rather, it is tacitly the judgment that the action under consideration is not wrong, not punishable in any respect.

If we consider, then, a fundamental issue of tolerance in modern society—that of permissible sexual practices between two consenting adults—it follows that any argument to the effect that it is nobody's business but theirs is quite invalid. That claim implicitly denies the right of others to judge—and such judgment is quite unavoidable except when the judge is completely unaware of the acts involved. Perhaps the desire that deviate sexual practices be kept utterly private, behind closed doors, and thus overlooked, stems from the wish to avoid judgment by fostering the unawareness that any judgment is called for. But once deviate practices are known to exist, then even their acceptance is a moral judgment—at least to the effect that any official act of censure would be wrong. The distinction mentioned above between the act and the person might well aid in clarifying the judgment required. But some judgment is called for, and must be made.

In cases where tolerance is of importance, we are dealing with actions we do not approve of; otherwise there is no need to speak of the need for tolerating them. In such matters, there is no question of reward or praise, only of punishment. The crucial question is whether punishment should be employed—that is, is it *right* to punish those who engage in such questionable activities? There is no way to avoid judging when the issue has been labeled a moral one, and principles of tolerance, whether sexual, religious, or moral, do precisely that. All we can do is limit our punishments to a minimum. And that is precisely what principles of tolerance implicitly ask us to do. Every judgment is itself the enforcement of a sanction, however slight. The principle of tolerance only asks us to weigh our acts and their consequences against the acts we are judging wrong. Although a given act may be wrong, nothing I may do in censuring or controlling it may be right. This is what seems to me to be the great insight of tolerance.

The problem can be put quite simply. If the issue is a moral one, we cannot *tolerate* immorality if this means that judgment should be avoided. It simply cannot be; and so we cannot accept a moral principle that we should do so. What we can be asked to do is to judge our own actions of reward and punishment in the light of their consequences. The only acceptable principle of tolerance must run something like: "Do not punish the actions of others unless it is valid to do so, taking all other possibilities and the consequences of the punishment into account." Tolerance is but another name for a perspicuous and farsighted view of acts in relation to their consequences, in the light of the recognition that every act—including moral judgments themselves—is itself evaluatable in terms of its consequences as well as moral principles. We may interpret the maxim, "Judge not lest ye be judged," not as a repudiation of judgment, but as a warning that judgments are themselves judgeable acts, and may not be right even when directed toward acts that are themselves wrong.

What is fundamental here is the universality of moral responsibility, and the attendant anguish of being unable to circumscribe our responsibilities. On the surface, the request that men abstain from moral judgments in certain cases is a repudiation of anguish, and that is no doubt the source of its persuasiveness. Yet since everything a man does may in fact bring him to failure and guilt, even his avoidance of judgment, then it is clear that a refusal to judge is only apparently that. It is rather a judgment that certain modes of action are wrong or invalid. This is a critical distinction.

6
Freedom

Introductory Remarks

There are a number of different senses of freedom that bear considerable relevance to moral responsibility: freedom from external restraints which I will call "liberty," as in civil liberties, political liberties, or putting the prisoner at liberty; freedom from causal necessity, which is often confused with liberty by equating the constraining effect of civil laws and natural laws, though they are quite different; and freedom to choose, decide, and act, which I will call "autonomy" after Kant, whose relationship to the other two must be examined, and which is the main concern of this analysis. It is autonomy which is essential to the ascription of moral responsibility, for to the extent that a man can and does choose his actions, he is responsible for them. If he is either constrained from acting, or rendered incapable of choice, he may not be held culpable for his sins and omissions.

The problem of freedom may be summarized in the following argument: (1) Men are often excused from condemnation for actions they perform when such actions are caused by external circumstances; (2) All human behavior is at least partly caused by external circumstances; (3) All human behavior may in principle be excused on the grounds that it was caused—that is, no clear and definite line can be drawn between excusable and inexcusable behavior once causation is taken into account; therefore, (4) Men are never to be held responsible for what they do. It is not possible to draw a line consistently and clearly between acts that are so out of a person's control as to be not his responsibility, and those for which we hold him accountable. The purpose of this essay as a whole has partly been to develop a view of moral responsibility which would provide for the solution to this problem. This will now be shown in detail.

Kant, through the notion of reason *a priori,* produced a criterion that could be used to distinguish sharply between men as responsible agents, and as members of a causal order. Human beings, possessing reason *a priori,* can know the moral law and be bound by it as a being who lacks reason cannot. Men are responsible for their deeds by virtue of their rationality. Yet Kant runs into the problem of freedom and determinism in the realization that reason alone may not influence the will. And although he introduces a will that can be motivated by reason alone, that acts out of sheer *respect* for the law rather than upon any motive with a particular goal in view, such a device ultimately fails to solve the problem. For whether a given man has sufficient respect for the moral law to follow it against certain of his powerful inclinations seems to be dependent on his education, and out of his control. Perhaps the Platonic and Kantian view that man is free and responsible when his inclinations are subordinate to reason is a valid one; but the problem of whether one is responsible for one's own being *as* a responsible agent is set aside, and unsolvable in this framework. If some men are responsible, in the sense that they know and follow the dictates of reason, and others are not, why may not the latter plead their innocence in never having been brought to sufficient respect for the law as to make them free? Kant's problem is that of uncritically bringing together freedom in *thought* and freedom in *action.*

The problem of freedom and moral responsibility has, it seems to me, been misinterpreted by many philosophers. The problem is not that in a deterministic world all human actions would be caused and therefore not free. (I shall, in due course, analyze the sense of freedom involved here.) Whether or not human actions are free in the important sense, we may hold men responsible for what they do. The apparent arbitrariness of this is not without foundation, since our societies are human societies, and our education is designed for human beings. We may hold all men responsible for what they do as men. Free or not, they are human, are educated and treated like moral agents, and may be expected to behave like them. They are given the privileges of membership in human society; they may also be asked to meet the responsibilities of that society. This is really the heart of the Aristotelian view of responsibility.

The difficult problem, however, arises because we do indeed excuse some men from blame for what they do. It is here that an *indefensible* arbitrariness apparently enters. For if it is not sheer humanity that is the criterion of responsibility, it is difficult to determine just what is. Rationality, though the most likely candidate, is possessed profoundly by very few men. Scientists and philosophers—surely men of rationality in some obvious sense—are not particularly responsible for their actions. Historically, insane men have been excused when they did not know the quality of their actions. But there is a strong trend today toward the realization that this criterion is insufficient—that men may know the quality of their deeds and yet may be driven by compulsions too strong for them to withstand. It seems quite clear that a responsible man, who knows what he is doing and has the strength of will to carry out his projects, is made responsible by an upbringing that causally brought him to this degree of freedom; while an insane man is not responsible for his actions by virtue of an upbringing that denied him influences that might have made of him a genuine moral agent. Men are not responsible for what they become. They do not choose to become capable or incapable of significant choice. Ultimately, a man is the consequence of causal influences upon him, over which he had no control. Those men who have control over their being are brought to this capacity by an upbringing over which they too had no control.

Half of the solution to this problem has already been touched upon. The intuitive sense that all men are responsible for what they do, *as a condition of being moral agents,* seems to me inescapable. Instead of asking why some men are not responsible for their deeds, which is misleading and has no answer, it makes more sense to hold them responsible and yet excuse them for not doing what they were responsible for doing, if adequate justification for such an excuse can be found. Responsibility must be separated from condemnation. An insane man may be held responsible for his acts by virtue of his humanity. But he is not to be condemned for them. This sense of responsibility identifies it with moral being. Men are responsible for what they do insofar as they are moral agents. Responsibility is not praiseworthy in this sense, but is a precondition of moral agency. Kant argues that men can act only under the presupposition of freedom. The sense of freedom required is very unclear. The truth is that men can act only under the presupposition that they are responsible for what they do and are. What freedom is involved here I shall discuss later.

The pervasive sense of responsibility I have presented here is much wider than the usual one. I have already discussed the vague and indefinite boundaries of the human self, the critical relevance of remote events to one's being. Insofar as men are responsible for what they are, they are indefinitely responsible toward the events around them, at least for taking some active stand with relation to them, and for which they can be brought to account in a pervasive and unbounded sense, with no limits or exclusions. Human experience is expansive, and what seems irrelevant may in fact be of critical importance. Men are pervasively responsible even for what is irrelevant, at least for recognizing it as such. There is nothing which cannot be brought to our account. As moral beings, we implicitly adopt an open and limitless stance toward the entire world as a potentiality for action, events and objects past, present, and future, insofar as our actions might in any way improve them or even be affected by them and our sense of them. Any attempt to circumscribe a narrower domain of moral responsibility excludes from the agent's consideration things very remote, that he may not know about, that he could only improbably affect, and amounts to offering an excuse independent of the determination of validity. We are responsible for the validity of our judgments, and nothing is in principle excluded from the determination of the validity of our actions. We are responsible in a pervasive sense for excluding nothing from our judgments and actions, for not failing in our actions though even the remote and unknown threatens failure. Nothing is in principle outside our moral being—though it is true that many events are in fact of negligible importance. In this sense, we are indefinitely responsible *to* our surroundings, a responsibility which cannot be denied. The pervasive sense of responsibility represents the obligation upon men not only to act to the best of their abilities, but to improve their abilities as well, to expand their powers without limit. To the extent that the human self is a focused order in the world, it has unlimited boundaries and range. (It is more accurate to say "responsible *to*," rather than "responsible *for*," in that we are all bound by our natures as moral agents to adopt a stance toward events of the world, an obligation we cannot evade. They unavoidably touch upon us and our responsibilities. We must respond to events when they occur, and if we can gain from them. But we are not necessarily blameworthy *for* any particular failing.)

This pervasive sense of responsibility is the precondition of morality. Given our unbounded responsibilities (and our consequent anguish and despair), we seek the most efficacious and valid choice of actions in a complex and interconnected world. Failure is always a threat. Our abilities are always limited, and we may have excellent excuses for not being able to meet some of our responsibilities. So we escape outright condemnation, if not guilt and anguish. Even in the more usual and narrower sense of responsibility, no one can fully meet *all* his responsibilities and obligations.

A human being is intricately and inextricably bound up with events that are remote from him, to such a degree as to allow nothing to remain intrinsically independent of his moral concerns. For this reason, men are not only responsible for "their" deeds in a narrow sense, but to other events without limit. Holding them so responsible, however, does not imply that everyone is guilty of immoral action to the point where punishment is justified. An act of censure, punishment, even implicit disapproval, is itself an act which must be evaluated on its own, taking its consequences and intended goals into consideration. Thus we refrain from the punishment of a child for a crime it could not be aware of in the realization that such punishment could not possibly succeed in producing anything but fear and hatred, without bettering the child in any way. Or we omit censure of a man who did not risk his life to save another's because the probabilities that we know of indicate that both were likely to have been killed, and we do not wish to hold it obligatory to act where the prospects are of greater harm. In this latter case, to deny the existence of *any* responsibility is a repudiation of the fundamental moral principle at stake—of the value and sanctity of human life, almost without qualification. Yet we also must balance in *our* moral judgments the value of the life of the agent, and determine that he should not be castigated for his omission. The point is that it *is* an omission. He did not save the man's life. We cannot even say that he *could not* have (was not free to), for there is a small chance that he might have been successful. But such failures do not warrant censure, for to condemn every failure would be to lay a permanent and irremovable moral guilt for all the evil in the world upon the heads of all men; and this would both be overly onerous and weaken the force of more specific moral condemnation.

I will extend this view in considerable detail in the final chapter. It must be pointed out here only that it does dispose of the theoretical problem of the relationship between freedom and responsibility by holding everyone pervasively responsible without limit, but not necessarily censurable for those acts that are either too far beyond the agent's capacities or entail too great a risk of an opposing value. The dictum "ought implies can" may then be rejected entirely. I ought to do whatever is necessary to render things better and more just, even where I cannot actually succeed. But if I fail to, I may well escape all but a minimum of guilt—the primordial anguish and despair of moral being—if censure is itself immoral. If I could not have prevented a crime, or even if preventing it would have been extremely difficult, I am excused and not condemned, though I am not thereby relieved of the obligation. We ought to do what is right, do good and forestall all evil, always and everywhere. But since we cannot at once do everything, what we fail to improve we may be excused *for* (not *from*) if we do something else as or more important. The precariousness of life entails mercy. A man's failure to carry out his obligations by no means obligates others to condemn him. In fact, many lapses are and should be condoned, though not justified, on the grounds that condemnation would itself be on the whole disadvantageous. Knowledge of our fellow man and his weaknesses permits us, even obligates us, to withhold censure at times when he has succumbed to injustice—on the grounds that to condemn him in no way improves the world, and may well harm him or others. I may decide to refrain from punishing a man who has once stolen some money, who has shown repentance, and who is in other ways estimable and worthwhile. To punish—meaning imprison—him is to harm, not improve him, and we are forbidden to do this without justification. It is true that the man is guilty; but he need not be condemned for it.

Before taking this very strong position, however, it is worth considering the relationship of moral responsibility to different types of freedom, for much confusion has been generated in this area, some of which may perhaps be eliminated.

Liberty

The doctrine "ought implies can" derives most of its force from the cases in which we have liberty in mind when we say "We can do this" —meaning, we are at liberty to do it; or where we deny that we are able to do something because we are not at liberty, and in that way deny responsibility. We often say that a man is not obligated to support his wife if he is behind bars in prison—though he may have arrived there by refusing to support her when he could. We also say that a man is not obligated to prevent a murder if he is constrained by the murderer at the penalty of his own life. With a gun pointed at me (unless I am some extraordinary commando-type), I am without the obligation to save another's life, however strongly I may feel about it, for I cannot due to the constraints upon me.

A moment's consideration, however, reveals that constraints upon our liberty depend for their existence on regular and causal relations in things, without which we could not be said to be inhibited or prevented from action. It is true that chains inhibit my movements, but only by virtue of the general causal relation between the structural properties of metal and human flesh. The statement "I am prevented from moving by these shackles around my ankles" can be considered credible only when it has a foundation in some general causal facts. If I plead that I am not free (at liberty) to help you because I am restrained by the clothing I wear, you will consider me either insane or joking, unless I can demonstrate rather peculiar properties of my clothing.

To be at liberty to perform a given task, then, depends upon the absence of causal conditions which render it physically impossible to perform. This view has led to the common political view that "political" and "social" liberty refer to the absence of physical or juridical constraints which render certain actions *physically* impossible; while the conception of physical impossibility rests upon the causal laws relevant to the actions and tasks at hand.

However, physical impossibility (and logical impossibility, which is an uninteresting case) is a rare consideration in situations of moral significance. On the one hand, as Hobbes pointed out clearly and implausibly but with a luminous insight into the unimportance of physical constraints in moral affairs, I am quite free in the face of a death penalty for political opposition to criticize my government. It is not physically impossible for me to do so. But we hesitate to condemn a man for submitting to fearful and desperate threats. Is it morally wrong for me to refuse to criticize my government's policy of cleaning the subways when I will be jailed for doing so? Is this a case worth the risk? Some moral extremists would say that it is, though most people I suspect would not, taking the position that I was not at liberty to criticize, for sanctions of a severe character had been imposed upon me. Such sanctions, though, do not create physical impossibility. What then do they render impossible?

An answer that comes immediately to mind, though a dangerous one from a moral standpoint, is that severe sanctions render it impossible for us to *reasonably expect* that men will act rightly in unimportant cases when faced with severe penalties. Though an occasional hero will risk his life and even forfeit it in the name of moral principle, the great majority of men will not. This is a causal law, of a probabilistic or statistical sort, relating the severity of punishment to the number and percentage of men willing to take a given risk. On the basis of it, we may say something like, "He could not speak up, for his fear of reprisal was too great," implying that it was *physically impossible* for him to do the right thing in the face of his fear. What we mean is that he, like the great majority of men, would not act rightly in such circumstances. By appeal to some notion of normality, we explicate "could not" in terms of what men *do not* do. The man's liberty was destroyed by fear of punishment—and we have left behind the notion of physical impossibility, since the law in question is related to inhibition or lack of liberty only through causal principles related to emotions and the will, and only for many or most men at that.

The appeal to causal constraints upon the will is a dangerous one, susceptible to much confusion. On the one hand, suppose that we have a man bound by a rope physically beyond his ability to break, forced to witness an immoral act that he could have prevented if he had been at liberty to do so. On the other hand, imagine that we have a man bound by a rope that he *could* escape from, at the risk of injuring himself severely in doing so. Suppose that the danger of injuring himself is very great, but not certain: is the man then "at liberty" to prevent the wrongdoing? Now take a third case, in which he is told that if he interferes, he will himself be killed, but he is unbound and left to his own devices. Is he now at liberty to interfere? If these examples are not further complicated (which actual cases always are), it seems very essential to hold them quite different. The man bound literally cannot, whatever his inclinations, break his bonds. In the second case, however, and in the last, he is left free to act, whatever the ultimate cost of his interference. In the first case, the man can at best *try* to escape ("can" in the physical sense). (Let me qualify this directly: we must be confident that his trial is genuine. If he vainly struggles to chew his bonds apart with his teeth, and fails to utilize a knife nearby, he "could have" escaped, and thus is culpable.) Only in this sense of *strict* physical impossibility do we have a complete excuse for actions a man ought to have but did not commit, without further analysis. This is the complete substance of the doctrine that "ought implies can." In the case of risk, severe penalty, or a low probability of success, however, we cannot use this notion of physical impossibility. What is demanded is perhaps dangerous, or unlikely of success, and we must in our evaluation of what is done in response take both of these into account. Responsibility for what happens is a pervasive fact of moral life, to be tested and appraised by considering the special circumstances that may have made the agent's decisions valid despite his apparent obligations. Thus, if I abstain from criticizing my government because it has threatened to kill my wife and children, I may have repudiated my obligation to my fellow countrymen, but rightly in the name of my obligations to my family. Sanctions are circumstances to take into account in evaluation, and thus differ from causal conditions which render a given act *impossible*.

Moreover, I fear that virtually no examples can be found of complete impossibility. There is always a small probability that a way can be found to accomplish what should be done. For example, a man who cannot swim may be able to find another way to save a drowning man. He may even be able to swim enough to help him to shore. The probability may be small, but it is not 0. It may be impossible for me in New York City to prevent a civil rights murder in Atlanta, Georgia today, but I might have been able to anticipate it and take steps last week or last year. If I had pressured my congressman to pass stronger legislation, that might have forestalled the crime. It is impossible for a man to prove that no means exist or existed to produce a particular goal, only that he considered all the obvious cases. Perhaps the only cases where we are justified in arguing that there is complete physical impossibility is in events completely past, and this is certainly a trivial case, precisely because the whole question is begged—begged in that our very conception of events as past depends on our recognition of them as done, finished, events which we cannot affect by anything we may do now. Nothing I could have done would have prevented the assassination of Lincoln—so far as we know. We think of an event as past precisely in such terms. On this basis we have no obligations to the past. But suppose we had a time machine and could affect the past? Far-fetched as this notion is, it reveals that we are released from obligations only on the basis of a conventional and mutual acceptance of events as outside our consideration. We may change our opinion on this matter at any time, as new information about efficacy is gathered. Complete physical impossibility is an empty notion, except for the cases we take for granted and agree not to try to do anything about. The key point of agreement, however, is not on impossibility—which is a factual matter and must be proved—but on the arduousness of attempting to change the situation. That is what is tacitly involved. Even where we could not have prevented a crime, we may be responsible for compensations and punishments many years later. Our actual obligations depend on our real powers and abilities; but nothing abrogates our obligations to face events with moral concern, and to use our powers to improve them.

The view that "ought implies can," then, is a trivial one, and has application only to cases of logical impossibility. It is never legitimate to argue that one could not (was not at liberty to) have accomplished a meaningful goal, only that good reasons exist for doubting the advisability of trying, considering everything. The very few cases that we consider to be cases of complete impossibility are such only by tacit agreement, not based on empirical proof. It was once thought impossible to run a four-minute mile. Is it impossible to run one in three minutes? Clearly we do not argue that it is truly impossible; rather, we agree that it is too much to ask of someone under present circumstances. So far as being able to accomplish their goals, men are almost never sure that they cannot. All cases of significance involve a tacit acceptance of some degree of possibility coupled with the argument that the risk is too great, or the probability of success too small.

Suppose, however, a psychologist wishes to construe a sanction causally. He proposes the following complication of the third example above: not only is our agent threatened with harm, but he is exposed to the harm directly by, let us say, having a finger pulled off by force. He is then told that if he interferes, all his fingers will be so treated. Is he now "free" or at liberty to interfere? Is it not more likely that he will simply be paralyzed, unable to move or even think about acting? Can we not deny that it is physically possible for him to make an affirmative action, whatever the cost? Is it not possible, that is, to chain a man's mind and will as well as his body? Is not the concept of liberty in this way reducible to the notion of causal dependence, in that the question of whether a man *could* accomplish certain goals depends on the existence of causal antecedents that enable him to reach his goal. Perhaps the "can" of "ought implies can" refers ultimately not to what is physically possible or impossible so far as what the agent is at liberty to do, but to whether he possesses the relevant causal powers to produce what he wishes to accomplish.

One problem that arises in appraising such cases is that it is very difficult to draw the line between physical paralysis which is due only to the pain experienced—which can indeed be so severe as to impair the functioning of the body—and the paralysis due to fear and anticipation of what might happen. Not only is it difficult to draw such a line, but no amount of evidence would seem to clarify our understanding. We might wish to say that pain and even threats can literally and causally inhibit action by rendering a person's body immobile, but we must distinguish such cases from those in which fear alone leads a man to *decide* that he is more eager to prevent further pain than to do what is right. A man under torture is more of a problem than Sartre seems to realize when he claims: "No matter how long he has waited before begging for mercy, he would have been able despite all to wait ten minutes, one minute, one second longer. He has determined the moment at which the pain becomes unbearable. The proof of this is the fact that he will later live out his abjuration in remorse and shame. Thus he is entirely responsible for it." First of all, a man may decide that he can wait ten minutes longer, but at the end of ten minutes be unable then to decide to hold out another minute. Eventually he will talk, because he must. On the other hand, there are men who withstand torture. Perhaps Sartre means that shame and remorse are and should be the result of succumbing to torture when others did not. But there are also men who can run a mile in under four minutes; should we be ashamed that we cannot? Do not men differ in their capacities to endure pain as they differ in their strength or swiftness?

Open the Pandora's box, however, and everything falls out upon us. If I can claim that I am free from responsibility for events I am physically unable to prevent, I can also claim that I am free from responsibility for any of my actions, for if I "could" have avoided doing them, I would have. A man who embezzles $50,000 from a bank for which he worked for twenty years may say that he succumbed to the temptation of all that money. He simply was not strong enough to resist—paralleling the plea of the man under torture. It may be this parallel that motivates Sartre to claim that both men "can" resist but choose not to. If only we could find grounds on which to distinguish causal impossibility from the failure of will when it is still possible to do the right thing!

The rule of thumb we sometimes use depends on causal knowledge embodied in well confirmed empirical generalizations, which we apply to particular instances before us. We may say that a man should not be condemned for succumbing to torture because almost everyone would so succumb. There are, however, two difficulties here. The first is that although the generalization "Almost everyone would succumb to this torture" may be true, it has exceptions. And if a man is one of these exceptions, we do not wish to excuse him from some degree of blame. We must therefore look at the details of his life and physical characteristics to determine if he might be hardier than most men and perhaps morally weaker too. Such an individual examination renders the force of the original generalization virtually without relevance to our particular case. Either our hero could have held out, or he could not. What the rest of the world does or can do is irrelevant.

The more important point, though, is that the awareness we have that someone withstood the same torture, when the information the prisoner possesses is of vital importance and it is imperative that it be withheld, may well lead us to claim that the man who succumbs *should have* held out even in the face of the apparently sincere plea that he could not help it. "You could have withstood it: John did. You should have held out. It was catastrophic for you to give in." The suggestion here of inconsistency is, it seems to me, an error, based upon the assumption that the giving or withholding of censure must be based only on the circumstances which constitute the deed in question. I suggest that there is little basis for such an assumption.

If it is impossible to distinguish causal impossibility from weakness of character, we seem to have no choice but to hold either *everyone* or *no one* responsible for evil. If we claim that a man cannot be held responsible (and perhaps culpable, though not necessarily) for actions he could not have prevented, we are vulnerable to the attack that in every case something must have deterred the agent from doing the right thing, and that therefore he was physically unable to do what he should. A man who has murdered his wife may plead that the strength of his desires to kill her must have outweighed his moral sentiments, otherwise he would not have done it. The fact that for most people such desires do not overcome moral inclinations is quite irrelevant. This particular man may well be one of the exceptions. The man who is prevented from saving a drowning man because he could not get to him in time though he tried is open to the attack that another man would have moved more quickly, which on the surface is quite irrelevant. Even the claim that at other times the same man moved far more swiftly is irrelevant, unless we are in a position to rule out contributing factors. I would like to note here once again that throughout the examination of responsibility and the ability or inability of a man to act in a particular case, intimate knowledge of the agent is presupposed and sought. It is impossible to avoid recognizing the relevance of knowledge of the particular person involved as agent in moral judgment.

The proposal that no one is responsible for his actions, in that some

cause prevented his doing as he ought, has been accepted with great en-
thusiasm in the twentieth century, partly, I believe, as an expression of
the dismay the ordinary man feels before the weight of obligation he
bears simply by virtue of being alive and human. Couple the everyday
demands upon a particular man to lie, refrain from lying, face political
realities, and oppose corruption whenever he encounters it, with the
often unjustified guilt he bears for acts and thoughts which are either
common or never even took place, and the overwhelming urge to be
free of his burdens and cares becomes quite understandable. Such an
urge is by no means new. The conformity and mediocrity of social man
is evoked again and again in Sophocles' chorus. The flight from heroism
can be found also in the quietude of Epicureanism and Stoicism as well
as Lao Tzu, and in the abdication of responsibility to the Church or
God captured in "The Grand Inquisitor" scene from *The Brothers Karamazov*. Many social scientists have adopted such a moral outlook on the
basis of their mode of understanding of the dynamics of human behavior, for some causal law can be found under which any given human act
can be subsumed as necessary and thus impossible to avoid.

It does not follow, however, from any formulation of causation or of
possibility that men are not responsible for their actions and never culpable for their transgressions. It is, however, one of two choices that remain if we grant that all moral lapses are caused in some sense. There
remains only the alternative that we recognize the perpetual and unlimited responsibility all men bear to what happens around them, for
all suffering, evil, and injustice, whatever the proximity of their relationship to it. Here at least is the source of the pervasiveness of guilt and
anguish, the conception embodied in Donne's Seventeenth Devotion:
"Any man's death diminishes me, because I am involved in mankinde,"
which is probably the only justification for our perpetual obligation to
consider not only the evil that surrounds us closely, but remote and distant events whether they affect our self-interest or not. The second formulation of Kant's categorical imperative—"So act as to treat humanity, whether in thine own person or in that of any other, in every case as
an end withal, never as means only"—despite its unqualified and over-
drawn character, is also an embodiment of the view that *all* men are
objects of moral concern. We do not escape our responsibilities and obligations by being unable to fulfill them. We only excuse ourselves from
being condemned for our failures. We do not escape judgment. We simply escape overt censure. A man's failure to rescue a drowning man because he failed to reach him in time may be construed as "unfortunate"—meaning wrong but understandable. Moral censure, praise,

condemnation, and approval are not attributes of actions of men. They are later actions undertaken by men in response to those earlier ones. The statement "You have sinned" is an expression or revelation of an action toward the act in question. "It was wrong to let the man die, but you did the best you could and so are not even to be castigated," is far more the appropriate response to the case above than "You are not at all responsible or culpable." The abiding of evil, even unknown, is immoral.

The recognition that an unbounded world and nothing less is the object of moral action for us, toward which we are fully responsible but with respect to which we often justifiably plead extenuating or mitigating circumstances, frees us to some extent from the problem posed above by causal impossibility, particularly when motives and emotions are included as causal factors. For example, a man under torture may well be held culpable of having broken silence, and guilty of betrayal, though anyone would also have succumbed, because of the nature and importance of his information. Yet culpability, when it is universal, merits neither condemnation nor punishment, since the universality of the success of the torture points out the uselessness of both of them. On the other hand, a man who succumbs easily to torture, on the plea that he is weaker than other men, may well be condemned and even punished in order to influence him and others to realize the importance of resistance. What has been omitted from the above analysis of moral condemnation is the realization that *all* the consequences of an act are relevent to its appraisal, and we may respond to a given transgression by punishment in order to forestall dangerous consequences. The judgment applied to a given moral act (which is itself a moral judgment) is necessarily a distinct appraisal, taking into account everything relevant at the time it is made as well as at the time of the original act. Condemnation and praise are thus to be given or withheld when valid or invalid in the widest possible sense. It is for this reason that condemnation of the form "That is wrong" takes circumstances and consequences into account, relieving a man from punishment (though not pervasive responsibility) on the basis of physical or mental factors. The criminal who pleads necessity in his life leading up to his crime may well be condemned and punished even when the necessity is admitted, as an act on the part of the state in which the encouragement of general moral attitudes is sought. On the other hand, an active member of a lynch mob may be freed without censure, or censured and not punished, which is rather more plausible, when the consequences of punishment would not be advantageous. Analogously, our complete repudiation of murder as immoral and evil need not imply that capital punishment is a good. Some actions are justifiable in condemnation where others are not. What is essential is that the entire context and set of consequences of our own actions enter into our judgments.

All of this will be taken up in greater detail in the last chapter. Here I wished only to sketch a way out of the difficulties that arise in determining responsibility when it is associated with liberty, and to criticize the implication of "ought" with "can." Further difficulties in this area associated with indeterminism will be taken up shortly. Before this, however, I wish to consider other relationships between liberty and constraint—particularly the necessity for constraints in order that liberty exist. That is, we must consider the need for structure in order that moral choice be possible.

Choice

The precise nature of a choice and how it differs from a mere act has never been adequately set forth, though one or another analysis has touched on important features of choosing as against merely doing, wanting, or desiring. One extreme of the spectrum of choice has been thoroughly considered, in a manner analogous to the problem posed in the last section concerning physically impossible acts: a man can hardly be said to choose if he is physically compelled to act in a given way, nor even if he is in the throes of an insatiable and irresistible passion—i.e., a physical addiction to narcotics. We are all aware of the expression, "You leave me little choice." When all alternatives but one have been ruled out, or when every one has been made impossible, we say that we have *no* choice at all.

The other extreme, however, is even more interesting, though it has been rather neglected. The problem is whether a man can be said to choose without qualification or restriction: can there be completely open or arbitrary choice? A man free from all compulsion, all determination, all restriction, literally has no basis for making a choice as against acting or moving haphazardly. If I am stunned or semi-conscious—perhaps just awakening from sleep—I do not *choose* to move or stand still, for there is no sense of selection from a restricted range of possibility. If *anything* is possible, what happens just does. It is only chosen if it is selected as an alternative from a given range of alternatives, subject to some specific conditions which I may determine myself.

Thus, suppose a man chooses to go to the movies rather than to stay home and watch television. First of all, we note that he chooses in this case from two alternatives, not from an infinite range of possibility. His act (going to see a film) is a choice with respect to the possibility of watching television, not with respect, for example to flying to the moon or going sailing on his yacht if he does not own a yacht. We may say that a choice exists only within a context that defines a very small number of alternatives to be relevant out of the whole realm of logical possibility. A context of choice must be given or presupposed in advance in order that any choice be made. The man may also stay at home and burn his books—that is physically within his power—yet we would not say that he chooses to go to a film instead of burning his books.

The point here is that the expression "A man *(X)* chooses to do *Y*" is elliptical. For example, a choice is an event, taking place under certain circumstances and at a specified time. We may not care to specify fully all times and conditions, but they are implicit in any statement about choosing (as well as eating, sleeping, and so forth). Thus, "*X* chooses *Y*" is incomplete, and must be finished with "at time *T* and in place *P*." This is still incomplete, however, for we must distinguish "*X* does *Y* at *T* and *P*" from "*X* chooses *Y* at *T* and *P*." At one time, appeal was made to the will, or reflective consciousness, entertaining the thought of *Y* prior to or along with, but separate from the act of doing *Y*. A man who falls down a flight of stairs does break his leg, but does not choose to do so, for he did not plan to or think of doing that before he did so.

Ryle and others have attacked this view of "the ghost in the machine," which contemplates, plans, or wills apart from the actions of the body. It is only too simple to find cases in which antecedent reflection is lacking, and yet where choices are made. The simplest example is where some standard of appraisal of an act as "good" or "appropriate" exists, setting it off from a "mere" or "arbitrary" act. A tennis player may return a ball quickly, effectively, indeed make a superb shot, yet without time for reflection or any other special state of mind. To characterize his act as without choice is quite implausible. He could have hit the ball off the court, missed it altogether, even ignored it. But he chose from the available alternatives, without antecedent reflection, to *make* (not to try, but to succeed) a superb return.

The notion that an antecedent thought is necessary to a choice derives its plausibility from the fact that choices are never arbitrary or unrestricted, but are always qualified by a range of possibilities from which the chosen act is selected. The tennis player chose to strike the ball "so" instead of "so" (missing it), or refusing it completely (and conceding the point). Some reference class must be stipulated as part of the very meaning of the choice undertaken. For example, we object to the accusation, "You chose to play golf instead of saving your home from burning down" when the man in question did not know that his house was on fire. He did not choose golf *instead* of rushing home with pails of water. He did choose to play golf instead of sleeping in bed that morning. And if he had slept in bed, he would have discovered sooner that his house was on fire. But the latter implication is separate and distinct from his choice. It belongs to a different context or order of judgment.

The specification of the reference-class from which the selected alternative is taken is not sufficient to constitute a choice. The statement "*X* chooses *Y* at *T* and *P* from class *C*" is still incomplete, for it fails to specify the further condition that all choices are made in a particular style or manner. One can never claim to choose *A* instead of *B*, and not be able to specify the basis for the choice, without succumbing again to the accusation that this is a blind and arbitrary act, and not even a poor choice. A choice unavoidably entails an act *undertaken*, therefore with some awareness of conditions and consequences, means and ends. I choose to go to the movies, because I like films—to give me pleasure. I choose to write rather than to type a letter, to be more intimate. I choose to read *Moby Dick* rather than *Typee*, because it is a far better novel. I cannot choose without at least the minimal end in view of conforming to certain rules—though I can choose to follow other rules.

Thus we may say that constraint, restriction, limitation, even necessity are essential in order that choice exist. I can never choose arbitrarily, though I can *act* arbitrarily or capriciously. I can only choose in accord with certain goals or principles. If I act in accord with principles, I may be said to choose to conform to them. A man who is hammering nails into a bench may be asked, "Why are you doing that?" He may answer, "It is Thursday; I do this every Thursday." Unless we thought he was joking or coy, such a reply would make us suspicious of his mental balance; it reveals very clearly that he has not made a choice. If he answers, however, "To build a bench," then he has chosen to do so, and chosen as well to use nails instead of screws. The choice may thus be defined as the taking or employing of a class of alternatives from a specified range of possibilities in accord with the constraints defined by a particular purpose, goal, or method. A football end, running downfield to catch a pass, chooses to fake to the left or to the right, in accordance with the purposes and goals of football. He cannot choose to bow to the crowd and still be playing the game. The method of football determines the particular range of alternatives he may choose from. Given his adoption of the method, his choices are then sharply defined. Note, however, that he may not choose the method, but have it forced upon him, as a soldier is sent to the front against his wishes, and must fight or die.

The method does not itself determine the selected alternative, though it does circumscribe the range from which the alternative may be chosen. What is important to realize is that the larger the range of possibility—the greater the arbitrariness of selection, and the less possible it is to determine the choice in advance—the less possible it becomes to "make" a choice. A football end told to "Do anything" may not be able to choose what to do at all, for his sense of football may well not allow for such choices. When the quarterback stipulates the play, then the end's position settles his general role, and his training to certain habits of running and faking allow him in a given time and place to choose the best act defined by these conditions. There exists a possibility of a "real" (that is, effective) choice only when strong limitations are imposed on possible actions. It follows, then, that a "free" choice that is anything more than an empty one exists only within a context of necessity—the necessity imposed by methods with particular constraints.

A further point to realize is that there can never be a situation or method in which everything is decided. However much the details of action are stipulated, some degree of liberty remains—the freedom to act within stipulated conditions either accepted or imposed. The mass, as ritualistic and confined a procedure as can be found, nevertheless permits deviations in stance, tone of voice, rate of delivery, and the like. Choices always remain, defined by the very procedures which rule out other possibilities. The more structured a situation is, the easier it is to make a definite choice as well as a "free" one, defined by the structure. Recognizing that human action is so often habitual, we can see that the very confinement of habits is their strength, for in confinement and structure they also introduce effective arbitrariness and openness. All structure has niches within which possibilities remain open. Here it is that choices are to be found.

How then are we led to deny a choice where no possibility remains open? Obviously, where the defining method stipulates the act in question. A chess player has no choice as to whether to move his rook in a straight line or diagonally. That is determined by the rules of the game. A man freely falling in space has no choice as to the rate he will fall, unless he has a parachute. The rate is set by the conditions of his situation. Even here, though he did not set the rules, he can modify them by the use of equipment properly chosen to fit means to ends. Moreover, he may choose to move himself around in different positions as he falls. Only in certain respects is his behavior completely set by the conditions in which he finds himself. Choices as to other aspects of behavior always remain. What cannot be chosen is defined by the conditions of the procedure or method under which the choice is to be subsumed, and is relative to it. In putting the pieces away, I can do whatever I wish with the rook, so long as it ends up in its box. I cannot, of course, do what is physically impossible, so that is a limiting case. It is difficult to see, however, how this limiting case creates any special difficulties, at least with respect to choosing. I can choose, within the limits of the procedure specified by the method adopted, any act that is physically possible. In general, the method itself will rule out those acts which are impossible to perform. For example, in parachuting I cannot choose to rise, not only insofar as it is physically impossible, but because it is ruled out by the method employed as well. What cannot be chosen is thus not a matter of personal idiosyncracy or whim, even of psychological determinism, but of the procedure specified which the agent has adopted. A man chooses in accordance with some procedure or specified rules. These eliminate what cannot be chosen.

Suppose, however, a man makes the claim that he has chosen to lift 300 pounds in a weight-lifting contest, but in fact *cannot* do that. We may reply to him that his choice is neither effective nor even genuine, for he must take realistic stock of his powers and means to achieve his ends. He possesses no method to achieve his goal. The question then arises: can a man claim that due to his psychic makeup, he "had to" choose to rob a bank? One difference here is that he did rob the bank (compared to the man who tries to raise 300 lbs. and cannot). He chose, in accord with conventional moral standards concerning stealing, nevertheless to steal. Perhaps, though, he meant to say that he "could not" have refrained from stealing. However, it is not obvious why it is supposed that the choice to do *x* always entails something more about the choice to do not-*x*, other than that it was not chosen. What is the source of the view that one chooses something only when one "could have" also done the opposite?

There is a definite confusion here between the methodic conditions which render a choice possible by defining it as one of a small number of alternatives, and the causal factors in a man's past which also (and in a certain respect, quite independently) rule out many alternatives, possibly all but one. A baseball player goes to bat when his time comes, in an open and direct choice, though he could not refuse to do so *as* a baseball player. He may choose to bunt or hit a home run (if he can), but he cannot choose not to take his turn at bat. Yet without doubt, he is not forced to bat, but does so willingly, in a deliberate choice. In this sense, a man can definitely be said to choose an act forced upon him by the method he has chosen, not merely because he has "chosen" the method with its restrictions and constraints, but because choosing is acting methodically, even where the method defines the act in question. A painter may feel compelled by an unfinished painting to place a certain color in a particular area to "finish" the painting. But he definitely chooses to do so despite the compulsion. And in fact, he may vary the size and shade of the color within his compulsion, as can the baseball player go to bat slowly or quickly, choose his bat, take one or another stance, and so on, indicating that no degree of constraint can eliminate choice. Methodic constraint is necessary to choice; within it, both restriction and decision necessarily play a part.

The baseball player may also, however, be viewed as a complex biochemical structure with ingrained patterns of behavior, the result of conditioning according to causal laws. In this sense, whatever he does may be viewed as *necessary,* as an outcome of causal sequences and forces. Here one may be led to say that men really do not choose, but act in ways which are necessary outcomes of their past. Since whatever is done by this baseball player is necessary, he can never do otherwise; he is not free, nor is he capable of choice. Robots and mechanical devices do not choose; neither do men, who are only devices of greater complexity.

The concept of choice which is implicitly assumed in this argument, and in the claim that recent psychological discoveries have shown that men really do not choose, is anything but clear. If what is meant here by a "choice" is an arbitrary act, without reason or intent, this would seem to violate our usual notions greatly. Consider expressions like, "I choose to die for my country," and "What system do you use in choosing your starting-point in attacking problems of this kind?" As the above analysis has shown, mere behavior may be spontaneous and unreasoned, but a choice can never be. In fact, as Hume showed with respect to punishment, arbitrariness and the absence of causal patterns can never be part of a choice, for the latter presupposes structure and method. Arbitrariness in action is a justification for the claim that a man did not choose, for he was not "rational." A man who chooses can always give reasons for his having chosen what he did, entailing a definite set of criteria upon which he based his decision. The rationality implicit in this choice in no way detracts from it or makes it less of a choice.

The intrusion of causal elements into the concept of rationality can have no bearing upon the sense in which we speak of a choice or even of a rational choice; therefore, it cannot affect a conception of responsibility based upon the existence or absence of choice. It can, however, raise rather important questions concerning the causal origins of a particular choice, and the control an individual may be said to have over his choices where they are rooted in distant times and places. Although I choose to write this essay, the causes of that choice lie apart from my reasons (though they contribute to them), are *inescapable* (an odd word, for one does not really resist causal laws that one employs, only those that one opposes), and came into existence under circumstances when my own powers were quite limited (when I was a child). May I not say, then, that whatever I choose, a causal explanation can be given which will demonstrate both the causal necessity of my choice, and its unavoidability so far as my powers are concerned? How then am I responsible for it?

I have already suggested any number of ways of construing this last question so as to preserve our acting upon moral condemnation, with or without profoundly analyzing the rather sophisticated notion of responsibility implied in such a question. Regardless of the causal origins of an act, as an act it relates to others, to good and evil, and thus carries with it a permanent and unbreakable responsibility, which can only be mitigated and never overcome by appeal to causal conditions, ignorance, or insanity. This pervasive sense of responsibility may be viewed, not as a property of some and not other actions, but as a property of all human actions. Here we find the source of anguish and despair, as well as the moral heroism that involves a perpetual concern for other men, whoever and wherever they are. The ongoing nature of moral judgment, however, permits us to differentiate cases where censure is necessary and valid from cases where this pervasive responsibility cannot be expected to promote action. We may also relate responsibility to choosing regardless of causal antecedents, by considering only the reasons given and motives presented.

However, some direct confrontation of causal determination as a source of moral responsibility is necessary, at least to face the demand that men must differ in some remarkable way from robots if they are to be considered responsible for what they do. I find it most remarkable that no one has sought to define the conditions under which robots would be considered moral agents. I suggest that consideration of the notion of self-knowledge presented in the last chapter provides a basis for such a notion, quite independent of the causal conditions of the agent's deeds.

Causal Determination

The view that moral responsibility is incompatible with causal determinism is much aided by the pernicious connotations of the word "determinism," which not only suggests force, but has an idiosyncratic sound which suggests some special mode of control under whose sway bound and regimented creatures move. An initial propaedeutic, then, is to to use the word "determination" in posing the problem, not only because of its freedom from ill-use, but because of its inherent suggestion of a variety of *modes* of determination. Not only may events be causally determinated, but they may be determined in innumerable other ways, each of which contributes some element or degree of determination to the event in question. Here we have no obvious conflict between efficient and final causation—at least, not one inherent in our vocabulary—but a merging of factors of determination into a holistic event.

If there is a problem of freedom, it arises not from the wealth of possible modes of determination, but from the achievement of a synthesis among them within a single event. Certain of these syntheses are no problem at all: an event may be determinate in both causal aspects and with respect to its character. There is no conflict between causal determination and the determination which is the predication of character or properties to an event, for we view the latter as part of the causal determination. The content of what is determinated by the causal antecedents of an event is the character or set of properties which are the nature of that event. There is also no apparent conflict between the determinateness of an entity contributed by others, and the determinateness it offers to itself when these become merged in a synthesis whose threads become a tangled skein, but which can—to the best of our limited knowledge—be separated, as we give the biography of a famous man and seek to show the origins of his fame and of his specific actions.

Nothing is more natural than this unification of different modes of determination within any single event. Every individual is a composite of varieties of order and circumstances, each of which provides its contribution to the determinateness of his individuality. We are faced with so obvious a truism here that it is difficult from the point of view set forth to see any basis at all for the view that causal determination can be so overwhelming (in some sense) as to nullify that mode of determination which is provided by rational deliberation and responsible decision making when they are present. Yet it is equally a truism that responsibility and even moral obligation entail some kind of freedom— and in many interpretations, a freedom from causal determination. The sheer absurdity of the latter notion is all too often overlooked—once again, based on the magic provided by the word "determinism."

For again, if we address the problem before us in terms of causal *determination,* then the notion of freedom from such determination is at its best obscure, and at its worst genuinely absurd. Do we mean by freedom from causal determination: (1) that other modes of determination can be found?—it would be foolish to deny it; (2) that causal determination is a specious mode of determination?—that is equally foolish, even in the human realm, as biographies testify; (3) that some events "just happen," without any determination by past events whatsoever? —that is not only metaphysically absurd, but is quite irrelevant to matters of moral import, which are the last things we may hold to "just happen."

The absurdities of interpretation (3) are, it seems to me, worth looking at more closely, for they are the most dangerous of the stumbling blocks offered in the discussion of responsibility. The first absurdity is revealed in the realization that in speaking of a causal order, we are speaking not so much of laws of science, or even of laws of nature (though we may have them indirectly in mind), but of the determination of an event by earlier events. In all cases where the past conditions the present, we have causal determination. Of course, such modes of determination may vary, in precision of determination, in forcefulness of determination, in character of determination, and in preservation of specific character. But what is most striking is that the notion of responsibility entails the determination of a present judgment by a past action. This is the substance of Hume's argument that judgments of responsibility entail a causal order. The second absurdity is that events which happen outside any systematic order are thought to have the character of responsibility attached to them. Yet, the nature of the agent, his links to his transgressions, and the plausibility of his rationalizations, are all rooted in a systematic order between past and present.

What, then, if the problem of the relationship of moral responsibility and freedom is so filled with absurdities, is the core of that problem—for it is by no means wholly absurd? It is, simply, that (1) some causal determinations serve as excuses; while (2) no rational criterion can be found for distinguishing between legitimate and illegitimate excuses on the basis of causal determination. We do indeed accept excuses based on causal inadequacy, even when they do not render the act in question *impossible*. Why not then admit every act to have a causal excuse? For in every event can be found some—and indeed, many—determinations which are cases of the past conditioning the present.

I am proposing a *principle* here, to aid in the clarification of the problem before us. That is, that every event is a synthesis of a multiplicity of determinations and a multiplicity of modes of determination; moreover, every event, which is necessarily located in space and time, is conditioned by its past and causally determinate. Does the acceptance of this principle entail the rejection of moral responsibility? Obviously, only if all causal determination provides an excuse for what one has done. Otherwise we have the very real possibility that causal determination may instead provide a *ground* for moral action, rooted in the agent's own being, and thus entail his moral responsibility.

Here, however, we can formulate the issue that is of critical concern. Since every causal determination marks the conditioning of a person by past events, may we not always consider his behavior not self-caused, or self-determined, but determined *externally?* How, then, is *he* responsible for what he does? Let me only add to this difficulty the remark that most of the other modes of determination of an event are conditions other than the event itself—circumstances, environment, the past, and even the future: why not then face the fact that all beings live in an interrelated world, that their determinate actions always are conditioned by their relations with other things, and that they then are never wholly self-determinate in their actions? We are beginning to reach a metaphysical ground for our discussion. Nothing is in itself. Nothing acts in itself. No one is therefore responsible for his "own" deeds, for there are none that are his alone.

The transfer of our analytic concern from ethics to metaphysics, however, is of great value in clarifying the problem before us. Indeed, we seem to have come up against a metaphysical principle of interrelatedness much like Whitehead's *Fallacy of Simple Location*. Nothing exists alone; *ergo*, nothing is self-determined in action; and moral responsibility is a vacuous notion. But the conclusion is bad metaphysics. It is not the business of metaphysical analysis to undercut distinctions, but to ground them—or, better, to offer secure grounds for the distinctions we make. On the level of greatest generality, nothing is self-determined.

Therefore, there are no *ontological* grounds for self-determination. We have no metaphysical basis for declaring some men responsible for what they do and others not.

But if there are no metaphysical grounds of responsibility that permit relative distinctions as to degree of responsibility among different men, there are equally no metaphysical grounds for claiming lack of responsibility. Either no one is responsible for what he does, or everyone is. On the surface, each of these alternatives is equally vacuous. But they differ in at least one major respect: to deny responsibility to everyone is to undercut morals altogether; to hold everyone responsible faces us with severe problems, but at least keeps us on moral ground. I prefer the latter version of these virtually empty principles concerning responsibility. What we must do is to transform our question from *whether* men are responsible for what they do, to a consideration of the meaning and consequences of the view that *everyone is indeed responsible for his actions*. This will be considered below.

We can, however, take a further step. The view that everyone is responsible for what he does has a severe problem at its core—that we have relinquished the conception of self-determination, and with it the notion of an action belonging to a particular person. It was precisely the difficulties that pervaded the concept of an action "belonging" to a specific person that underlay the complexities of moral responsibility revealed in the body of this essay: we have now recognized these difficulties to be inherent in a rather fundamental metaphysical principle. How, then, are we to provide a ground for the obvious fact that we do hold some people responsible for what they do, and others not? Have I capitulated to the principle that if everyone is guilty, then no one is?

In one sense, I have indeed capitulated—by affirming the view that everyone is responsible for what he does, and by recognizing that no actions are wholly self-determined. A particular conception of responsibility follows from these notions, and I believe it to be inherent in our moral tradition. In another sense, however, it is clear that a ground must be found for comparative judgments of responsibility. All I wish to do is to point out that this entails *another* conception of responsibility, not to be confused with the first. The confusions which have permeated most discussions of punishment have had their basis in the failure to distinguish *two* senses of responsibility, both of which provide grounds for punishment, but only one of which provides grounds for praise and is of moral worth.

The key to the second mode of responsibility is the concept of *self-determination*. We have found that this notion has no *metaphysical* basis:

nothing is inherently self-determined; everything is determined by its relations to others. The world is social in this sense. But it does not follow from this that all modes of determination are equally without specific focus, realized purpose, or self-knowledge. Put another way, if nothing is self-determined in being wholly without determination by other things, is there not another notion of self-determination—*the realization of oneself as one knows oneself to be?* Can one come to sufficient self-awareness *as* related to other things to realize oneself most completely as a synthesis of all the conditions upon one? This is what I call "autonomy," and it is the ground of specific responsibility as against the unconditioned and pervasive responsibility that belongs equally to all men.

The range of possibility defined by a causal order of determination is relatively slight. Causes lead to effects of a similar nature to themselves, and perpetuate constancy and recurrence. Hume's analysis of causation is limited in many respects, but most obviously in his sense of unlimited possibility available within a causal order. A simplicity both of possibility and of recurrence is essential to causal determination. Where complexities of indefinite range and novelty arise, we seek other modes of determination in addition to causal ones. Pervasive structures and adaptive mechanisms make us turn to biological and organic tools of analysis; end-oriented activity makes us speak of method; complex and interwoven systems of events lead us to linguistic and symbolic forms of determination.

Causal determination is not deterministic in its ability to *force* its determinations upon events, but in the limited range of possibility it provides for its determinations. The past offers itself to the future in the mode of causal determination; insofar as the future is determined by that past, it is so without the consideration of alternatives. Intuitions are always multiple, and never singly determinate; language contains within it a wealth of possibility and of means of expression.

I have shown that consciousness is never a single linear sequence of events and behavior, but resides within a range of systematic interconnections and associations. An object of which we are conscious calls forth multiple possibilities, just as a word in a working language calls forth multiple possibilities of response. Language fleshes out our encountered world; consciousness fleshes out our encounters with what is before us. The determination provided by consciousness is necessarily loose and somewhat unsettled, because of its complexity and interrelatedness. Here the conditions of human freedom are to be found.

Consciousness and causal determination are not competitors, but different types of determination, with different degrees of complexity. Causation is linear where consciousness is multidimensional. Causal determination minimizes alternatives; consciousness unfolds them; language revels in them; and self-consciousness orders and controls them. Yet in no case does one choose to be conscious or self-conscious; conscious or linguistic; or likewise, conscious or caused. Causation is the relatively direct course of events from past to future; consciousness is the consideration of multiplicity as a factor in the universe. One sense of freedom is precisely to be found in the multiplicity that resides in the universe along with the linearity of causal determination. Freedom here is the alternatives that remain after we have stipulated what is done. Consciousness is the entertainment of that possibility, not *as* a possibility, but within the multiplicity of determinations in human life. It is therefore a freedom *in itself,* though a freedom of possibility and not of achievement or action.

What is required for this freedom of multiple determination to become actualized rather than merely possible is for consciousness to turn upon itself and to control itself. Self-consciousness must determine within the alternatives of conscious life the order of action that can be efficient purpose. Consciousness entertains possibility; methodic self-consciousness can actualize it, and can render freedom a fact. This latter freedom, fully actualized in determinate activities, is autonomy.

Autonomy

Autonomy prevails when a man makes decisions that are fully "his," and are not the decisions which he is forced to carry out, or the consequence of a sequence of events outside his control. The freedom that is autonomy is the identity of an individual manifested throughout his actions. This sense of freedom is also the one involved in making choices, where we say that although external events often compel a man to choose as he does, sometimes he can make his choices freely and responsibly. Modern psychoanalysis reveals unmistakably that a man without external constraints may still be at the mercy of compulsions beyond his control. Autonomy is the freedom from control by one's hidden self also. In fact, autonomy is more properly a property of actions than of persons, since a man may act autonomously at some times and compulsively at others. It is a way of acting, a method, in which choices, decisions, and activities may properly be deemed to belong to the agent in question: "his."

Autonomy in no way violates causal determination, Kant notwithstanding, for in order to call an act "mine," I must be in a position to influence it causally. It is mine only insofar as a determinable relation can be found between my character and the act. Otherwise it is mere caprice, and I may deny it to be mine, though it was performed by my body. The concept of a coherent will is the traditional basis for claiming actions to belong to a particular person. Hume showed that the consistent order of self necessary to such a claim is founded in a causal order. What a man does is related intelligibly and causally to what he has done and been; otherwise it is his only inexplicably. The reasons I give are only apparent unless rooted in my character, which has causal structure. A bare act independent of causal order is not more "mine" than it is anyone's. We might take the position that all actions and events are a man's insofar as he accepts responsibility for them. But this global view of responsibility must also take into account the connection of means and ends, insofar as the methods of autonomy are capable of achieving ends by known means. The autonomous acts of a person are at least his in that they are effectively produced by methods he employs.

The need for some conception of freedom represented by "autonomy" is unmistakable. At least two important senses of freedom may easily be discerned: what I have called "liberty"—the freedom *from* external coercion, threats, force, or fear; and the freedom that is the ability to make decisions, to choose among alternatives, to face the anguish of moral conflict, and to hold steadfast in the face of despair—in short, the freedom *to* act, decide, choose, and determine. This latter sense of freedom can be found in the chapter "The Grand Inquisitor" of *The Brothers Karamazov*, where Ivan makes the case that men desire to give up their freedom completely and be treated as children or sheep—not their liberty, but the anguish and torment they suffer as moral agents freely choosing their destinies. The release of external sanctions and controls leaves men empty-handed and forlorn, unable to appeal to rules and conventions for their decisions, yet called upon nevertheless for decisive action. The triumph of democratic thought, and its repudiation of traditional authorities, leaves men in democratic societies nowhere to turn for help in their decisions but to themselves, where they stand in loneliness and fear. If men are to have the fortitude and strength, the capacity and will, to render moral judgments in the face of both adversity and alienation, they must possess some unmistakable character of determination that is autonomy.

Analogous to the Greek sense of virtue, autonomy is acquired. It is not a native talent or capacity. It represents the fruits of a method applied to judgment and behavior, in which decision is made possible, and valid or right actions sought and achieved. A right action done by chance or mistake has no moral worth. At best it pleases an observer, who can approve it without concern for its antecedents. It is in the method which leads to the act that purpose, intent, and autonomy are all to be found.

Kant's moral views lead to the conclusion that an autonomous act is necessarily right. Such a position corrupts the meaning of "autonomy" by reducing it to "right" or conformity to moral law. A man must be capable of autonomously doing wrong if he can act autonomously at all—that Aristotle makes quite clear. Perhaps it is this that has led to that strange view wherein determinism is held antithetic to autonomy. But I suspect that the difficulty lies primarily with viewing "right" and "good" as properties of actions, when they are more properly located in judgments directed toward those actions. A man who endeavors to make a valid choice, to act rightly in a difficult moral situation, who weighs the possible consequences and his own needs in the balance, may be found by himself or another *at a different time and under different circumstances* to have acted wrongly. The method he employed in the determination of what is valid could not guarantee eternal validity, always and everywhere. However, if his decision was based on adequate knowledge of himself, on the consideration of possible consequences, on careful and meticulous examination of relevant facts, feelings, and needs, then his action is autonomous even when wrong. He made a justified and methodic decision, based on rather definite knowledge of himself and circumstances. No method can *guarantee* validity; it can only maximize its possibility. An autonomous action is not free from causal influences and tendencies; but it is the fruit of a method wherein the various influences, tendencies, and moral principles are balanced and weighed against each other, and taken into account in the decision to act. In this "taking into account," the influences are not overcome or nullified, but are channeled into a moral judgment reflecting on all of them. The self-awareness and self-reference of the method employed in this kind of moral judgment is the source of its autonomy.

A strong resemblance holds between logical thought and autonomous behavior, though the latter is much more complex. Kant's mistake lay in reducing the latter by analogy to the former. In logical demonstration—for example, the solution of a problem in mathematics—although the agent acts in learned ways, causally determined by past influences and education, his solution is rational only insofar as it is determined as well by rules of demonstration distinct from the causal influences in his past. Of course, his thoughts are a causal consequence of his past conditioning. But that is true alike for rational and irrational thought. What is distinctive about rational thought is its determination by standards and rules, rather than past events or things. Rationality does not eliminate causal determination; it simply provides events with a greater degree of complexity in having multiple determinations. Without causal determination there can be no rationality. In calling a proof "rational," we point out its special properties which call for other than causal analysis, and indicate our particular respect for that mode of determination.

Autonomous action is at least rational in the same sense, but it goes a step further in that the rules of the method utilized are possibly in question. A moral agent, particularly in a moment of conflict, must in principle rewrite the canons of morality and redetermine his own priorities and scale of values as he decides to take action on the basis of them. The double question here marks a level of self-reflection that does not overcome the influence of the past—for nothing can—but renders assured prediction impossible as well as inappropriate. A rational act may be predicted to be in accord with the rules of logic. An autonomous act has no specific rules that may be taken for granted. Autonomy is the reflection of causal determination upon itself to transcend its limitations. The responsible moral agent is left completely alone, with knowledge of himself and of ordinary conventional principles of morality, which can in a definite way only take him so far. Beyond this, he must methodically but unroutinely decide what is right, attempt to make a valid decision in terms of all the factors relevant to that decision, and take responsibility for what he does. His appeal to any authority, either the state, convention, or even reason, is intrinsically forbidden. His act remains his alone, incapable of subordination to any larger scheme of things. No wonder it is so appalling and fearful; no wonder men try to escape their moral condition. However, it is inescapable. Every moral agent is bound inextricably to anguish and freedom. Anguish can be escaped only through the abdication of morality altogether.

The autonomous act is an act of passion, residing in conflict and anguish, and sufficiently grounded in self-knowledge to escape predictive determination. It resembles a creative leap in any domain of human judgment, even that of science. A scientist, in proposing a new theory, must overturn some of the sacred canons that have become part of the common and unquestioned store of knowledge. This is why a new theory is so earth-shaking: it challenges principles that no scientist could have dreamed of questioning before. The thought that we may someday have a science of sciences, predicting the future of science, is as farfetched as the view that individual human actions can in principle always be predicted. In both cases, there is a reflexive and critical self-awareness that promotes a novel rejection of older forms and procedures that cannot itself be predicted in detail, due to its novelty. To have predicted relativity theory in advance would have eliminated the nature of its discovery. To be able to foretell a man's autonomous act is to reduce it either to moral law or to the outcome of his passions and desires. But it must be something more than either of these to be autonomous, since the agent knows the facts on which prediction is based as well as the observer, and can take them into account. Something new is generated in this self-reflection—new in the order of antecedents and consequents. The multiple possibilities of conscious thought are realized and acted upon. The linear order of causal determination is overwhelmed by the possibilities it has unleashed at the level of complexity where autonomous self-awareness can be found.

Autonomous action is founded upon sophisticated self-knowledge, without which the agent's actions would be subject to unknown and perhaps uncontrolled inclinations. I may be willing to go along with my passions in an act I consider moral, but I must know what they are in order to be able to decide responsibly whether to accept or reject them. Not to know who I am, the kind of person I am, what I want and the means that I tend to employ, is to risk being completely dominated by unknown and therefore uncriticized and unintended habits and desires.

Of course, complete self-knowledge is never possible, nor is it usually necessary to moral action. Moreover, self-knowledge is not always on an articulate and verbal level. Consider a man who possesses what I earlier called "moral wisdom," or a skill of making valid moral judgments, but who lacks anything like psychological self-knowledge. Is he to be considered an autonomous agent, or a man acting according to blind and uncontrollable habits of thought? Only a dialectical answer seems possible here, differentiating between an act which is alone the consequence of inclinations, without reflection or concern for future goals or moral principles except as they are followed unthinkingly, and an act given by the method of ethical decision and action, which is ruled by ceaseless evaluation. It is true that in the latter case, causal determination is present as much as in the former; but it is also true that causal determination can promote autonomy as well as hinder it—and in fact, is necessary to it. A valid moral act is one which synthesizes the various elements within a moral situation into a resolution faithful to the agent's self-identity, one consonant with his moral duties as well as his self-interest. A valid act minimizes remorse, and maximizes the self as a rich and consistent factor in moral action. A valid act must be one that implicitly reflects both the agent's character, his needs and desires, his temptations and inclinations, his sense of morality, and the social determinants of moral thought surrounding him, which are exemplified in the attitudes and actions of others. When a man's moral convictions are sufficiently strong, he may act on them in a relatively direct and unconsidered way, without complex deliberation. Such a mode of decision can be valid if, for example, it is the expression of a moral compulsion which allows one to do nothing else—like Antigone's obligation to bury her brother. The difference between a valid action and an unthinking and habitual moral response rests upon the way in which the moral principles followed are viewed in the two cases. When the agent views a moral rule as *absolute,* incapable of qualification by circumstance, the suffering of others, or even his own self-interest, it is untestable for him. He is, in effect, quite unresponsive to what surrounds him. Nothing could happen to make his judgment wrong. He is capable of no more than an irrational and unresponsive morality. His principles represent absolute authority. Such a man is not at all responsibly moral, for he does not employ any method of judgment—he does not face the future consequences of his actions with the same moral attitude as he faces his immediate actions, though they are intimately related. He unwarrantedly rules out consideration of the possibility of failure, and is unresponsive to the needs of the situation, therefore irresponsible and not autonomous. He seeks implicitly to free himself from moral responsibility in the most profound and risky sense.

The responsible and autonomous moral agent recognizes that every consequence of an action bears upon its value or rightness. He must know not only the consequences of his actions in external respects, but with respect to his own feelings of satisfaction, guilt, even revulsion. He must be highly responsive to the possibilities and nuances in the situation, aware of what they might lead to and how they will affect him. If he can predict that his present decision will continue in the future to remain consonant with what he becomes and believes, when he has faced and continues to face the unavoidable prospect of failure, then and only then can he responsibly call his action right or valid. He may be wrong; some humility before the omnipresent possibility of failure is essential to moral wisdom. But when his self-knowledge is adequate, when his awareness of his own moral convictions is strong enough, he may be justified in acting on the basis of his judgment of validity. Thus, a man who acts out of supreme conviction—for example, in refusing to fight in the army—and who recognizes that his refusal may cost him and others a great deal, but feels that it will not in fact be so great as to render his refusal a mistake—though it could be—can act autonomously in terms of his own moral being.

It is the risk of failure that defines the difference between rational morality and blind adherence to law. An autonomous person makes a choice that affirms his being, one in which his whole existence is at stake, for he may *fail*. His decision is valid when he does not fail, when he knows himself and the world well enough so that his decision remains valid under later conditions. He must face the prospect of failure in order to make an autonomous decision, or else he risks having acted uncritically and blindly.

Blind conviction, however faithful to common moral principles, is always uncontrolled and irrational. A pacifist may refuse to fight the enemy out of sheer obstinacy, never dreaming of the price he may have to pay, unable to consider the terrible consequences that may follow if his country is invaded. A continual inability to weigh the moral impact of events on one's actions, even in imagination, marks the absence of autonomy and the binding of men to moral principles which are external to themselves. If a pacifist refuses to fight a particularly vicious enemy, who if victorious will assault his wife and murder his children, and refuses without any regard for his feelings toward the possible consequences of his refusal, then he lacks foresight, is blind to the reality of his decision, and is at the mercy of habits of thought not open to his own modification. A pacifist who can test and evaluate alternatives by facing them directly in terms of other feelings is in a position to modify and transform blind moral principles into tested and coherent rules for his own conduct. What is remarkable in valid moral judgment is that the determination that an action is valid is implicit testimony to the effect that it is the best action within the sphere of judgment that constitutes the total being of a human person in the world, with his loyalties, moral sentiments, personal needs, loves and hates. A valid act transcends its past as a manifestation of the present self in its complexity and relation-in-the-world. It nullifies its past as a factor in judgments, and looks solely to the future as a test of its own validity. It comes out of the past, for its rationality depends on the fact that the agent has learned to make valid moral decisions in a causally coherent manner. But its methodic control of the elements that enter into a judgment of validity surmounts that past as a fundamental mode of determination. There is an implicit prediction within the act that it will enhance or conserve the self. The method at work in providing such validity is autonomy.

Consider again the pacifist who seeks a valid decision. If he refuses to fight without complete assurance that he is not doing so from coward-ice, his act is not likely to be valid. If it is to be valid, his decision must embody adequate knowledge of his own feelings and fears, and his tend-encies to shirk pain and death. Suppose, now, he is a man whose gen-eral pattern of action indicates cowardice, so that an observer predicts, "He will refuse to fight because he is afraid." In order to act validly, the agent must directly face this prediction and its possible double truth. Upon doing so, he may well decide to fight, thus falsifying the predic-tion. Suppose, however, he is morally convinced beyond all changing that killing is wrong. He may be so convinced as to refuse to fight re-gardless of his fears or possible cowardice. Indeed, he may, provided he "knows" of his cowardly tendencies, refuse to consider them relevant, and make his moral decision on the basis of principle alone. If he can claim that it is a valid decision, he is implicitly asserting that he has considered all possibilities relevant to the situation; and if he truly has, then he may claim that his act is autonomous as well. Autonomy pro-vides the justification for a claim of validity—though it may not guar-antee it. On the other hand, a man may act validly without methodic awareness—though that validity will not be justified.

An autonomous action may well be anticipated—for example, if we know the great strength of the agent's moral convictions. My point, however, is that insofar as the act can be claimed in advance to be valid, it involves a degree of self-reflection that renders predictability impossible on the basis of past events alone. An autonomous agent's ra-tional method and self-knowledge transcend his past, and become de-terminative in their own right. New principles may be generated, new discoveries made. The pacifist above, in facing his own disposition to cowardice, and balancing it against his pacifistic beliefs, may come to a new realization about the consequences of principled pacificism. The rationality of the method which provides autonomy provides the pros-pects of a new outlook, coming from but not locatable in the agent's past. So complex and controlled is methodic activity that prospects of novelty are enhanced, and a new future becomes a likelihood, new in the most transcendent sense, as a creative leap in science or art tran-scends the possibilities inherent in the situation prior to the creative act.

It is indeed difficult to distinguish between a principled act wherein the principles become "right" by definition, and one wherein the agent recognizes the possibility of error, yet acts rightly on the basis of what he knows of himself. It is in the importance and respect for pervasive responsibilities and the prospects of failure that autonomy resides. However, the greater the agent's self-knowledge, the more he can be said to act upon it and not be bound by unknown influences. In an action wherein conviction is great, and the agent knows himself "on the whole," he may claim valid decision, autonomy, and thus responsibility, quite apart from the kind of empirical knowledge anyone else may possess about him.

A moral decision can be wrong in different frames of reference—the agent's and various observers'. In the latter case, another person makes a judgment, founded on his own self-knowledge and sense of right and wrong, directed toward the agent's actions. Such a judgment can be offered without regard to the autonomy of the agent, though usually the agent's methodic abilities are important factors to consider. But in the former case, where the agent reevaluates his earlier decision, he is affirming or denying his prior conception of himself and what things meant and now mean to him. To say he was wrong is to admit that he judged his being in the world wrongly. But no method can guarantee validity in action; failure is always a prospect. It follows that autonomy, when encountering unforeseen circumstances, may entail the transformation of the self—though self-directed, and not through manipulation by other people.

A man is autonomous when he makes a judgment according to methods which maximize his prospects of gaining validity. When he fails to gain validity, he may find himself culpable, as may others, for not knowing enough of himself and the world to gain such validity in action. He is required to change, either in what he knows or in what his general attitude is toward the world. He may continue to judge his actions valid, not from blind habit (which reveals heteronomous ignorance), but as an assertion of deliberative validity. Perhaps such a personal moral conviction will be repaid by punishment. But it is nevertheless the pinnacle of moral capacity—the adherence to oneself and one's moral vision on the basis of methodic control of events and circumstances.

A tacit reference is made, in the case of an autonomous action considered valid by the agent, to his entire person, the causal determinants of his behavior, the remote and immediate consequences of his actions, the principles he espouses, the strength of his loyalty to them, the reactions of others, and the consistence of his personality through time. In this sense can he alone claim the action to be truly his—his by virtue of its having been chosen methodically in such a fashion as to bring into a unified order the entire course of his life. Insofar as a man fails to understand the hidden reaches of his person, he may be unable to take them into consideration, and though methodically autonomous in his actions, he is not a whole self in his decisions. He is implicated in events in ways which he cannot entirely assimilate or control, perhaps due to ignorance. Only an action valid to the agent, and valid by virtue of a methodic choice made from self-knowledge, can bring into focus the entire being of a person. An act is valid insofar as it reflects the complete realization of the competing tendencies within the agent and the situation in which he finds himself. In this sense, the unified self is not the source of a valid action, but rather the valid action unifies the self in its rejection of some of its aspects as irrelevant, and in its recognition of what is essential to it.

In a general sense, every person is a unity amidst plurality, insofar as the various elements of his experience are brought together in his personality. This sense is too general, however, to reflect the self divided and torn before a difficult moral choice, as well as the denial of an agent that his deeds are actually his ("I was not myself then"). It may be said that there exists a unity of the person captured in the course of his experience viewed from past to future. This is the unity of a person's life and actions as a causal inheritance from past to future. This is the unity of character provided by psychoanalysis in knowledge about the patient in therapy. This unity is neither autonomous nor valid.

There is, however, a unity which is the outcome of a project to make oneself unified in one's actions as the autonomous agent responsible for them. Psychoanalysis may bring with it a transformation of the patient as he overcomes the divided nature of his being and projects himself as a unity into the future. I constitute myself before the world and into an indefinite future as I make a valid and autonomous choice. The freedom here is not a freedom from causality, but a freedom within a causal order that defines an indefinite future for a unified self. An autonomous agent knows himself to the point where his actions reflect a pattern of his being that dismisses as irrelevant to the validity of his actions all sorts of causal influences. It is in this sense that an autonomous individual transcends causality: he so methodically encompasses what he is that he can break with part of himself to realize himself in a new unity of action. A creative realization of the self is involved in the autonomy of the moral agent. In an autonomous and valid act a moral agent realizes and reaffirms himself. He either accepts what he has been, or changes from it into someone new. Only by virtue of this realized unity in his projected actions does an agent gain the right to claim an action as his. Autonomy is the freedom to realize oneself in one's deeds and the right to bear responsibility for them. When a man denies his responsibility, he denies his autonomy, his self-knowledge, and his unity of self. He views himself as at the mercy of unknown forces, a divided creature. Since all men seek a unity of self in their lives, one may say that they continually and implicitly seek autonomous validity, but fail the powers for achieving it. They remain alienated and divided. Such validity is the harmony within the soul that Plato called "justice," but a unity realized within actions performed. An autonomous man, by virtue both of his self-knowledge and self-unification, defines his unity in the validity of his actions. He succeeds in subordinating to the unified order of his person those elements of his experience that are inessential, irrelevant, unimportant to the decisions he makes. He reaches the self-assurance that is the knowledge that he has done all that he can do out of the depths of his being. He comes to a synthetic unity of his being with the world out of a completeness of himself that renders circumstances unable to violate him. Autonomous validity is the realization of oneself which is the result of having found exactly what one is and being willing to live with it. An autonomous man is so secure with himself that it literally makes no sense to raise the question of whether he has chosen freely. He did exactly what he had to in terms of the methods and powers available to him.

Unfortunately, the autonomy described here is not only merely an ideal: it is in large measure vain. For human life affords a variety of types, degrees, and styles of order and unity, but no complete unification of all aspects of experience into a single order. Failure lurks everywhere, especially in what is hidden and remote, in those regions of the world which encroach upon us suddenly and unexpectedly. No method and no self-knowledge could provide a man with complete control and possession of his actions, many of whose consequences are so public and remote as to be beyond any agent's sphere of influence. Autonomy is, then, less a state than a project, of so continually expanding one's powers and authority through interrogative methods that the likelihood of validity may be maximized, though failure is a permanent possibility. We cannot expect to unify all aspects of ourselves, but only to create new and expanding orders of synthesis. Autonomy requires continual renewal. Freedom in action is always tentative and evanescent. Yet without seeking it methodically, we cannot find it, and remain mere creatures of habit and movement rather than responsible agents creatively organizing our energies in action. Autonomy is less a possibility to be actualized than an obligation residing in our moral being to be pursued. Our moral imperatives obligate us to seek autonomy methodically and unceasingly. Their fruit is to be found in the attainment of validity in action, though no methods can render such validity completely secure.

7

Moral Responsibility

Pervasive Responsibility

Many of the problems that arise in conventional ethical theories stem from the assumption that, in the main, every man looks out for his own self-interest, and that if he can be held culpable for a moral failure it must be proved that he and he alone is responsible for it. This approach, in other words, takes for granted that without adequate grounding of morality in something other than itself—religion, science, or philosophy—moral obligation is no more than a fiction. The deeds we perform simply happen, superficial products of ourselves, and do not attach to us so completely as to make us responsible for them. Independent of prior moral commitments, it is impossible to draw a definite line between an agent's deeds and the actions of others. A man may have failed to prevent a heinous crime. Others likewise failed to prevent it. In what sense is he particularly responsible?

I have developed the position that such responsibility is derived from an initial acceptance of a moral commitment such that every would-be moral agent is *prima facie* responsible for or to what takes place around him. What is to be determined is whether an agent will be excused from some of his obligations and responsibilities. What is remarkable in moral affairs is not that men are held responsible for their deeds, but that they are sometimes released from responsibility. As Kant has shown, the call of duty renders an agent's inclinations and self-interest completely irrelevant. In encountering a moral situation, however near or far, I cannot look away without concern, for the evil within it bears on me.

This sense of responsibility I call *pervasive responsibility*: a man is pervasively responsible to events surrounding him, and these responsibilities are of indefinite range and constantly shifting focus. Nothing in the world is wholly devoid of moral significance, insofar as it may be employed to generate goods or evils, to the extent that its causal impact may bring about valuable consequences, or in virtue of its capacity to be known with the powers that knowledge provides. Pervasive responsibility is the precondition of moral commitment, in that it defines the purview of moral values to be without limits. The method of moral judgment has no theoretical limits: everything in the world is a potential for evaluation—though in practice human powers are quite limited. The range of moral principles is without limit; the number of relevant consequences indefinite; the prospects of failure never circumscribed by well-defined boundaries.

Pervasive responsibility rests on two conditions of the moral life: the indefinite and expanding nature of the human self, so that its powers are open to ever new prospects; and the capacity which the rational methods of science and morals share—to encompass all things without exception as objects for consideration. Pervasive responsibility is analogous to the condition in science that everything in the world is a potential object of scientific knowledge. Fundamental laws of science are without intrinsic boundaries, and all events and objects come under their purview. So also, a moral action has no clear boundaries; failure may come from any quarter.

Pervasive responsibility is the condition of belonging to the world in an interrogative mode. A man is called upon to be *responsive to* his surroundings, and potentially to *anything* that could have significance for his actions, if he is to avoid failure. Our moral selves are so adaptable, and moral failure so pervasive, that anything may become a factor of moral importance—either in terms of remote consequences, hidden meanings, or new connections. Pervasive responsibility reflects the flexibility of human experience, so that nothing is assured of remaining outside its province. Pervasive responsibility is a gross condition of responsibility, to the extent that the world in a general and undefined sense is an object of moral concern. There remain details which have no moral significance—though they can be discovered only after the fact, and on the basis of information seldom available to us. They have almost no relation to conditions of pervasive responsibility, for failure lurks even within them, to the extent that we may have overlooked another of their aspects which is relevant, or to the extent that we may simply be in error concerning them.

By all of this, I do not mean to imply that a man's abilities and position do not affect later judgments that may be made about him, for the claim that whatever one could do would have had little effect on events in question is of vital importance to moral evaluation. The point is that one's moral world has indefinite and constantly expanding boundaries, and cannot be escaped. Anything in the world may become of critical moral importance, and we may be called upon to make moral judgments in terms of it. What may have been irrelevant in a given context may be relevant in another, or become so in a third, especially where the conditions of human life are transformed. No specified and limited context is the *correct* or *right* one in moral affairs. Men are responsible where there is evil and misery for changing themselves or the world—or at least for trying to do so. No event, no matter how remote from us, is, because of its remoteness alone, morally irrelevant to us. The rejection of a single event as "not bearing on me" entails the *right* to ignore that part of one's responsibilities. The mere consideration of the concept of responsibility indicates that one can only choose *how* he will meet his responsibilities. They are his regardless.

For example, responsibility in law generally is the *instrument* by which events enforce certain consequences. A man marries and becomes responsible for the support of his wife; when he has children, he is responsible for their upbringing; if he owns land, he is responsible for taxes on it and conformity to zoning regulations. It is never appropriate in such cases to plead ignorance or inability. A man is responsible for his taxes employed or not. He cannot evade responsibility by pleading his inability to meet it. It is true that in the cases I have mentioned, men make the original decisions which create responsibility, but this is not necessary. A man who wills his land to his son makes him then responsible for it, a responsibility the boy can transfer but not deny. Legal responsibilities place specific demands on men, quite independent of their powers to meet them.

There are two ways of meeting such demands without affecting oneself—by transferring them to someone else through sale, divorce, or the equivalent; and by denying that one is the party in question. In both cases, the agent denies the responsibility to be his, and claims it to be another's. However, the remarkable feature of *moral* obligations is that it is impossible to ascribe them to one man rather than another. Moral obligations confront everyone equally. This is but another rendition of Kant's categorical imperative. If anything is wrong, I am responsible for doing something about it. There is no way of relieving myself of this responsibility by shifting it to someone else. All I can do is to find someone who may be more effective in action than I am. But I am obligated to seek him out. And since there are an infinite number of things I might do, and ways I might perform them, nothing I do can relieve me of the possibility that another choice might have been better.

However a man may plead his inability to have prevented a wrongdoing for which he has been called to account, there is always something he might have done that he did not do. A white businessman who closes his eyes to the struggles of black people, even those a thousand miles away, cannot plead that it is none of his concern. There is much that he could do, in voting, seeking legislative remedy, even by directly involving himself in distant affairs. It is necessary to separate the claim of pervasive responsibility, which is a moral demand made upon a man to respond in his ethical judgments and actions, from the subsequent judgment that a man has met or abdicated these demands. Built into the nature of the demand that one be responsible is the recognition that demands sometimes cannot be met, particularly when they conflict. The point is that they cannot be ignored.

The concept of responsibility is like other moral concepts—such as "good" or "right"—in being fundamentally instrumental in character. Its primary meaning resides in the *act* of making a judgment about the person in question. It makes no reference to an isolable property of the agent or his deeds. The substance-attribute quality of our language suggests that the statement "John is responsible" in some way describes a property of John, when in fact it is thoroughly the act of uttering the statement in response to what John has done that possesses significance. I do not mean to imply that responsibility is independent of facts about John. But the facts form only part of the context involved in ascriptions of responsibility. What is necessary is to discover the grounds for the legitimacy of statements of responsibility. This is nothing less than ascertaining the conditions for validly blaming and punishing a man for what he has done.

Moreover, there is another point to consider here, concerning the role of responsibility in moral affairs. Corresponding to the use of "responsibility" in law to require particular attitudes, moral responsibility functions as the instrument whereby moral attitudes are enforced. This was Kant's great insight, though he subverted it with notions of *a priorism* and freedom: what renders an attitude moral rather than scientific, frivolous, or artistic, is the recognition that moral demands are inescapable except by denying one's being as an agent altogether. A man cannot consider himself a moral agent and yet abdicate his responsibilities. He is responsible because he has accepted the commitment embodied in the moral life, a commitment with no beginning and no end, no boundaries and no restrictions. We are obligated by the demands of moral commitment to certain actions, and when we fail we are responsible for our failures.

The man who leads a life of quiet contemplation may refuse to face the fact that people are starving elsewhere, yet live in peace, even with dignity. But he lives with the unrelenting possibility that he may have made the wrong choice. The mere remoteness of events from him does not render them outside his concern, or make him not pervasively responsible for them. On the other hand, the dedicated revolutionary, whose conviction that evil in the world must be eliminated through straightforward action, considers human suffering something to oppose at every turn, and battles at great personal sacrifice for a new world of plenty for all. His failure to affect the world positively, and the adverse consequences of his actions, neither increase nor decrease the number of his responsibilities. They only reveal his choices also to have been wrong. He must face the danger that in his war for humanity he has deserted the people close to him, even been untrue to himself; that loyalty to mankind may not outweigh the loyalties to his own needs and to people who are close to him. Every moral choice brings with it the possibility that something else might have been done instead, something that might have had far better results, even when one is convinced that he has acted validly.

The function of the notion of pervasive responsibility is to attack blind and uncritical action by representing the principle that nothing is devoid of moral significance. The habitual moralist, who acts without uneasiness because his life is stamped with unswerving assurance, can never justify his actions as valid. However much in adherence to moral principle they may be, his choices are valid only by chance. The man to whom every choice is a risk, every conflict fraught with the danger of error, cannot but feel the pressure of all things upon him at least providing him with possibilities of action. A man may hold that he has considered the problems and made valid choices only on the assumption that he has not overlooked important possibilities. It must be implicit in the purview of the general principles which define the conditions of action. Pervasive responsibility is the basis of the demand that the moral life be a perpetual questioning and responding, testing and retesting, evaluation upon evaluation, in which nothing is finished or irrelevant. The most remote events are least within my power, and it is not likely that it would be right for me to engage all my energies in trying to influence them. But to deem them wholly outside my moral concern is to distort the moral attitude.

It will be noted that I have introduced no temporal reference into the claim that one is pervasively responsible for everything. It may then be questioned whether one actually can be held responsible for past events, when nothing one could do could possibly affect them. Yet it will be recalled that today blacks in the United States have demanded reparations from white churches as indemnity for past injustices—reparations from people who may themselves have never acted unjustly toward blacks. The point of pervasive responsibility is that the moral life does not permit escape, that moral judgments have no definite boundaries. Moral action calls upon us to expand our powers and to overcome our limitations. We may always be held to account for what we have not done. We are responsible *to* past events insofar as they set the conditions for our future actions. It is only by virtue of our adaptive sensitivity even to remote and apparently irrelevant events that we can achieve valid choices in terms of our own powers and needs. The claims of Germans who supported Hitler that they did not know what was happening in the concentration camps, so they cannot be held responsible for it, or that they were incapable of bettering things, can only be rejected if we recognize that ignorance and powerlessness are but elements upon which we deliberate in determining what kinds of condemnation to enforce. They cannot in any way affect a man's pervasive responsibilities. The world makes its claims upon us regardless of our attitudes toward it, so long as we accept moral commitment. Even where we do not, the commitments of others bring us to account just as forcibly. A past event —a massacre, for example, or the gas chambers—not only must affect our moral feelings, but must compel in us the realization that another crime has gone unpunished, and the conviction that this must never happen again. The force of the responsibility we bear for facing such past events is small precisely because of the needs of the present in which we must act. But it is real nevertheless.

The moral judgment of culpability is very complex, and will be taken up in detail shortly. Here I only wish to emphasize again the point that pervasive responsibility and the power to act are separate notions, each of which must be taken into account in judging a man guilty. I am pervasively responsible for every murder because life makes its claims upon me which I cannot escape. Murders, past and present, will force themselves on me, in the character of my world and the attitudes of men around me. But the cases in which my powers to effect remedies are greater are more important in my moral judgments. A responsibility which cannot be acted upon is still a responsibility, but it cannot give rise to a valid action. The notion of validity in moral action involves a commitment to pervasive responsibility, but must not be automatically equated with condemnation or punishment.

The existentialists, Sartre in particular, have emphasized man's absolute and inescapable freedom, attempting to ground it in his being. Such a view, I have shown, cannot be substantiated in its implication that a philosophic proof of freedom can be given. In truth, man is pervasively responsible for the world he lives in, but only as that is a characteristic of a moral being. The man who admits no moral claims at all escapes nothing. He is simply despicable from the point of view of men who do. He too can be accused and brought to account for his failures. On the other hand, a man who accepts a moral commitment cannot weaken it at will. The attempt to circumscribe the moral environment is misled from the start, operating under the misapprehension that one is free from responsibility where unproved. Such a view permits retreat from commitment and isolation from moral conflict, precisely the elements of morality that brook no compromise. Insofar as a man is a moral agent, the responsibility rests upon him to treat everything morally, just as the rational commitment to empirical knowledge commits one to rational methods of investigation directed toward everything in the world, though not all at once, nor need one be only a scientist. The point is that to a scientist, nothing is intrinsically unintelligible. To a moral agent, nothing is outside his responsibilities. The inescapable call to moral confrontation is pervasive responsibility. The obligations which we have, though we cannot meet them, are the result of our pervasive responsibilities.

Perhaps it will be replied that so pervasive a sense of responsibility simply leaves no room for ordinary moral distinctions. If everyone is responsible, no one in particular is. If the fate of six million Jews in concentration camps during the Third Reich is everyone's responsibility, how then is it particularly the fault of the German leaders? Such a reply misses the point of separating condemnation (itself a moral action) from the ground of moral commitment. The former is an act within the moral life; the latter is a pervasive quality constitutive of it. In truth, if the concentration camps were horrible, each of us should have done all in his power to abolish them. The magnitude of that crime rests on the shoulders of everyone in the world, both in the actions they might have performed that would have prevented the atrocities, in the appalling fact that men could live with such events and even contribute to them indirectly without knowing of them or opposing them, and in the continual burden men bear afterward to make the world a place where such atrocities will never again occur. Ignorance is no excuse in a case like this, nor does it eliminate responsibility and even guilt. But pervasive responsibility does not entail punishment.

Pervasive responsibility may be viewed as an essential part of the order within which the moral judgment is made that a given person is guilty and should be punished. Within the moral life there is a permanent and unavoidable obligation to expand our knowledge and powers in the light of all events and prospects, for we may be held to account for any of them. But knowledge does not come automatically upon obligation, and our powers are limited. We differentiate between lack of knowledge as a function of the inability to read of a farmer many miles from any concentration camp, from the claim of the residents of the town Dachau that they did not "know what was going on," or the claim that fear paralyzed even the rational faculties of many Germans. Perhaps in the latter two cases, the Germans involved really didn't "know" of the crimes; they never consciously thought about them. But such a refusal to know marks nothing more than the rejection of their moral obligation to face what was happening around them. The actual circumstances in the life of a particular person constitute the background of the judgments we apply to him in holding him culpable, and condemning him for his actions. A man may be held responsible and even guilty for not knowing what he ought to have known.

We are all pervasively responsible for the killing of the Jews in Germany, as were the Jews themselves, for such events are of undeniable moral concern. They cannot be ignored, even after the fact. But such pervasive responsibilities in no way entail that all men are equally guilty, that all should be punished, nor even that none should. The latter claims are moral judgments without any basis at all, either in human actions or in the means we must use in generating moral consequences. Among the wide range of obligations facing a Chinese peasant during the Nazi reign, his ability to help the Jews, compared to the events he could effectively influence in his own country, is so slight that it would have been wrong (invalid) for him to try to do so. Yet it forms a part of the moral world in which he lives and against which he must make his choices. Men can almost wilfully blind themselves to evil in order not to feel the force of their moral duties toward it. Pervasive responsibility reflects the moral obligation we all bear to remain open to and knowledgeable about what surrounds us. German officers, judges, even the self-blinded citizens of Germany paid for their denials of responsibility dearly. They cannot plead the extenuation that other moral obligations took precedence, only that they succumbed to self-interest and convenience. This is their fundamental guilt. The only relief from pervasive responsibility is a conflicting responsibility; and the resolution of conflicts among responsibilities is the heart of moral judgment. But the abdication of all morality out of fear should not be confused with moral judgment. It is simply self-denial. The pervasive and inescapable character of pervasive responsibility provides the basis for the perpetual demand that we go against our fears and need for security in the name of morality.

Pervasive responsibility has one consequence which is somewhat unnerving, and which is revealed by Kafka and Dostoievski to an almost uncanny degree. That is the implication that where in Anglo-American law one is innocent until proven guilty, in morals one must always consider himself to have failed. Since we can never wholly avoid failure, even our excuses do not completely redeem us. Among our pervasive responsibilities, the question is not whether we are obligated to meet them, but how. Those we cannot meet we stand accused by. Responsibility cannot be escaped or put aside. It is a perpetual challenge, an unavoidable part of every moral situation. Every choice incurs risk, and even when valid is taken at the expense of other obligations and responsibilities. There is always some way in which I have failed, however validly I have made my decisions. I cannot affirm innocence; I can only plead justification for what I did in terms of some other obligation.

The source of the difference between legal and moral responsibility rests on the connection of failure with blame. In law, the judgment of guilt almost always entails punishment. This guilt demands far greater assurance than does the failure which stems from pervasive responsibility. In the latter case, failure is a fact of moral experience for everyone. It follows that punishment is often quite inappropriate. In *The Brothers Karamazov*, Dostoievski sets Dmitri's trial against the reader's almost-divine knowledge of what actually happened. Moreover, Dmitri has undergone a transformation through the confrontation with his failures that makes further punishment absurd—yet the State has no choice but to punish him. The burden of pervasive responsibility is an e: of moral consciousness. We may well demand that moral agen... ... this consciousness, and punish them if they do not. But often the mere consciousness of failure and of pervasive responsibility is enough. It does not follow that judging all Germans guilty for the crimes of Hitler obligates us to execute or imprison them. The mere acceptance of guilt may prove moral awareness to us. The acceptance of guilt, however, is necessary to signify that a fearful lapse in moral being took place. We ask men to accept their pervasive responsibilities for everything in order to arouse their sensibilities, and make them responsive to what surrounds them. The best will in the world cannot overcome blindness. Pervasive responsibility is the call to see what can and must be seen.

Complete Responsibility

The notion of pervasive and inescapable responsibility arises from the need to affirm the breadth of the moral commitment, the continual and permanent demand of our moral being that we view everything in the world to be potentially relevant to our moral concerns. We are pervasively responsible to our world, and bear it on our shoulders at every turn. It is the potential ground of all our failures. It does not follow from this that we are guilty of wrong actions when we choose to act upon only one of the many claims before us. The world cannot be confronted in detail at every turn, though whatever we fail to manage with may prove our failure. Here is the source of anguish. The need for choice among inescapable obligations is the fundamental moral imperative. The key to moral action rests in its resolution of conflict, not its adherence to rule or routine application of principle. A moral problem without conflict never broaches the problem of responsibility. What is right is straightforward and direct. But life is never simple; every choice, however straightforward, involves the rejection of some alternatives that might have been better. The notion of pervasive responsibility brings to awareness the perpetual confrontation within our moral lives.

The notion of pervasive responsibility is derived from the fundamental interrogative posture a moral agent bears toward the world he lives in, and the unavoidable obligation he has to *respond* to the questions that arise by *seeking* answers. Pervasive responsibility is the precondition of obtaining answers. It is the attitude of *being obliged to respond,* of standing before events interrogatively and accountably for the actions we undertake or omit. It is the condition of having events carry moral significance, which may call forth actions of significance in return. We are pervasively responsible as we are obligated to face the world morally, choosing and acting on our choices. Holding a man so responsible is nothing more than declaring him a moral agent, demanding from him the awareness and consciousness of what being moral entails—the need for choice at every moment, the perpetual reemergence of moral confrontation, the obligation to continually transcend what he has been.

However, there is another conception of responsibility, in which we go beyond the affirmation of a moral commitment of perpetual interrogation and response, to the awareness of the methods needed for the resolution of moral conflicts. We not only wish to *hold* a person responsible for what he does, but also wish to commend him for the responsibility he has shown. Praise is often given to men for being responsible for their deeds. This cannot involve a responsibility which is pervasive and inescapable. There is required a second notion of responsibility, according to which some men are responsible for what they do while others are not. I shall call this *personal* or *complete responsibility*.

Etymologically, "responsibility" may be thought of as meaning "answerability," and this may be understood not alone in the sense of being compelled to answer, nor even of seeking answers, but as *able to answer*. The method of ethics is an interrogative method. A moral agent, beset on all sides by demands, obligations, and questions as to what he will do, seeks answers in his actions. The difference between a responsible and irresponsible man is that the latter acts without thought or analysis, without any sense of questioning or answering. The former sees the fundamental questions present in all of his choices, and recognizes and affirms that he is called upon in his actions to find the most valid answer to them. He is able to answer the questions the world poses for him, insofar as he possesses valid methods of finding answers. Since questioning once begun never ceases, he must continually seek to resolve the problems of his existence by determining who and what he is, and what he is living for.

Also etymologically, "responsibility" may be associated with *responsiveness,* in the sense that a responsible man is alert to the world surrounding him, and sensitive to his own needs and ideals. An irresponsible man refuses to answer the questions posed to him by significant and rich events. He fails to respond where and as he should. In exactly the same sense, he fails to be responsive, fails to be alert to the demands of others upon him, even to his own deeply rooted needs and confused thoughts. A completely responsible man is one whose responsiveness to things and events is as great as is humanly possible, by virtue of his methodic powers. He is highly sensitive to others, for their needs and feelings are part of the situations in which he is responsible. As seldom as possible does he close off possibilities of response. Although he may choose to ignore others' needs, or at least take no overt action toward them, he is not blind to them. His responsiveness makes every action of his a significant choice. A choice made by a person who sensitively considers everything potentially relevant in the situations before him is a choice for which he is fully accountable (completely responsible). No common excuse such as "I didn't expect this to happen" is available to him. He should have looked into its possibility. His responsiveness is grounded in a sensitive knowledge of himself that provides the most secure ground possible for valid action. The personally responsible man methodically seeks to understand where he himself is at stake in the events that surround him, and how to respond to them to conserve himself.

This kind of responsiveness is not to be interpreted as mere activity subsequent to the presentation of a stimulus. We have no stimulus-response theory here, with responsiveness thought of as a complex response to simple stimuli. Given the method of ethics, the perpetual interrogation of the world entailed by pervasive responsibility, then complete responsibility is the responsiveness inherent in the capacity to find answers to the perpetual questioning—an alertness to anything that might have significant bearing on the making of valid decisions. "Responsiveness" here is the sensitivity to events and knowledge of what they entail for oneself and others such that validity in action is rendered most probable. A completely responsible person maximizes the likelihood of valid action by virtue of his control of the method he employs. Sensitivity and responsiveness are fundamental traits of such powers.

The conception of a moral agent as standing before the world in an interrogative posture—"What must I do?"—to which he must respond and find answers, leads to both conceptions of responsibility. What I have called "pervasive responsibility" is the condition not so much of being able to answer as standing in an interrogative stance, *ready* to answer, whether one knows the answers or possesses the tools to find them. A man is responsible here in attitude, in stance, if not actually in the methods he uses. The readiness is all. The method of ethics raises unavoidable questions—unavoidable, that is, to a moral agent. The entire world asks, "Can you save this child?" "Will you punish this man?"

Dmitri in *The Brothers Karamazov* undergoes a personal redemption when he ceases the pursuit of the satisfaction of his own needs, and realizes how he is part of the world, how he is responsible for what happens everywhere in it. When he accepts that responsibility—though he has no answers to give, nor means to employ to discover them—he becomes a different kind of person. He recognizes the importance of the questions, "Why is the babe starving?" "What can be done about it?" He becomes an active moral agent, who considers something more than his own willful desires. He sees that as a moral agent he stands before the world beset by questions that mean his very life. A man is pervasively responsible not so far as he has answers, but insofar as he is accountable for the struggle to find the answers that create what he will be from what he was.

If responsibility is the response to questions posed, however, then there is a natural sense of complete responsibility that comes to mind— the methodic ability to answer the questions posed, at least where answers exist. A man is personally responsible when his actions represent his methodic reply to the conditions of life as he confronts them. He has weighed himself before the world and its obligations, has responded to the depths of his being to them, and is willing and able to stand by his choices as they define what he has and will become in answer to them. To the extent that his actions are valid, what a man is and what he does come into unison here. He grasps who he is and how he is part of the world, and his deeds mark this validly. He stands by his deeds because they sum up what he is and what he will be. The world asks a moral agent, "What will you do?" A completely responsible man has maximized the prospects of his learning the answer.

A man is personally responsible for an action which is uniquely his, which cannot be laid to anyone else's responsibility in quite the same way. It differs markedly from the pervasive responsibility which is everyone's. Pervasive responsibility belongs equally to all men; complete responsibility varies, as we say that one man is "more (completely) responsible" than another. The concept of pervasive responsibility is logically prior to that of complete responsibility in that it provides the ground of holding a man bound by his moral commitments. But though pervasively responsible, men may sometimes not be blamed for what they do wrong. And even when they meet their pervasive responsibilities, we may refrain from praising them. A compulsive advice-giver may be thought to be so out of control as to be criticized for not being completely responsible for what he does, though he gives good advice most of the time. This is the sense Kant emphasizes concerning the man whose act is morally praiseworthy, but which is performed out of great personal need or inclination. A man who fights and dies bravely in a war in a suicidal attempt to prove himself may be pitied, however noble his valor, for his inability to act otherwise. That is, he was not completely responsible for his actions. Lord Jim may have saved himself; but he may also never have known just what he was doing.

The critical point, then, is the realization that we have two kinds of responsibility, related to moral obligation in an intimate way, but distinguishable from each other. Pervasive responsibility reflects the very foundation of moral thought—the world to which we are accountable, and to which we must modify our actions and even our very natures. There is a global obligation inherent in the very fibre of the moral attitude, expressed in the view that a man can never be released from his moral obligations, but can only be excused for his failures. The pressures of the world upon men and the inescapability of evil are reflected here. Pervasive responsibility reflects the implicit demand in every unnecessary suffering that it be prevented or eased, a demand with no particular time or place. However, it cannot be expected that men can persevere in continual moral torment. They must discover ways of judging among their pervasive responsibilities those which call for action and those which do not. Continual response to every evil leads to the elimination of none. Special powers and skills are needed to meet one's pervasive responsibilities effectively. We are committed by the notion of pervasive responsibility at least to the ideal notion of a man who can respond deeply and powerfully to the demands placed upon him, and take particular actions selected from the indefinite range of alternatives before him. Such an ideal is the notion of complete responsibility.

A man who is pervasively responsible for a crime may not be blamed for his actions if he lacks the capacity to act validly. To hold a man completely responsible, however, is to declare him in some sense a fullfledged moral agent who is without excuse. He may have reasons for having done what others disapprove of, and they must be weighed. Excuses concerning his weaknesses, background, physical incapacities, and the causal influences upon him are irrelevant. The question then becomes that of determining when a man may be thought to be such a full moral agent—*or*, of determining when no excuse except that of an alternative obligation may be considered legitimate.

There are various kinds of excuses that are given to relieve men of responsibility. A man may plead that he could not physically have prevented a man from drowning, for he had already drowned by the time the agent reached him. One major kind of excuse is that an agent is not responsible for an event when he could not have prevented it no matter how hard he tried—it was not within his physical powers to do so. A simple way to undercut this excuse, however, is to hold a man at least responsible for trying to the best of his ability. For example, suppose a man strolls along a pier and hears a cry for help. He notices a man drowning, figures the distance, and decides that the probability is .8 that he will not reach the man in time. Do we not hold such a man guilty for not making the effort? We might not if it was winter and the cold might well have killed them both, but where the risk to the agent is small—that is, where there are no major conflicting obligations—we demand that action be taken. Of course, we do not blame a man for not trying if we could be *sure* that nothing would help—but such certainty is extremely rare: moral rules of conduct function in an unassured world. It is no excuse to say that "Nothing I could do would have helped." The appropriate reply to this would be, "You couldn't have known that in advance, and even if you did you couldn't be sure." Knowledge can modify our responsibilities, and help us to decide among conflicting alternatives by giving us information as to which of them is most likely of success. But such information is not decisive. If I must choose between trying to save a drowning man where the probability of success is small, and getting home to supper and not inconveniencing my wife where the probability of success is very high, I ought to do the former. One must always try in cases of serious moral significance, whether or not he has a good chance of succeeding.

Moreover, even those cases in which we are helpless are not without moral force upon us. The danger inherent in the claim that we are not responsible for a given domain of events is that we will then ignore them as irrelevant to ourselves. Pervasive responsibility provides the ground of accountability, wherein we are called upon by events to chart our moral course among them. We may be able to influence some; we may be influenced by others; we may be led to try to influence some of the rest; but we may ignore none of them, for they all contribute to the world for and to which we are responsible. Not trying is often equivalent to denying.

Trying is not to be thought of as wishing. Standing on a river bank and wanting to save a drowning man is worth very little. Trying is relating means intelligently to ends where there are good grounds for supposing that the means that one employs are capable of accomplishing the goals in mind. A man who assumes that no means can succeed bears the burden of responsibility on his shoulders for proving that claim. Pervasive responsibility demands of him that he try unless he can show forcefully that he was able only to fail. No one can ever be sure of this, and we judge men according to a graduated scale of risk and gain. A man is held less blameworthy if he pleads physical inability in the case of a fire in which he might be hurt, than in a case merely of throwing a life-preserver to a drowning woman. A man who stands on the bank with a stop-watch counting off the seconds as the man goes down for the last time to prove that he couldn't have saved him if he had tried is the epitome of one kind of evil, and his excuse is scorned. Physical incapacity is not a complete excuse in and of itself, but a factor to consider in weighing the moral judgment under consideration. We accept the plea "I tried but couldn't succeed," but never "I did not try because I knew I couldn't succeed"—at least, not in important cases.

Trying is a genuine act, and where there is no way of trying, we accept the excuse. One can be unable even to try—as a man paralyzed from the neck down cannot try to prevent another from drowning except by calling out to attract others' attention. So also, the prevention of past crimes is impossible, and not demanded as such. Neither of these cases call for a serious judgment of complete responsibility, nor condemnation for failure. The force of pervasive responsibility is directed from such events toward others performed in their shadow. Where we cannot act, our pervasive responsibilities obligate us to learn, and to build our powers for the future.

But if we accept physical impossibility as an excuse in some cases, do we not undercut the whole basis of personal responsibility? Do the environmental and external factors constitutive of the human self give rise to the legitimate claim that no one is completely responsible for anything? Can we accept the plea that no criminal is ever completely responsible for his deeds, because they are always indirectly the result of events partly independent of him, and out of his control? In other words, can a man not always plead some excuse for his inability to try, such as cowardice, passivity, even lack of moral conviction?

In contrast to the commonly accepted view, I suggest that often such an excuse is legitimate for denying complete responsibility. Since it never eliminates pervasive responsibility, we may still judge the agent involved, and punish him if it is right to do so. A man who has in a fit of passion murdered his wife's lover may well be considered to have been so overcome by hatred and envy as to completely ignore his moral sentiments. Another man might not have been so overcome, perhaps because of stronger moral convictions or weaker passions. But the man in question may not have been able to help himself. Sometimes we say that such a man "was not in control of himself," but that expression implies too particular a view concerning the nature of self-control. It is sufficient merely to recognize that feelings can indeed be too powerful to resist. We cannot describe such a case as one where the agent "tried" to resist his feelings but couldn't. He simply didn't try, because he couldn't.

We can extend this kind of example almost indefinitely, so that almost every immoral act can be explained as the result of a pre-existent condition. Whatever a man does may then be thought to be a mechanical, habitual response to circumstances for which he is not responsible. Yet somewhat more clarification is required, for though a man may deny complete responsibility, he cannot claim to be a moral agent and escape from pervasive responsibility. Perhaps men do not wish to be moral agents. Unfortunately, that is somewhat irrelevant, since they either are and think themselves to be agents, or we demand, coerce, and educate them to be agents, and condemn them otherwise. There is no good moral reason why one must be a moral agent—but it is by definition wrong not to be one. The very foundation of normative terms includes the recognition that they may be applied indiscriminately and wholesale, entailing pervasive responsibility. The problem, however, is that if we *are* pervasively responsible, does this entail that we are completely responsible? Obviously not. The criminals mentioned above are pervasively responsible for their deeds and everything else as well. Within that context, we judge means and ends, and may well punish them for their crimes. But they may still not be completely responsible, for they are not full-fledged moral agents, but act on blind feelings and desires.

The question then arises whether men can ever be full moral agents, who can consider themselves and be considered by others completely responsible for what they do, for whom and by whom no excuse is possible, and by whom none would be given. In general, men are willing to be excused from their obligations unless they are heroes; and heroism is not common. Yet surely there is a state of being wherein men not only deny themselves the right to excuses, but are of such moral capacity to render it inappropriate for anyone else to make excuses for them. We often make excuses for others, even when we deny them the right to excuse themselves. We can say of the impassioned murderer that he lost his head, but we resent his appeal to the same excuse. It seems to me that a moral condition exists for men in which no excuses are legitimate. This state of being I have called "autonomy," and it is identical with complete responsibility.

A man is completely responsible for an action which may be considered properly "his"—if he possesses a genuine claim to it. Now, there are a number of different ways in which a claim to an action can be grounded. A man may claim an event to be his if his behavior is causally related to it. It is not clear if we wish to demand that his behavior be a sufficient condition for the event—causal necessity may be enough. But the question then arises whether every person whose behavior constitutes a necessary condition of an event is responsible for it. If so, we would be approaching a modified form of pervasive responsibility, without considering the possibility of withholding blame on the basis of some excuse. A man either is or is not a necessary factor in the occurrence of an evil event. Generally, almost everyone is, at least negatively; for there is almost always something one might have done to prevent the event from taking place. It would then be impossible to admit that a man contributed causally to an event and yet deny him responsibility; yet this is exactly what is entailed in our treatment of addicts, children, and the insane. Children in particular are considered a special case, regardless of the actions they perform.

Another possibility is that an act be thought to belong to whoever claims it, so that a confession is the perfect example of proof of guilt. However, not only are there compulsive confessors, but there are cases in which we deny that a man who has committed a crime and confessed to it is completely responsible for it—when he is not sufficiently aware of what his actions mean. It is possible to make a claim that must be denied, particularly with respect to actions—and even more particularly when the claim is to a praiseworthy action. If a mere claim will not suffice to gain praise, it will not suffice to promote censure.

The third sense in which an action properly belongs to an individual, rather than being but a consequence of various happenings, is when it is the result of a method. A mathematician may take credit for the discovery of a proof when he has utilized a method for reaching it, and may not if he employed no method at all—in which case we consider the discovery an accident, and without significance as to responsibility—or where the method he employs could not have led to the discovery. A well-defined method utilizes means to achieve ends, is reproducible, and is always employed by an agent. A claim to "know," "own," or "have committed," something is a claim that is based on a method of achievement. A man "owns" property if he has utilized a definite method of acquiring it, either by purchase, settling on it, receiving it in inheritance, or by force. It is his by virtue of the method utilized, and nothing else. If some of these methods are considered unacceptable by others, they may be repudiated, and the ownership repudiated as well.

An act belongs to a person by virtue of the method he employs in performing it. A cook may claim that a souffle is his and that he deserves credit for it because he made it in such and such a way. We laugh at the proprietor who may, in a moment of self-grandeur, claim that the souffle is *his* instead, for there is no way in which he can produce it at will. If, however, he can, through manipulation and cajoling, lead the chef to make it whenever the proprietor wishes, perhaps his claim is legitimate. What is important is the method utilized. When a demand is made to prove a claim, some method of proof must exist, though it need not be the method originally employed.

In ethics, methods are employed to accomplish valid acts. Unvalidatable actions are not methodic—or at least, they do not employ methods of test and criticism. There is no way here to test a claim of responsibility, and it is without significance. A man accidentally topples a lamp which burns down a house. If we are convinced of the accidental nature of the act, we declare it not his personal responsibility (though it was his pervasive responsibility). What we do in such a case is to deny the orderly relation of means to ends, thus the use of a method. On the other hand, even the faintest suspicion of a connection of means and ends would make us wonder about the presence of intent, and intent entails method. Mere wishing is not intending, which exists only within a context of methods for achieving ends. The pervasive responsibility all men bear for all their deeds bears on their general moral condition. But they can respond to this responsibility blindly and without method, in which case the results of what they do simply are not fully theirs, since they neither intended nor foresaw them.

Complete responsibility may be thought genuine only when we literally can find no excuse for relieving a man of that responsibility; and this can come to pass only when the agent's actions are under the aegis of methods which eliminate the possibility of any excuse. When the likely alternatives are weighed against others, when an indefinite range of consequences enter into every judgment, when the danger of submission to other intentions than defined by the method is reduced by careful and systematic analysis of oneself, we have autonomy and complete responsibility. A man dominated by hatred, who utilizes means to achieve terrible ends, may well be thought despicable but irresponsible, precisely because his choices are so dominated by his overpowering passions. He acts intentionally and methodically, but without the capacity to control the passions that set his orientation. Complete responsibility obtains when passions are viewed as but one of many competing factors, accommodated together in a coherent and self-critical method. This is precisely the state of autonomy. When ultimate goals are themselves not susceptible to critical analysis, they are outside the domain of intelligence at work. This is no more satisfactory or responsible a condition than insanity or physical coercion. When a rational method of critical self-examination and the analysis of circumstance is utilized, in which every feeling is weighed, every consequence noted, every value and principle considered, then the resultant is truly an achievement—and that is personal responsibility.

A completely responsible person is one who employs the method of moral judgment with great skill, rendering it most likely that his actions will be valid—though nothing could guarantee that. Certain very important properties of complete responsibility follow from this:

(1) In a very special sense of "rationality," a completely responsible person is eminently rational in a manner that is at once paradigmatic for all conceptions of rationality and offers the widest possible sense of the word. Narrower conceptions of rationality, such as that utilized by Hume in his famous attack on the rationality of causal inference, borrow methodic techniques from special domains of thought and apply them wholesale. In logic and mathematics, empirical considerations are either wholly irrelevant or at least have only a very indirect bearing on the structure and form of logical order. Nevertheless, a perfectly legitimate sense of "rationality" may also be found in the procedures and methods of the physical sciences, in which both logical rigor and empirical adequacy are taken into account. Both may be viewed as cases in which a valid action is called for, on the basis of the methods employed and procedures adopted. In mathematics, a theorem which follows from axioms under consideration is valid as enacted under the restrictions of the logical method employed. In physics, a law is set forth in its particular form on the basis of both logical and empirical constraints, as the best or most valid generalization possible under the circumstances. The writing and presentation of either law or theorem is an act undertaken by an agent as good, right, or valid under the special conditions of method and accepted goals.

While neither physicist nor mathematician may take everything into account in deciding whether a given law or theorem should be accepted, it is perfectly legitimate *from a moral standpoint* to ask them to do so. Although perfectly valid actions may be undertaken within relatively confined orders, there obtain quite naturally questions concerning the general validity of the same actions in other contexts or orders. The method of moral judgment utilizes an expanding and unrestricted order of judgment, wherein the entire world is potentially

implicated in a choice made and acted upon. The consideration of the
consequences of one's actions as well as their origins, the ways in which
action undertaken affects both others and the agent himself, the bringing together of the questions that arise, and the creation of a synthetic
response to them in the action undertaken, is probably the paradigm of
rationality. This is particularly true insofar as questions which arise of
the form, "What shall I do?" and "What will happen if I do it?" are
given defensible and valid answers. A completely responsible person
acts as he must in his responses to the world and its imperatives. As he
acts, he continually responds to his own needs and the consequences of
his actions upon himself and others. The unremitting interrogation and
reinterrogation of the world before which one stands, and the continual
answers found in the actions one seeks to make valid, are the paradigm
of rationality.

Too restricted a conception of rationality must be avoided. Logical
rigor is part of the method of ethics insofar as various possibilities of action are weighed against each other. But sheer logical order is not sufficient—thinking that it was led Kant to his most serious error. On the
other hand, empirical information alone provides no basis for valid action, which is rooted in the character, attitudes, and ideals of the agent
himself. It is the inescapable requirement that one *must* act, coupled
with the unceasing consideration of everything that might bear on the
decisions involved, that generates answers in actions undertaken on the
basis of evidence offered, yet which are never reducible to a straightforward and routine calculation. Here we have rationality as the grounding of action in the knowledge of traits of things, as well as in knowledge
of oneself as agent undertaking the action in question. An act for which
one is completely responsible is one grounded rationally and methodically in all the knowledge one can have of the world and its relation to
oneself.

(2) Self-knowledge is fundamental to personal responsibility. A man
who must deliberate upon and respond to the perpetual confrontation
of events before him must ultimately let his own most fundamental attitudes and ideals determine his actions. He may consider everything before him, but he must fashion from that consideration an action which
is the only legitimate or valid one possible for *him*. He manifests in such
an action his very being as he knows it to be, a being intrinsically bound
to an indefinite number of things that he must therefore take into account. By choosing in accordance with his realization of himself as
agent and the ideals he lives for, he creates from his past a new self
which is completely responsible for the actions it has chosen. The act is

a man's by virtue of the fact that it completes the being of the self-in-the-world which undertook it, in terms of that person's most fundamental conception of himself. A person maintaining consistency and integrity amidst temptations and corruption will act as he "must" to preserve himself, in line with what he wishes to be. A person struggling to generate a new self from ambivalence and personal disorder, may generate integrity by acting as he truly wants to in but a single instance. He wins a new being by acting validly, and generates the conviction that he is no longer at the mercy of the "worst part of himself."

Where causal determinants of personality, even those recognizable only as undiscerned patterns of response, "compel" certain kinds of behavior, then a person who does not know of them is at their mercy, and can never be completely responsible for what he does in response to them. He becomes completely responsible only by virtue of a knowledge of how he is disposed to act and be influenced that provides him with the tools for acting either in accordance with his disposition or in opposition to them. A completely responsible person may be held to account for what he does only when he knows himself sufficiently that no excuses of the form "he couldn't help himself" apply. He has sufficient knowledge of what is most fundamental to his own nature as to be able to do as he wants most basically to do. This knowledge is not merely *about* himself, but is also a skill of reconstituting himself. It is what I have called "autonomy."

(3) A completely responsible person not only knows himself and employs a rational method directed toward valid action, but is responsive enough to himself and his surroundings to render validity most likely. It is difficult to exaggerate this quality, for it is a luminous concern for others and a sensitivity to them and their needs that makes the responsible man's actions likely of success. The self-knowledgeable man may well fail in his actions if he is not sensitive to underlying currents in the behavior of others. However praiseworthy his intentions and goals, however deeply he knows his own ideals and needs, he will fail if he is not deeply responsive to the needs of others where he must act, insofar as those needs reflect on him and what he does. Not only must a responsible person know himself as he has been, but he must know how he is and will be at stake in his relations to others; he must be highly responsive to others as they affect him. This is most obvious in the case of parents who may be deeply concerned about their children, profoundly aware of their own shortcomings which they struggle to overcome, yet who fail to go beneath the surface of their children's rebellion to grasp what their deepest needs are. The degree of sensitivity involved in valid

action is enormous. It may well be that only men who have suffered from most kinds of torment are capable of genuine sensitivity to the sufferings of others. This is part of what Dostoievski tried to show in emphasizing that even Alyosha is a true Karamazov—i.e., a sensualist. Perhaps sensitivity and responsiveness to others come naturally with an assured knowledge of oneself and what can really harm one. That would have to be shown.

One of the difficulties inherent in moral analysis is that the principles of evaluation utilized by autonomous and responsible men may not lead to unanimity or agreement. It is possible to find that a completely responsible act is nevertheless one which someone else cannot condone. A man may choose to leave his wife and children to go off to a Pacific island and to develop his talents as an artist. He may become a Gauguin, but he may also fail. Another person, not so sympathetic to painting, and one who takes personal responsibilities very seriously, may condemn the first for his choice even when made with deliberation, care, and concern. One of the fundamental characteristics of moral decisions is that an autonomous act, which is the consequence of a rational and determinate method, may not be valid by the standards of another person who judges it, nor even by the agent himself at a later time. That a man is completely responsible for what he does, then, does not make him praiseworthy or virtuous in any other sense than that he has applied a method of evaluation, taken everything he could into account, and understood the risks he must take. The element of personal risk, however, increases with complete responsibility, since there are no available excuses left. If a man is completely responsible for what he does, but has chosen wrongly by the standards of others, then condemnation is demanded. Only in this way can words like "right" and "wrong" have any definite meaning. The application of a method, however interrogative or rational, is not sufficient to guarantee validity and eliminate totally the chance of failure. The results of what one does always leave one's own narrow domain of action to enter the larger framework of world events. This is the permanent source of anguish and despair.

What the method of moral judgment provides is autonomy and responsibility, in the sense that the agent evaluates the situations in which he finds himself in all their dimensions, and makes the best choices he can in terms of himself. He relinquishes the right to plead ignorance, overwhelming passion, or causal inefficacy, and takes upon himself the moral obligations of autonomy—that he must know of the consequences of his actions, that his passions are but a part of what he must consider in moral decision along with other present and expected feelings, and that he has adequately calculated means and ends so that what he can do has been weighed not only for its desirability, but for its possibility of success. In so doing, he risks the opprobrium of others, and their punishment as well—that is the consequence of accepting responsibility. But he at least can claim that the choice was his, and that he struggled with it. He may fail, but it will be a failure of responsible action, rather than the failure of escape or flight.

The method of moral judgment is rational, deliberate, and unending. The wise man, whose actions are a clear and unquestioned manifestation of his being, appears to avoid both the difficulty and the torment of complex decision making. Yet he does possess a definite method of making decisions, one compatible with his simplicity of soul. The contrary view is the result of construing the interrogation of method too linguistically or superficially. The professional golfer who plays in a tournament in a habitual and unthinking manner is by no means without an interrogative method. He may have so incorporated his questioning into his total game of golf that he can trust his body and its habits, at least throughout the tournament, without discursive control. So the wise man, though completely secure in his convictions, nevertheless may also be completely committed to the possibility of failure which he will avoid only by persevering in himself through trial and judgment, or by changing as he wills. The method at work here is a method of retaining assurance and the validity of one's actions by preserving oneself before the exigencies of circumstance. Because I am what I am, and accept myself completely, I am completely responsible for what I do. I cannot be relieved of responsibility under any conditions, for I know fully what I am and act as I must. A man who asks to be relieved of responsibility always views himself as divided. What he has done and what he is are not part of a unified order. The division within him makes him feel that he deserves to be excused. The other part of him, which fought his evil act, is the "true" part of him. The good man, however, who has fully come to terms with himself, and who accepts himself on the deepest and most visceral level, simply must be held personally responsible. He achieves the highest possible degree of responsiveness to the needs of others. He differs in this respect from the fanatic, who may have complete assurance in his decisions, but has lost the quality of responsiveness to others and follows a narrow and unresponsive pathway to destruction. Responsiveness and sensitivity to others are essential to valid action. That is because one's personal being is at stake in the judgments and actions of others.

Personal responsibility, when it achieves validity in action, is a form of unity of self. It can be a synthetic unity which is the outcome of a highly deliberate and self-conscious method of critical interrogation. But the development of certain habits of thought that bring with them a complete assurance and acceptance of oneself renders most stages of criticism implicit rather than explicit. An autonomous and responsible action brings into being a unity of self and deed that may not have hitherto existed. One way of achieving this is through discursive and explicit appraisal. Another is through a sense of self that renders explicit analysis unnecessary, provided it is accompanied by a deep and abiding sensitivity to other men and the character of the world in which one lives. Deliberation becomes implicit, in the pervasive sense of the possibility of failure which is never lost. Tests continue to bear upon the validity of actions; but they are passed successfully by maintaining oneself throughout the test as having done what one *had to do* in a sensitive awareness of the environing conditions. One "had to" here, not in terms of causal necessity, but in terms of other compulsions within one's being—namely, the autonomous revelation of oneself before the world that is methodic and intentional in its ability to maintain validity. The wise man realizes both the possibility and the risks of failure. But he avoids it through a prevailing acceptance of himself, and through a profound responsiveness to others. He has done all that he can do, and he knows it. Could anything more be asked of him? Most men who ask this doubt themselves. The wise man does not because he knows who and what he is, and maintains his integrity throughout everything he does.

Condemnation

A major dimension of moral censure will be rather neglected in the present essay—that involved in the meaning of and basis for judgments of the form, "that is wrong." The analysis of all that is involved in the making of moral judgments, affirmative or negative, would render this essay cumbersome and diffuse. Nevertheless, it is important to consider at least one aspect of such an analysis in order to grasp the nature of condemnation, particularly as this relates to responsibility. Whatever else may be involved, whether or not the responsibility and freedom of an agent are of great significance, condemnation is not a passive characteristic of an event, but is itself an act, with its own moral characteristics. The act of taking money from a counter is not in itself "wrong" or "right." It is, like a stone rolling downhill, merely an event, in this case interesting only because it is an act of a human being, and judged by another. Hume compares the destruction of seedlings by the shadow cast by the parent tree to filicide, to demonstrate that the mere event is not in itself of moral concern. Censure does not accrue to events or human actions merely by virtue of their occurrence, but resides in the subsequent judgments and actions they promote. Hume oversimplified the issues involved by conceiving of moral judgments in too simple and immediate terms; they are considerably more complex and ramified than he realized. But the basic fact is that condemnation and praise are themselves actions, to be analyzed in terms of everything relevant to the making of judgments as moral actions, not merely as qualities "in" objects apart from everything else. Perhaps a comparison with other properties might be useful, for colors do not belong to things independent of other things, like properties of light, vibration, or the spectrum. And human actions are censurable or wrong only in the context of the moral judgment of condemnation.

Various consequences of this recognition follow that are quite important. For one thing, the view that a particular act can be judged wrong on the basis of limited information becomes impossible to maintain. Too often the position is taken toward punishment that it is a direct consequence of an immoral act; the punishment is entailed by the transgression; the punishing agent acts virtually automatically in his response to the wrongdoing. It is the act of theft alone that entails the incarceration of a thief for a number of years, and the act of murder alone that entails the execution of the murderer. The doctrine, "an eye for an eye and a tooth for a tooth" embodies within it a dogmatic and virtually unethical (if not immoral) attitude toward punishment and revenge, based solely on actions long past.

The fact is, however, that some person must be agent for the judgment, even according to the strictest rules of vengeance, and he cannot escape the responsibility for his own actions that being an agent carries with it. A country which enforces capital punishment cannot take refuge from criticism in the plea that the punishment fits the crime. The original crime is only one of the many factors a judging agent must consider, including consequences and ultimate goals. Nothing automatically relates an act and its condemnation. The condemnation is itself another act, and must be judged by its place in the scheme of things, including its consequences for the agent. Under the most straightforward and automatic system of punishment, the punishing agency is, as its name indicates, *agent* enacting deeds for which it is responsible.

Even the man who has committed the original act cannot hold that act itself to be "wrong" in some sense independent of consequences, other events, and above all the act of condemnation in which he finds it wrong. The agent is *found* guilty. He is not guilty until the further judgment of condemnation is made by an external agency or by the agent himself. The point is that we cannot escape the *judgmental* character of guilt. The responsibility for the condemnation rests somewhere, and may itself be wrong. That is the basis on which we hold that neurotics should not feel guilty when and where they do—their own acts of self-condemnation are invalid. It is also revealed in courts of law where either the judge or the jury must reach a decision concerning the defendant's guilt. That guilt is never a property of his actions—it is dependent on the act of judgment itself.

Moral statements are primarily *acts* of utterance, rather than propositional in character. It is quite true that moral statements are meaningful, and express something—perhaps a proposition, though not a verifiable one. But as *moral,* they are themselves acts, utterances to be sure, sometimes of censure or punishment, and are open to the same modes of judgment applicable to all acts. The statement, "you did wrong" is never merely a description of a property of an isolated event, but is itself an act which calls for further judgment from the parties involved. The claim "that was a cruel thing to do, but I'll forgive you" is, therefore, never as innocent as it sounds, for it embodies an act of judgment which is condemnatory. The statement "I forgive you" implies that the excuses given are sufficient, or that condemnation is not called for by the act in question; but the utterance as a whole denies it. The self-righteousness inherent in such statements marks them for the specious acts they are.

It follows, then, that if there is such a thing as innocence, it can be validly responded to only by the complete withholding of censuring actions and utterances, rather than by giving excuses. More particularly, if we accept excuses based on physical or mental impossibility, we must avoid utterances of any form that suggest even weak condemnation. Where we censure a man for his actions, even indicating that we accept his excuses, we are in fact somewhat condemning him. If each of us is pervasively responsible for everything, then we can be judged to be completely innocent (though still responsible) only by abstention from all condemnatory response. Statements of the form, "you ought not to have done what you did, but under the circumstances we will excuse you," given in cases of extremity, are not judgments of innocence. They are mild forms of condemnation. Only silence is without a small degree of censure or praise.

The point I am making is that although the force of pervasive responsibility cannot be evaded, the silence that must follow the decision to avoid moral confrontations which will have only undesirable consequences suggests that it can. I choose not to send all that I own to Iran, despite my awareness of the poverty there, for I hold that my own interests are of moral significance also. All my friends may approve of my decision, and avoid any mention at all of my distant and weak obligations. But it does not follow that such obligations do not exist. They are, however, inexpressible without being utterances of some degree of censure, and that is precisely what my friends wish to avoid. It may appear that pervasive responsibility does not hold under those circumstances where negative judgments are inappropriate; but this is an error, based on a miscalculation of how condemnation is a public act with moral characteristics.

Like all purposeful actions, utterances of censure have consequences, and when intentional and directed are the employment of means for the accomplishing of definite ends. Since nothing is wrong in and of itself, but only wrong in a context of moral judgment and action by some definite person, all the many consequences of such actions become part of the condemnatory judgment, rather than of the original act alone. Every judgment of an act as wrong must be viewed in its full range of consequences and goals if it too is to be judged as valid. We cannot pretend that in the consideration of another's act, we are free from moral scrutiny or not responsible for what we do. Personal judgments of condemnation include the implicit judgment that *all in all* some condemnation and perhaps punishment is desirable. If a man has stolen money, but made full restitution, and if to punish him openly is to harm his wife and children more than can be justified, then it would be wrong to condemn him in a way that would make it known that he is a thief. Private censure may well be sufficient condemnation to punish him as strenuously as can be justified. If it is felt that in such a case the innocent people affected should go unharmed, then even subtle and implicit innuendos of public condemnation must be avoided.

An act of condemnation, precisely because it is an act and not the discovery of an antecedent property of an event, exists amidst complex situations of judgment, like all actions. It is notable, however, in that it is the predominant means, with its counterpart of praise, for developing moral ideals in men—and I speak here in both the psychological sense of conditioning and training and in the logical sense that moral invalidity resides wholly within condemnation, whether the agent's or someone else's. With respect to the former, the educational effects of moral judgments are vital consequences of their utterance, and when we seek justification for severe condemnation we must consider the effects of our actions on the men we judge as well as on others. Spoken condemnation is a powerful means of persuasion in the moral realm. The thief above, if left totally unpunished, may not understand that he has done something wrong. Often it is only by the overt expression of disapproval that moral principles can effectively be made part of an individual's basis for judgment. At least part of the moral environment within which we come to grasp moral laws is the repugnance of others. An act of condemnation, then, must be considered in its capacity as education, and must be weighed in this regard against the other considerations that are relevant to it. A wide range of judgments is always possible. That which is valid is such by virtue of its place amidst all the alternatives.

Setting the educational effects of condemnation aside, however, it is nevertheless apparent that the judgment "that is wrong" derives its meaning from contexts of moral judgment, and that the making of moral judgments entails either praise, censure, or abstention from judgment. Abstention from judgment is itself a moral act, and must also be considered in the wide range of its moral consequences. It is true that men often compete and differ in their moral judgments. But they far more often abstain from any moral involvement whatsoever, preferring to tend their own gardens rather than to beat their heads against stone walls. However, patience and fortitude can be disgracefully wrong, particularly when they mark the refusal to condemn others when condemnation is called for. The whole doctrine of pervasive responsibility can be undermined and nullified if condemnation is withheld whenever some degree of remoteness obtains. There is at least this basis for general moral principles which condemn passivity, self-interest, and cruelty without qualification. As moral beings, we are obligated without limit for the alleviation of suffering and the fostering of goodness and strength. We may refrain from some actions insofar as they conflict with others. And when we do this, it is inappropriate and even wrong to condemn us. But if we extend this principle of withholding censure in all cases which are remote, or cases of abnormal difficulty, only the most obvious cases of moral condemnation remain. It is not that distant evil ought not be opposed, but that our powers are more effective at home.

If none of our actions is directed toward the moral improvement of life, the claim that it is sometimes permissible to passively withdraw from involvement has no meaning.

The omnipresence of failure amidst our pervasive responsibilities continually raises questions of condemnation which themselves cannot be ignored, particularly when men are reluctant toward their obligations, and weak in their hearts. Sometimes men are self-righteous and uncharitable, and condemn others far too easily. Sometimes they are passive and unconcerned, and require the overt condemnation of others to call them to their pervasive responsibilities. Condemnation itself never follows automatically upon failure, but is an open and risky act like all others.

Punishment

All acts of condemnation are some form of punishment, whether overt acts of physical constraint and cruelty or merely the utterance of censure. The few men to whom mere criticism means nothing directly are still subject to social disapproval if not restraint. (And there are very few such men, for we are concerned about social appraisal—Hume was quite correct that morality rests at least partly on the fact that others often mean quite as much to us as we ourselves.) The crucial question becomes: when is punishment justified, and under what conditions? I have already suggested that the answer to this question can serve as the basis for a solution to the problem of moral responsibility.

It is important to realize that the problem of moral responsibility as it is usually understood is not the theoretical problem of whether men can or cannot be held responsible in some abstract and obscure sense for what they do, but is the very practical and moral problem of whether punishment is ever justifiable, and on what grounds. The completely responsible man who has committed a misdeed is punishable where the child or idiot is not, seemingly because his responsibility for his action renders retribution appropriate. However, why may not every man, when brought before the tribunal of justice, plead the excuse of empirical necessity? I suggest that the only legitimate answer to this question is the obvious one that there are some cases where punishment is right and others when it is wrong, and that some actions deserve punishment regardless of the pleas of the agent that he could not help himself. If we emphasize the fact that our moral judgments commit us to (and indeed, often are) some form of punishment, and that deeming a man "not responsible for his crime" frees him from most forms of the punishment that usually accompanies recognition of that crime, then we may turn from the context of responsibility to that of moral judgments which require punishment.

We must also consider the sense of moral responsibility as a positive virtue, in contexts where praise and not condemnation is likely. Just as the commission of an immoral act is not always sufficient to justify condemnation, so the performance of a worthwhile act does not always entail praise. In particular, praise seems in Kant's eyes to depend solely on the motive for the action. Worthy acts done for selfish purposes do not merit our moral praise of the agent, though they may be judged worthy on their own. In the analysis of this essay, moral responsibility as a positive characteristic of an action and of an agent depends on the *method* employed in reaching the act in question, not alone on the quality of the act or the feelings, rules, or goals of the agent. That is, since it is impossible to follow a synthetic *a priori* law for its own sake, respect for moral law for its own sake can be manifested only in a method devoted to achieving valid judgments in moral action. A man who commits a worthy deed from force of habit, for selfish reasons or mere caprice, merits no particular approval. But if his deed is the result of careful and deliberate consideration of the consequences, the weighing of alternatives, knowledge of himself and his deepest needs and desires, then we may heartily endorse the method he employs as being so complete and reflective as to free him from the bondage of any particular set of prejudices and unwarranted passions. This method warrants (or validates) the relevant feelings and desires, and that is all that can be expected of a method for making moral decisions. A man who is in this sense completely responsible for his deeds merits praise and gratitude. He is fully and completely a moral agent, endowed with feelings and desires like all men, but nevertheless in possession of and committed to a method of judgment whereby his sentiments are placed in their proper relationship to his principles and duties. What this proper relationship is, of course, is precisely what each moral judgment is an attempt to determine. But only when the method of considered judgment and rational analysis is employed can we actually speak of the determination of that relationship.

Although it would seem that moral praise and blame are essentially symmetric—that is, that a censurable act is one which is wrong and committed by a responsible agent, while a praiseworthy act is one which is right and committed by a responsible agent, responsibility being the same in both cases—I proffer the claim that they are not. The hope that they are has led to much of the confusion that surrounds the analysis of moral responsibility. Complete responsibility is the characteristic that entitles us to praise an agent for his virtuous actions. Without complete responsibility he is but flotsam and jetsam on the sea of moral decision. But it does not follow that a completely responsible act which is judged wrong or invalid is thereby rendered particularly *punishable*. In fact, we may decide that a man who chose with sensitive awareness of consequences—who made careful judgments on the basis of what he knew, thought, and expected to come to pass, but who erred nevertheless in his realization of what the future would bring—should not be punished as well. He came to know the errors he made by himself. He did make mistakes; but his commitment to the moral life may be so complete as to make his failure punishment enough. When a man is punished for a misdeed, it may well not be because of his method of decision, his *complete responsibility*, but on some other basis. On the other hand, a controversial act undertaken by a completely responsible agent, with which we are in strong disagreement, may obligate us to punish him severely. Such judgments can only be made upon the consideration of the function and purpose of punishment.

As I have already indicated, moral condemnation serves two major functions: that of education and persuasion, in which social pressures are brought to bear to induce a person to follow generally accepted moral principles; and that of expression of the moral attitude itself—for without condemnation it makes no sense to speak of something being wrong. The latter point is of such fundamental importance that I shall return to it. But first let me consider the educative function of punishment which has at times been taken to provide a solution to the problems of moral responsibility.

When we punish a man, we do so in order to educate him toward being a better member of society. Whatever the motives and circumstances of a crime, we punish the criminal when there is reason to suppose that such punishment will change him for the better. The problem of responsibility does not arise, nor does that of indeterminism, since the methods employed in reeducation must themselves be causally related to the behavior of the agent. The only questions we need consider are whether the deed before us is right or wrong; and if wrong, what we can do that will most effectively render repetition of that misdeed unlikely. To say that a man is morally responsible is to say nothing more than that he deserves punishment because he can be changed for the better.

This educational or rehabilitational view of punishment and moral responsibility is a very powerful one, because it reflects fully half of what punishment may be expected to accomplish, and also because it is a much more enlightened view of punishment. In exactly the same sense, Plato points out that punishment is never intended to harm the person punished, but to improve him. Otherwise it is unjust. Modern practices of penology fail when they corrupt and injure prisoners. The enlightened viewpoint that punishment is never intended to be retributive, but is always educational, in its own way expresses a part of the solution to the problem of moral responsibility: we never seek to harm a man, but condemn his actions and educate him to avoid such actions in the future.

However, the enlightenment of this view may well be its major limitation, since it is doubtful whether most men would agree that the *sole* purpose of punishment is rehabilitation. The kinds of penal methods which men have utilized throughout history suggest a far more vicious sense of the relationship between culpability and punishment than the rehabilitational view is capable of portraying. Though I share the sensibilities of the latter view, it seems to me that there undeniably exists a further role for punishment, found in the Biblical doctrine of an eye for an eye, in all forms of capital punishment, and in all retributive views of punishment. The question is whether retribution can in fact be justified—which is but another way of stating the problem of moral responsibility.

I suggest that the solution to this problem may be found in considering punishment as the sole means for expressing the moral attitude of censure. It is not that "stealing is wrong" *means* nothing but "You will be punished if you steal." That is far too simple-minded a moral view. But a statement of censure must be related to contexts of punishment if it means anything at all.

A man who lacks moral attitudes or principles can come to grasp their nature only on the level of genuine confrontation, which is essentially linked with punishment. If awareness of a transgression is not accompanied by genuine regret, then the nature of the transgression as such is not understood by the agent. The fostering of remorse is without question the most important goal of punishment. A genuine moral confrontation demands some degree of condemnation or praise, and where condemnation is ineffective other forms of punishment must be at least implicit as possibilities, if there is to be a moral confrontation at all. That is why Antigone had to die, and Creon's life had to be ruined. Mere talk without genuine and critical consequences is not moral. An

immoral act which no one is willing to repay or condemn is tacitly condoned, for moral confrontation takes place on the active level. Although
it may be wrong to punish a man for a wrongdoing, not to punish or
condemn him at all is an acquiescence in his deed. For this reason guilt
and remorse are not easily to be dispelled from moral life. Moreover,
the engendering of guilt is one of the most powerful instruments for the
creation and enforcement of moral attitudes.

In demanding that moral judgment be accompanied by condemnation or praise, it by no means follows that harsh or cruel punishments
are the best, either in educational effect or in moral expressiveness. The
crimes of Adolph Eichmann were so great as to surpass any method of
punishment that could be employed. He might well, then, have been allowed to live after conviction, as proof of his having transcended ordinary moral judgment. That would by no means have been without its
expressive effect. On the other hand, in the face of his continual protes-
tations of innocence, a means had to be found for expressing the moral
view that he was horribly guilty.

Like the educative, the expressive function of punishment is but another side of the obvious and well-known fact of morality that one's
moral judgments are active, not simply mental or passive observations
about things. The thoughts "That was wrong," and "You should do
that," are without moral significance if they do not commit the speaker
to action on the basis of them. Sometimes that action may be no more
than the open and public utterance of condemnation—that is often
punishment enough. Sometimes, however, further forms of punishment
are required. Without any punishment, moral conflicts cease to have
meaning. If both parties are eminently tolerant and gentle, their moral
convictions are without effect. If a moral agent seeks to make a valid
judgment in the context of a tolerance that is so great that, regardless of
his decision he will never be punished, the only place left for him to find
the possibility of failure is within his own self-regard. And although this
is very important, it is seldom of sufficiently definite structure to exhibit
within it true moral conflict. A moral man will consider the consequences of his actions, and recognize through his anguish and possible
guilt the problem of valid moral choice. But a large portion of the influences surrounding him and constituting his choices will be eliminated if everyone refrains from punishment and censure. Why then
should he care? Moral conflicts are always confrontations of different
views on an active level. Without concern or active response, there can
be no conflict, and nothing really matters.

The expressive and educative functions of punishment, although relatively distinct, nevertheless almost always implicate each other in practice. In effect, the educative function of punishment is predominant when the agent may be changed by the punishment and may be brought to a better understanding of moral obligations. The expressive function of punishment, however, emphasizes the punishing agent's own view of morality, and is an active form whereby he expresses his moral convictions toward the actions of others. It should be noted, however, that the expression of moral outrage may serve an educational function both for a person condemned, and for other people who are made conscious of this moral outrage as well. It would not be misleading, then, to say that the expression of moral attitudes is fundamental in punishment, but that among the consequences which must be considered in determining how such outrage should be expressed are the educative results both for the agent being condemned and for all other men as well.

The dual function of punishment, when it is recognized to be necessary to the very nature of moral decision, creates a very complex situation for a moral agent. In every case he must weigh both the educational and the expressive functions of punishment against each other, as well as his own moral ideals concerning cruel treatment of his fellow man. The expressive function of condemnation is not alone sufficient to justify severe punishment. Punishment can be judged valid only in a balanced and organized consideration of the various elements constituting the moral situation. When it is clear that a man feels definitely remorseful and contrite, and recognizes the invalidity of his own actions, it may well be unnecessary to punish him further. Mere verbal condemnation may be sufficient, and perhaps even extreme. On the other hand, when a man denies guilt, either overtly or in action, perhaps the educational function becomes predominant, and once again the expressive function of punishment is minimized. In both cases, retribution may well be thought to be minimized by the overall considerations the judging agent brings to bear on his own actions. In fact, the entire notion of retribution seems abhorrent to a rational morality wherein the consequences of moral action are considered vitally important. Going back to the original act seems irrelevant and without justification. We are more concerned with general consequences and results of principled actions.

But it does not follow even from such enlightenment that all punishment is educational. Some degree of overt censure, of punishing import, is essential in order that there be any morality at all. Nothing would rehabilitate Eichmann; yet some punishment was needed. In the case of the typical German after World War II, punishment in the sense of jailing or execution seems inappropriate, both in terms of the numbers of people involved and the magnitude of the crimes. Yet to leave Germany without punishment of any sort was to condone her deeds, tacitly if not overtly. Crimes of the horror of the Nazis demand remorse and atonement, if not permanent suffering. Where some Germans admit guilt and horror, that may be punishment enough. But where many admit only to Hitler's error in losing the war, no degree of condemnation can be sufficient. The question of responsibility does not arise here. The scorn and censure represent and express our general moral attitudes independent of degrees of responsibility. The judges who violated their principles to save the German state chose dangerous and risky actions. When these failed, bringing horrible atrocities rather than progress, mere censure was not enough. The greater the moral risk, the easier it is to succumb to some kind of rational temptation, then the more necessary is open punishment.

Where in this view of the central role of punishment in moral action is there room for excuses? Can a man ever plead innocence or lack of responsibility? The answer to the first question is "everywhere"; and to the second, "yes." Since punishment marks both educational and expressive elements in moral judgments, many excuses can be found for mitigating and eliminating punishment. The incredible complexity of moral judgments concerning punishment leaves room for excuses everywhere. The sanity, age, condition, and history of the agent before us may be of vital importance. If he cannot understand moral censure, even the point of physical punishment, then these serve no expressive or educational purposes for him, though they may for others. In the context of society as a whole, we may punish as an expression of our moral point of view for others to understand. But here too we must be very clear as to what we are doing, and be capable of justifying the punishment of one man for the good of others. Where such deterrence is weak or ineffective, or even where the threat of such severe punishment weakens the morale of the majority of men, it cannot be defended. Mercy is always possible and worthy if overt censure has been definite and clear. The cases where punishment as an expressive act is without mitigation are bound to be rare and infrequent.

The plea that everyone is innocent insofar as he causally couldn't help himself comes to naught where the total context of the punishing situation is concerned. Simply in order to support and strengthen general moral attitudes, the censure and condemnation of men who submit too easily to temptation is necessary. Though we may agree that causal

factors played a special role in a given person's life, if direct recognition
of such factors weakens moral stamina and will, we may well be unjustified in openly affirming them. On the other hand, arbitrary and capricious punishment, harsh and cruel measures, cease to be of significant value where we take into account the definite causal antecedents
in an individual's life.

There remains to consider only the notion of complete responsibility
in the context of punishment. If a man with complete responsibility
commits an immoral act, has he lost what I have called the "right to excuse himself"? The answer, it seems to me, is a clear "yes": but it does
not follow from this that he must necessarily be punished overtly. The
expressive function of punishment may not always require overt forms.
In the case of a completely responsible person, the very fact of his complete responsibility and his acceptance of his own moral failure may
well be considered far more than enough to justify not imposing external sanctions on him.

It would seem, then, that from the point of view of a censuring agent,
complete responsibility makes no difference in principle, and small
difference in fact. In terms of gross qualifications and distinctions, such
as that between severe punishment and the total absence of overt condemnation, this is a legitimate conclusion. But there are many important facets of complete responsibility that must be considered with regard to the question of punishment. For one thing, neither the agent
nor the judge can "excuse" the agent by the expression, "he could not
help himself." Whether or not the act in question was causally determined (and in some sense, it almost certainly was), the autonomous activity involved in examining and evaluating the act removes it from the
sphere of mere causation, and makes it appropriate to judge it on moral
grounds alone. Only the intent and procedures of analysis that determine validity are important—and, of course, the judgment that marks
the determination of that validity. A completely responsible man rests
on his deeds completely as testimony of himself and his decisions. He is
completely responsible by virtue of the methods he adopts, which render causal analysis meaningless; nothing need be considered in defense
of his behavior but the validity of his actions. A completely responsible
man stands on the validity of his actions independent of their history,
by virtue of the methods that he brings to bear upon them. Neither his
own needs, dispositions, nor desires are omitted from consideration. No
consequence is too remote to be thought irrelevant. With such a
method, no possibility exists of excusing a man for invalid actions.
Moreover, the method itself merits our praise and respect, as does a

man who employs it, since it reflects a moral agent acting to the limits of his rational and moral capacities.

The heteronomous man, who lacks complete responsibility either by virtue of a refusal to constantly criticise and confront all aspects of the situations in which he finds himself, or because he fails to understand his hidden desires and habits and succumbs to temptations inadvertently, is and may be excused precisely because of his ignorance. In the first case, we may want to know why he is ignorant of appropriate methods of deliberation, and accept an explanation of his impoverished childhood as sufficient. This does not eliminate all possibility of punishment, especially educative punishment, but it certainly weakens the force of moral contempt. A mentally defective person may be the agent of a particularly vicious crime, yet with a sense of horror at his deed, we may excuse him on causal grounds. It does not follow that censure is wrong, only that we must separate the man from his crime. He committed it, but in one important sense it was not "his," for he could not employ the methods that would make it so. In the second case, the capitulation of men to feelings that are unconscious and little within their control—perhaps a violent anxiety with its accompaniment of desperation—is also an important excuse: without adequate self-knowledge, which can free them from blindness, men act in uncontrolled ways. Such actions also do not fully belong to the agent, for he "could not" avoid them deliberately. Punishment, however, may be quite valid, at least for the development of stronger moral feelings to overcome blind urges, and perhaps to create an impulse toward self-knowledge in the agent. Expressive punishment also can play a role here, in that the necessity for self-knowledge can be made clear only where failure is felt so strongly as to demand adequate control of unknown feelings.

In one sense, educational punishment is inappropriate in cases of complete responsibility, for the completely responsible man has affirmed his decision to be valid for him. Wrong or right, it is his decision. If right, especially concerning the judgments of other men, he is willing to defend what he has done. The personally responsible man declares himself to have acted validly as he had to in terms of himself and his sense of what is morally right. If he errs—and failure is always a risk, even, and more poignantly, for a completely responsible man—he will come to know it through subsequent events and through the actions of others. Facts always escape us, especially concerning long-range consequences and the emotions of other people. A completely responsible man may come to a sense of his own failure—and, of course, the need to change in some important respects because of it: to learn more about the world, to be more circumspect in his judgments, to be more sensitive to others. Educational punishment, understood as manipulative in the sense of controlling impulses and reactions, has no place here. The rationality of the methods employed by a completely responsible man makes only persuasion justifiable. Among completely responsible man, who would inhabit a rational kingdom of ends, the disrespectful coercion of educational punishment is inappropriate. If information is lacking, it can be provided as among equals in rational capacity. Of course, complete responsibility is in this sense only an ideal.

However, precisely because the rational capacities of a completely responsible man are so admirable, and controlled manipulation by others inappropriate, expressive punishment becomes far more important. The convictions of others are no proof of a man's failure, but their attitudes and willingness to condemn his actions are essential to the validity of his decisions. If no punishment followed a critical decision, only guilt would remain as the determinant of failure. This may simply not be adequate in the case of complete responsibility, for here the agent has minimized as far as possible the likelihood of failure in terms of his own convictions and feelings. Unless the social constituents of moral judgments are made manifest, it may not be possible to take them sufficiently into account in seeking validity in action, and the needs and concerns of other men may be ignored. The desires and values of others, insofar as they genuinely care, are necessary to an individual's sense of right and wrong. Without the reactions of others, my willingness to sacrifice myself becomes gratuitous, my willingness to sacrifice others indifferently unimportant. The very blood of moral decision, its despair and anguish, stem from our inability to isolate ourselves from the judgments of others. However we try to do the right thing, we may fail, particularly in the eyes of other men. Because men differ in significant respects, their concrete decisions based on universal principles will differ at times, when interpretations of general principles in the light of their personal characters differ in significant respects. Expressive punishment provides the only condition whereby differences among men may be channeled into universal principles. In this sense, expressive punishment has educational dimensions. Those failures which stem from insensitivity to others can be realized only through the reactions of others —entailing in many instances overt punishment. The tests of moral fortitude and validity rest on the willingness of men to submit to condemnation and judgment, or otherwise to conform and compromise. Without genuine prospects of punishment, the major dimension of tests of validity would fall into nothingness.

Three possible outcomes can be envisaged for the actions of a completely responsible man: (a) His actions may be valid, for himself and for others. The method of judgment he employs maximizes the prospects for such validity, especially to the extent that he is sensitive to the reactions of other people. Unqualified praise is warranted here. (b) His actions are invalid, as he comes to understand clearly his own failures. We must suppose such a man to take his failures very seriously. That is what the method he is employing entails. Neither form of punishment seems justified here—though overt condemnation might be. In an ideal sense, the completely responsible man can learn from his failures as much as others can teach him, provided they express their otherwise hidden reactions. (c) His actions are valid in his own terms, though others find them reprehensible, even other completely responsible men. Such an outcome is the result of the unavoidable differences among men, the possibility that there are genuine emotional differences and convictions. The method of moral judgment may in part reduce the likelihood of moral confrontation, since the differing views of others are presumably taken into account. But where differences are not eliminable, they become exacerbated to an extreme.

In this last case, after others have indicated their revulsion, which if accepted by the agent as a sign of failure would reduce to outcome (b), there remains only expressive punishment—and it remains here not as a possibility, but as a necessity. We may respect and praise the rationality and sensitivity of a completely responsible man, but having found him adamant, we can express our own moral convictions only by severe punishment. Moral conflicts are unavoidable in human life, even among responsible men, and their differences cannot be tolerated where the concerns are vital. Men who make unjust war, however honorable their motives, deserve our most drastic punishments if they never come to see their errors, and we are sure of them. If we tolerate their actions as well-meaning, we tolerate that blind honor which can bring about destruction without justification. If we would express our moral convictions so strongly as to bring about conformity to them in the future, so that all men would know the strength of our revulsion, we must punish wrongdoing, even where we respect the agent who performed it. A completely responsible man who denies failure when others are convinced of it is therefore *the kind of man who does that sort of thing.* If we cannot tolerate that kind of action, we can only react strongly to it. And if we are completely responsible ourselves, we may feel secure in our stringent punishments—though such security is never without its great risks.

In this sense, the completely responsible man cannot but respect punishment, as Antigone goes proudly to her death, and Oedipus seeks the truth at any price. We may almost say that the test of moral character rests in the prospective punishment that failure entails, and that without this test there can be no moral strength. If we all agreed on moral ideals, and could be sure of them, then expressive punishment would have no meaning. But given the differences among men, and the variety of moral convictions, only through genuine confrontation—that is, open and passionate moral action—can the test of moral principles be found. Unless men are willing to suffer for their moral beliefs, they cannot be said to have any. If we respect a man for his moral responsibility and the strength of his convictions, and respect ourselves as well, then we must be willing to judge his failures and perhaps punish him for them.

However, we must keep in mind that failure is itself a form of punishment, and sometimes a very effective one. Moreover, a completely responsible person suffers a double failure in his performing an invalid act—he fails both in what he does and in his judgment of that act as valid. He has indeed made a deliberate and valid choice, and if he comes to see its invalidity, his whole being may well be at stake in that revelation. Because he has chosen with full cognizance of what is at stake, for himself and others, he suffers a vital blow to his acceptance of himself. Since he has done what he took to be fully commensurate with his moral being, his discovery of failure calls for a reevaluation of his total self. Nothing is more thoroughly painful than the process of self-transformation; nor is anything more fully the goal of punishment. In this sense, if a completely responsible man accepts his failure, he is already punished, and probably more than enough.

Nevertheless, some moral action is necessary to moral judgment; merely thought condemnation is nothing. Whether we will imprison, execute, torture, or exile a completely responsible man depends on too many factors even to begin to determine in general. A felt sense of guilt may well be sufficient punishment. Sometimes we will refrain from punishment, if the consequences are extremely undesirable. However, moral wrong demands judgment and condemnation. Completely responsible men declare themselves willing to be judged by their deeds. We as moral agents cannot but take up their gauntlet. If we fail to do so, we scorn their actions, and implicitly reveal that nothing matters enough to us.

Index

*Stephen D. Ross is associate professor of philosophy at the
State University of New York at Binghamton. In addition to*
The Nature of Moral Responsibility *he has written*
The Meaning of Education *(1966);* Literature and Philosophy:
An Analysis of the Philosophical Novel *(1969);*
The Scientific Process *(1971);* and Moral Decision *(1972).*

*The manuscript was edited by Carl Fernelius. The book was
designed by Gil Hanna. The text typeface is Linotype Baskerville designed
originally by John Baskerville in the eighteenth century; and the display
face is American Baskerville.*

*The text is printed on 60 lb. Nashoba text paper and the book is
bound in Holliston's Novelex linen finish cloth over binders' boards.
Manufactured in the United States of America.*